Buchan's War

JOHN BUCHAN

AMBERLEY

First published 2014

Amberley Publishing
The Hill, Stroud
Gloucestershire, GL5 4EP

www.amberley-books.com

British Library Cataloguing in Publication Data.
A catalogue record for this book is available from the British Library.

ISBN 978 1 4456 4310 6 (print)
ISBN 978 1 4456 4326 7 (ebook)

Typeset in 11pt on 14pt Minion.
Typesetting and Origination by Amberley Publishing.
Printed in the UK.

Contents

	Maps	5
	Editor's Note	13
	Prologue: At Serajevo	15
1	The Battle Joined in the West	19
2	The War at Sea Begins	43
3	The War on Commerce	55
4	The First Battle of the Marne	61
5	From the Aisne to the First Battle of Ypres	75
6	The Battle of Coronel	99
7	The Battle of the Falkland Islands	107
8	The North Sea Raids	113
9	The Naval Attack on the Dardanelles	123
10	The Battle of Loos	149
11	The Blockade and the Commerce Raiders	173
12	Verdun and the Somme	183
13	The Battle of Jutland	203
14	Germany and the United States	229
15	The Battle of Arras	239
16	The Third Battle of Ypres and Cambrai	249
17	Last German Offensives	269
18	Zeebrugge and Ostend	281
19	The Turning of the Tide	295
20	The Surrender of Germany	305

Maps

The Balkans in 1914, showing Serbia and Austria-Hungary, including
Sarajevo.

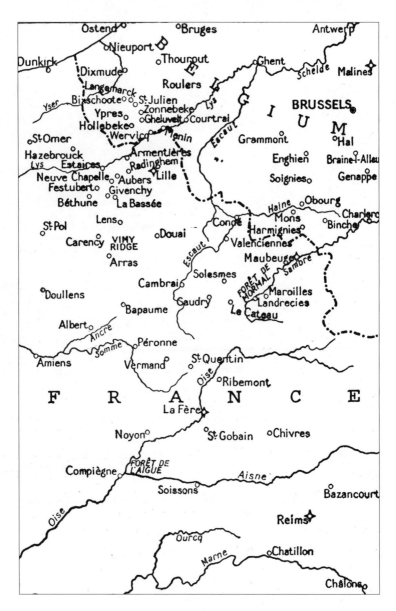

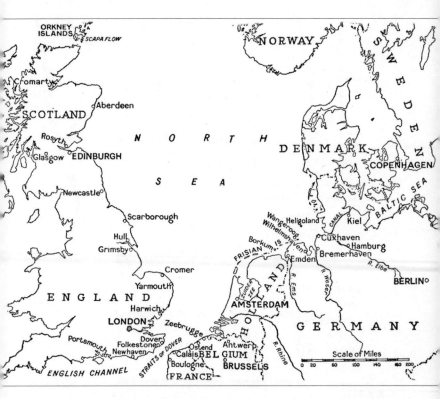

Above: The North Sea, showing the Royal Navy's bases at Scapa Flow and Rosyth, and the German naval base of Kiel.

Left: The northern Western Front, from Paris to the Channel coast.

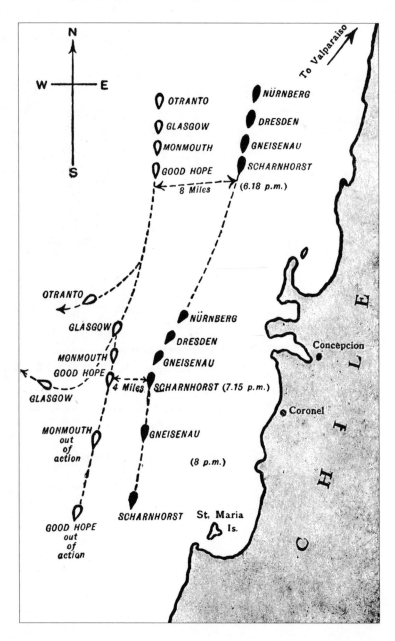

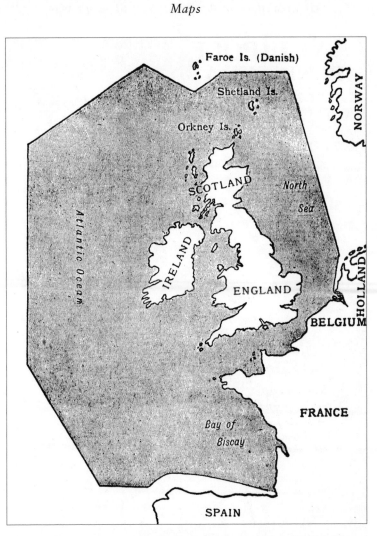

Above: The German maritime exclusion zone around the British Isles.

Left: The Battle of the Coronel.

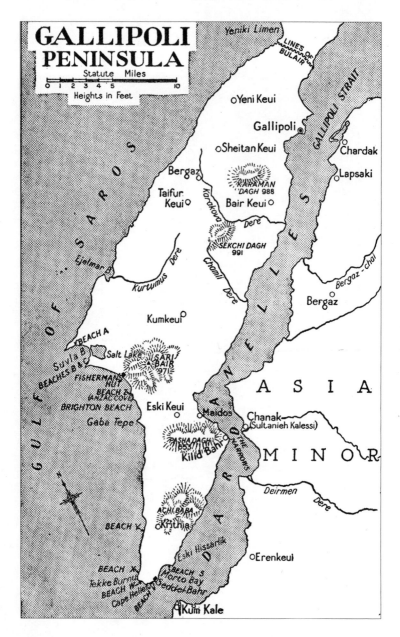

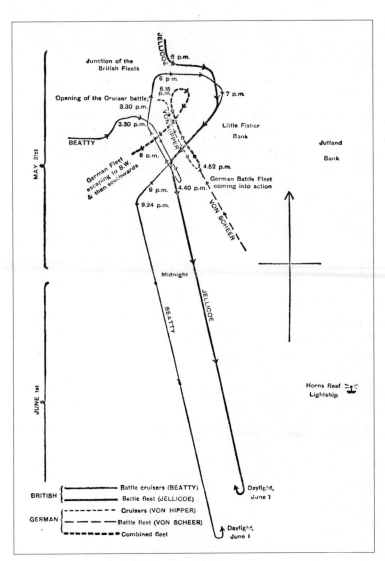

Above: The Battle of Jutland, 31 May 1916.

Left: The Gallipoli Peninsula and the Dardanelles.

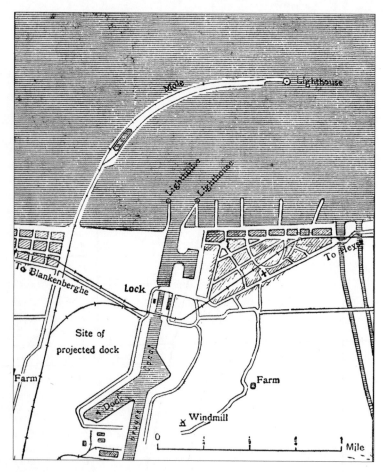

Zeebrugge Harbour.

Editor's Note

This volume consists of an edited series of chapters from two histories of the First World War, *Episodes of the Great War* and *Naval Episodes of the Great War*, published by novelist John Buchan in 1936 and 1938 respectively. These were in turn compiled from a twenty-volume history of the war written by Buchan between 1914 and 1919 and published in the form of a monthly magazine. At the same time as he was pursuing this project, Buchan was serving in the British Army intelligence corps and writing speeches and communiqués for Sir Douglas Haig, commander of the British forces in France. In 1917, Buchan would be promoted to Director of Information, working to coordinate propaganda efforts overseas. His official position made it difficult for Buchan to be critical of the decisions of Haig and his generals and other British commanders, but it also meant that he was in an excellent position to describe the grand strategy of the campaigns he wrote about, working with the men who had formulated it. He wrote, too, with all the style and skill of one of the best-selling novelists of the age.

The author of *The Thirty-Nine Steps*, Buchan was ennobled as Baron Tweedsmuir in 1935 and appointed as Governor General of Canada. He died in Ottawa in 1940.

We have preserved Buchan's original spelling, so for instance Sarajevo appears as Serajevo.

Prologue:
At Serajevo

28 June 1914

On the morning of Sunday 28 June, in the year 1914, the Bosnian city of Serajevo was astir with the expectation of a royal visit. The Archduke Francis Ferdinand, the heir to the Hapsburg throne and the nephew of the Emperor, had been for the past days attending the manoeuvres of the 15th and 16th Army Corps, and had suddenly announced his intention of inspecting the troops in the capital. The visitors drove in motor cars through the uneven streets of the little city, which, with its circle of barren hills and its mosques and minarets, reminds the traveller of Asia rather than of Europe. There was a great crowd in the streets – Catholic Croats, with whom the Archduke was not unpopular; Orthodox and Mussulman Serbs, who looked askance at all things Austrian; and those strange, wildly clad gipsies that throng every Balkan town. But the crowd was not there to greet the Emperor's nephew. It was the day of Kossovo, the anniversary of that fatal fight when the Sultan Murad I destroyed the old Serbian kingdom. For five centuries it had been kept as a day of mourning, but this year for the first time it was celebrated in Serbia as a national fête, since the Balkan War had restored the losses of the Field of Blackbirds.

The heir to the Austrian throne was not a popular figure, a morose, silent man whose ruling passion was for holocausts of game at shooting-parties; and his federalist politics were anathema to the Austrian governing classes. But he was an intimate of the German Emperor, and only a fortnight before they had pledged their friendship.

The royal party proceeded slowly towards the Town Hall. Motoring in Serajevo is a leisurely business, and there was a great crowd along the Appel Quay. Just before they reached the Chumuria Bridge over the Miliatzka a black package fell on the open hood of the Archduke's car. He pushed it off, and it exploded in front of the second car, slightly wounding two of his suite and six or seven spectators. The would-be assassin was arrested. He was a compositor called Gabrinovitch, from Trebinje in Herzegovina, who had lived some time in Belgrade. 'The fellow will get the Cross of Merit for this,' was the reported remark of the Archduke. He knew his real enemies, and was aware that to powerful circles in Vienna and Budapest the news of his death would not be unwelcome.

Arrived at the Town Hall, the Archduke was presented to the Burgomaster. He was in something of a temper. 'What is the use of your speeches?' he asked. 'I come here to pay you a visit, and I am greeted with bombs.' The embarrassed city dignitaries read the address of welcome, and the Archduke made a formal reply. He then proposed to drive to the hospital to visit his wounded aide-de-camp. Some small attempt was made to dissuade him, for in the narrow streets among the motley population no proper guard could be kept. But Count Potiorek was reassuring. He knew his Bosnians, he said, and they rarely attempted two murders in one day. The party set out accordingly, the Archduke and his wife in the same car with the Governor.

About ten minutes to eleven, as they moved slowly along the Appel Quay, in the narrow part where it is joined by the Franz-Josefsgasse, a young man pushed forward from the crowd on the side-walk and fired three pistol shots into the royal car. He was a Bosnian student called Prinzip, a friend of Gabrinovitch, who like him had been living in Belgrade. The Archduke was hit in the jugular vein, and died almost at once. His wife received a bullet in her side, and expired a few minutes later in the Government House, after receiving the last sacraments.

The tumult of the fête-day was suddenly hushed. The police were busy in every street laying hands on suspects, and in an impassioned proclamation to the awed and silent city the Burgomaster laid the crime at Serbia's door.

1

The Battle Joined in the West

The New Factors in War – The German Plan – The Attack on Liége Forts – Early French Failures – The British Expeditionary Force – Mons – The Retreat

As the minds of both soldiers and civilians bent themselves to the great contest, it was inevitable that they should be busied with forecasts. All agreed that the war would be of a magnitude never known before in history, and that most of the problems would be different in kind from those of the past. During the last half century, revolution had succeeded revolution. The invention of the internal combustion engine had provided motor transport and airplanes. Field telephones and wireless telegraphy had altered the system of communication among troops. The cannon had passed through a series of bewildering metamorphoses, till it had reached the 75 mm field gun and the mighty siege howitzer. No single weapon of war but had a hundredfold increased its range and precision. The old minor tactics, the old transport and intelligence methods were now, it appeared, as completely out of date as the stage coach and the China clipper.

There was general agreement that the existence of new factors made war a venture into the unknown. Perhaps the chief of these factors was the vast numbers now destined for the battlefield. It was the first instance in history of large bodies of men operating in a closely settled country; it would not be easy to find the wide and open battlefield which it was believed that great masses of men would require. For it was almost universally assumed that the coming war would be a war of movement and manoeuvre. The principal reason for this view was that men's minds could not envisage the long continuance of a struggle in which the whole assets of each nation were so utterly pledged. It was believed, too, that modern numbers and modern weapons would make the struggle most desperate but also short, since flesh and blood must soon be brought to the breaking-point. Such a view was possible, because no belligerent had recognised the immense relative increase of strength given by modern weapons to the defence over the attack. Of the impregnability of field entrenchments no combatant was aware till the third month of war.

The gravest of the new problems was scarcely grasped at the outset. What provision could be made for the Supreme Command? Obviously, even in the case of the army of a single nation, the task of the commander-in-chief would be most intricate. But what of the superior direction of the whole Allied strength? There would be national pride to reckon with, and diverse political interests; different Staff methods; different, perhaps conflicting, theories of war. That this problem did not trouble the minds of statesmen more acutely at the start was due to the fact that the contest was regarded as not likely to be a long one. No man foresaw that presently the whole strength of every belligerent would be involved; that scarcely a corner of the globe would be free from the turmoil; and that the supreme need on each side would be some central direction, political, naval, and military, such as in the Seven Years' War the elder Pitt gave to Britain.

All the world in that early stage failed, it may fairly be said, in prescience. Men looked for too little from the new factors in war, and they looked for too much. And yet in other matters they

To a German commander-in-chief the general strategy of an invasion of France was determined by two considerations. The first was the nature of the *Aufmarsch* imposed upon him by the lie of the frontier. The second was the necessity for that immediate disabling blow – that 'battle without a morrow' – consequent upon a war waged simultaneously in two separate theatres. Germany therefore arranged her *Aufmarsch* in three groups. In the north, moving against the French left was more than one-third of her total forces in the West – her I and II Armies, comprising thirteen corps and a mass of cavalry. Directed through the Ardennes against the middle Meuse was the central group – the III, IV, and V Armies – amounting to fourteen corps. On the left were the VI and VII Armies, eight corps strong, based on Metz, and destined for Lorraine. The supreme direction of the Army of the West, as of the whole armed strength of the German Empire, was vested in the Emperor as War Lord, but in practice the command was in the hands of the Chief of the General Staff. At the moment this post was held by Lieutenant-General Helmuth von Moltke, a nephew of the victor of 1870. He was known to the world as a learned and accomplished soldier and a successful commander at manoeuvres, while to his countrymen his name seemed of happy augury. The first Moltke had broken the French Empire; the second would shatter the French Republic and the Empire of Britain.

But the peculiar situation caused by the attitude of Belgium compelled Germany to send an advance guard to make ready the path through the northern gate for her great armies of the right. This force was placed under General von Emmich, the commander of the 10th Corps, and directed to seize Liége by a *coup de main*. At the same time the 2nd and 4th Cavalry Divisions, under von der Marwitz, were ordered to the north of Liége, and in the south the 9th, 5th, and Guard cavalry divisions moved into position in the Ardennes and along the Meuse to protect the concentration of the

II and III Armies from the interference of French cavalry. On the morning of Tuesday 4 August, Marwitz had seized Visé, crossed the Meuse, and entered Belgium, and late that evening Emmich's scouts came into touch with the Belgian pickets.

The chief routes into Belgium from the Rhine valley are four. There is the ingress through Luxembourg into the Southern Ardennes, and so to the central Meuse valley; there is the route from the German frontier camp of Malmédy to Stavelot, which would give access to the Northern Ardennes and to the Meuse at Dinant, Namur, and Huy; there is the great route from Aix *via* Verviers, by the main line between Paris and Berlin, down the valley of the Vesdre to Liége; and, lastly, there is the direct route by road from Aix to the crossing of the Meuse at Visé, on the very edge of the Dutch frontier. All four routes were requisitioned. But for Germany's immediate purpose the vital entry was the gap of 10 miles between the Dutch border and the Ardennes, the bottle-neck of the Belgian plain, with the fortress of Liége in the gate.

Liége itself lies astride the main stream of the Meuse and the second channel which receives the waters of the Ourthe and the Vesdre. It occupies the flat between the northern plateau and the river, spreading eastwards down the valley, and climbing westwards towards the plateau in steep, crooked streets. Obviously such a position had great capacities for defence, and these were made use of in the series of forts constructed by Henri Alexis Brialmont for the Belgian Government between the years 1888 and 1892. Brialmont's typical fort was largely an underground structure. His ordinary design was a low mound surrounded by a deep ditch, the top of the mound hardly showing above its margin. The mound was cased in concrete and masonry, and roofed with concrete, covered with earth and sods. The top was broken by circular pits in which, working like pistons, the 'cupolas', or gun-turrets, slid up and down, with just enough movement to bring the gun muzzles above the level of the ground. Internally the mound was like a gigantic molehill, hollowed out into passages and chambers. The whole fort was like a low-freeboard turret ship sunk in the ground, and it was fought much as the barbettes of a battleship are fought in action. The Liége defences consisted of six main forts of the pentagonal type, and six lesser forts, or *fortins*, triangular in shape. The forts made an irregular circle around the city, the average distance of each from the centre being about 4 miles. In theory they formed a double line of defence, so that if one fell its neighbours to the left and right should still be able to hold the enemy.

On 4 August the Belgian forces were still in process of mobilisation on the line of the river Dyle covering Brussels and Antwerp. The church bells were still ringing their summons at midnight, and the dogs were being collected from the milk carts to draw the mitrailleuses. The 3rd Division was rushed to Liége, and the civic guard of that city took their stand by the side of the regulars. At full strength the force should have numbered over 30,000 men; but as the mobilisation was incomplete, it was little more than 20,000. The defenders of Liége were in the same position as the attackers – an improvised force, hastily put together and imperfectly equipped. No stranger medley of colour could be found in Europe than such a field army which lacked a field dress – the men of the line in their blue and white; the *chasseurs à pied* with their peaked caps, green and yellow uniforms, and flowing capes; and the Civic Guard, with their high round hats and red facings. Little could be done in two days to improvise defences; but gangs of colliers and navvies were set to work to dig trenches and throw up breastworks, and the village of Boncelles and various houses, spinneys, and even churches, which obviously obstructed the line of fire, were levelled to the ground. By the afternoon of Tuesday 4 August, the Belgians held the line of the south-eastern forts from Boncelles to Barchon, and cavalry patrols covered the gap between Pontisse and the Dutch frontier.

The army of Liége was under the command of General Leman, an officer of engineers and commandant of the Military School, who had worked under Brialmont on the Antwerp and Meuse defences, and was regarded as the foremost living representative of his views. His business was to make such a stand on the line of the southern forts as would delay the enemy for a day or two. Then the city, in the absence of either redoubts between the forts or a strong field army, must inevitably fall, but its fate did not necessarily mean the end of the resistance. The northern forts could still hold out till the enemy should force the plateau from the city, or, advancing from Visé or Huy, should take them on the flank. This meant time, and till they fell there was no progress by rail from Liége towards the Belgian plain. It was Leman's aim to hold on as long as possible to the forts commanding the railway between Liége and Namur, for by that road the French would come. If three days were gained it would be something; if a week it would be much, for daily, hourly, the little Belgian army looked west for the arrival of its allies of France and Britain.

Germany did not rate Belgian valour high, and believed that Emmich's advanced guard had an easy task before them; for in spite of her elaborate intelligence system, she seemed to have no instruments delicate enough to gauge the spirit of a people. She did not realise that Belgium had acquired an army, and something more potent than armies – a vivid national self-consciousness and a stalwart patriotism. When the hour came Belgium was ready, and her faith was found in the words of her king: 'A country which defends itself cannot perish.'

On the night of Tuesday the 4th, as we have seen, Leman's pickets came into touch with Emmich's vanguard, and about 11.30 that night the citizens of Liége heard the beginning of a great cannonade. The artillery duel went on through the night, and on the morning of Wednesday the 5th a flag of truce was sent to Leman demanding a passage. The Belgian general refused, and an infantry attack was launched forthwith between Embourg and Boncelles. It was beaten off with heavy loss to the assault. That afternoon the Germans, hard pressed for time and now strengthened by a supply of medium heavy pieces, opened a new bombardment. All night the German infantry attacked, regardless of losses, and by the morning of the 6th had filtered through the circle of forts, and was marching on the city. By that afternoon the Belgian infantry and artillery were falling back on Liége. The retreat was necessarily hurried, and there was no time to destroy the Meuse bridges; but Leman succeeded in his purpose, and himself took up position in Fort Loncin, which commanded the plateau and the railway line to France.

That night the 14th German Brigade encamped on the heights of La Chartreuse, overlooking the city. Its general having fallen, it was led by the deputy Chief of Staff of Bülow's II Army, who had been sent to accompany Emmich. His name was von Ludendorff. It is a name which will appear many times in the course of this history, and now his quickness of conception and high personal courage were mainly responsible for the German success. On the morning of the 7th he went alone with the brigade adjutant to the citadel of Liége and received its surrender. Terms were arranged with the Burgomaster and the Bishop, and the Germans marched in.

The line of the southern forts had been pierced, though none of them had yet fallen. But it was the forts on the north hank of the Meuse in which lay the chief strategic value; for, so long as they were untaken, the great railway lines could not be used, and for the German advance Liége was a terminus and not a junction. Emmich had had enough of frontal infantry attacks and inadequate bombardments. He suffered Leman in the north forts to remain in peace till he had brought up his siege train. Meantime, to the east and west of the city, the German advance continued. Stores of all kinds poured into Liége, the pontoon bridges at Visé were completed, and the great batteries of Kluck's army were brought on to Belgian soil. Two German cavalry divisions advanced to test the crossings of the Gette, along the western bank of which lay the main Belgian force of five divisions.

During this time detachments from the II Army, which had concentrated south of Kluck, were feeling their way up the Meuse valley towards Namur. On Wednesday the 12th its advanced guards seized the town of Huy, which stood half-way between Namur and Liége, and was out of the danger zone of the forts of both cities. The capture of Huy put the invader astride of the main line from Aix to France by way of Liége; but at present it was of little use to him, since the northern forts of Liége still commanded its most vital point. It gave him, however, a branch line, running directly north from Huy across the plain to Landen and the heart of Belgium.

On the 11th the main siege train began to arrive at Liége. Barchon had already fallen on the 9th, and Evegnée on the 10th, to the German field pieces, and at midday on the 12th the final bombardment began. That day Boncelles was summoned to surrender, and on its refusal was bombarded for twenty-four hours. The electric light apparatus was destroyed, and through the night the defenders fought on in a suffocating darkness. By six o'clock on the morning of the 15th the concrete chambers began to fall in, several of the cupolas were smashed, and shells penetrated the roof and burst inside the fort itself. Surrender was inevitable, and the gallant commander hoisted a white flag, after a resistance of eleven days. Nothing was left of the fort but a heap of ruins.

Meanwhile the bombardment of Loncin, which General Leman stubbornly held for Belgium, was continued without rest. The heavy shell fire, as at Boncelles, smashed the cement framework and the cupolas; and seems to have exploded the magazine, for at 5.20 p.m. on the 15th the whole fort blew up. The few defenders left alive were half dead from suffocation. Only one shot was fired – by a man with his left hand, his right having been blown away. General Leman was found unconscious, his body pinned by falling beams, and his life in grave danger from poisoning by noxious fumes. He was carried to Emmich, whom he had met two years before at manoeuvres. His captor congratulated him on his heroic resistance, and gave him back his sword. 'I thank you,' was the answer of this soldier of few words. 'War is a different sort of job from manoeuvres. I ask you to bear witness that you found me unconscious.'

For eleven days the forts of Liége had stood out against the enemy and blocked his main advance. It may fairly be said that their resistance put back the German time-table by at least seventy-two hours, and by that space of time hindered Kluck from reaching the main battlefield. Of what immense consequence was that delay this narrative will show. On it depended in all likelihood the salvation of the Entente armies and the defeat of the German plan. Without it, the British Army and the French Fifth Army might well have been destroyed. That was a great thing in itself, but those eleven days of fighting made an impression upon the world out of all proportion to their results. The true significance of the Belgian stand was that it pricked the bubble of German invincibility. The triumph was moral – an advertisement to the world that the ancient faiths of country and duty could still nerve the arm for battle, and that the German idol, for all its splendour, had feet of clay.

***

The war preparation of France began at 9 p.m. on 31 July with the moving of the covering troops, a task completed by midday on 3 August. The mobilisation proper started on 2 August, and the concentration at midday on 5 August. By noon on the 12th the more urgent transport movements had been completed, and between that day and midnight on the 18th the main work was accomplished. The French forces faced Germany on the ancient frontier line of the Vosges, the Moselle, and the Meuse.

The commander-in-chief was Joseph Césaire Joffre, an engineer officer sprung from bourgeois stock in the Eastern Pyrenees. He was an anti-clerical and a strenuous republican, but he allowed no intrigues of party or sect to bias his judgment. He was not, like Foch, a great military student and thinker. He represented character rather than mind, and, as it happened, it was character which France needed most in the hour of crisis. We shall see him unchanged both by sunshine and shadow, in good and evil report the same bluff, shrewd, wise paternal being – one who, as Bossuet said of Turenne, could fight without anger, win without ambition, and triumph without vanity.

On 10 August, after an abortive raid in Upper Alsace in the course of which troops from the Belfort Garrison penetrated as far as Mulhouse, preparations began for that Lorraine offensive which was the first step in the French plan. The object of this advance was to turn the left of the main German force advancing through Luxembourg and the Ardennes, to secure the Briey coalfields by the investment or capture of Metz, and by the seizure of the bridgeheads of the upper Rhine to interfere with the communications of the German V, VI, and VII Armies. The offensive was a costly failure, but Joffre, although he was aware that considerable German forces were moving north of the Meuse, and every argument seemed to point to a strengthening of his left wing, tried the second of his alternatives and gave orders for an advance by his centre into the Belgian Ardennes. The enterprise was short-lived and disastrous. Almost at once the advance came up against strong prepared positions, which in that tangled country were hard to detect, and was at the same time taken in flank by enemy columns marching from the east. There was insufficient connection, too, between the corps of the attack, so that each unit fought a separate battle.

Meanwhile Joffre, aware of the German advance into the Belgian plain, had pushed his Fifth Army into the angle between Charleroi, Namur, and Dinant, on the Sambre and Meuse. Namur he considered to be capable of making as stout a defence as the Liége forts, and he held that it would form a good pivot for an advance into Belgium by Lanrezac, and the British army, now in process of concentration, which, if successful, would gain the line Namur–Brussels–Antwerp. It was clear to his mind the enemy could not be equally strong in Lorraine, in the Ardennes, and north of the Meuse, and his forward policy would search out the weak spot.

He had miscalculated the speed of the German advance, as he had underestimated its weight. We left the Belgian army still holding the crossings of the Gette against Kluck's vanguards. But once the last Liége forts had fallen, and the trunk line was cleared for traffic, there came the real impact. The invasion swept on like a tide, the cavalry screen fell away, and the Belgian field armies realised what was before them. Their one hope was the French, but the French infantry were far distant, though part of Sordet's cavalry was then across the Sambre and in touch with the Belgian right somewhere near the field of Waterloo. On the 17th, Kluck reached the Gette with three corps flanked by two cavalry divisions. During the morning of the 18th the river was forced at Haelen and Diest, and by the evening its whole line was in German hands. There was nothing for the Belgian command but to retreat behind the Dyle and seek sanctuary. It withdrew, therefore, on the 19th, and by the 20th, as Brialmont had always foreseen, was inside the Antwerp forts, leaving the open city of Brussels to the enemy. On

the 20th, M. Max, the burgomaster of the capital, arranged with the Germans for a peaceful occupation.

The occupation in force did not last long, for Kluck had no time for parades. On the morning of the 21st the bulk of the I Army was swinging south-westwards from Brussels, having reached the line Grammont–Enghien–Hal–Braine-l'Alleud; while the whole of von der Marwitz's cavalry moved westwards in the general direction of Lille, looking for Sir John French. Kluck's huge wheel was behind the German time-table, but far in advance of his opponents' expectation.

Bülow's II Army had less ground to cover. We have seen that on the 12th he had seized the bridge at Huy, and was rapidly transferring part of his troops to the left bank of the Meuse. On the morning of the 21st he had the better part of five corps north of that river, with their right in touch with Kluck about Genappe, their centre at Gembloux, and their left a mile or two from Namur. Meantime the mysterious III Army had moved swiftly through the northern Ardennes, where the leafy cover seems to have screened it completely from the French airmen. On the morning of the 21st, therefore, the I, II and III German Armies were bearing down on the angle of the Sambre and the Meuse in an arc 70 miles long. Before them lay Lanrezac s Fifth Army, as yet only of four corps, now getting into position on the Sambre, the fortress of Namur, garrisoned by the Belgian 4th Division, and on Lanrezac's left the British army of two corps, the concentration of which was expected to be completed that day.

Saturday the 22nd saw the main Battle of Charleroi in which Lanrezac after a gallant fight was defeated. The battle was lost before it was joined through the mistaken theory and imperfect intelligence of the French General Staff, and under no conceivable circumstances could Lanrezac have succeeded. He had to fight before his army was in position, and when his centre was already tottering he found his flank turned.

On Sunday afternoon, the 23rd, the Germans entered Namur singing their part-songs.

We turn now to the doings of Sir John French and his Expeditionary Force. The state of war with Germany, officially declared by Britain on 4 August, did not in itself commit her to sending an expeditionary force to the Continent; but the unmistakable trend of public feeling, and the assurance of France that she counted upon our military cooperation, gave the Government no choice. It was resolved to dispatch four infantry divisions at once, to be followed by two more at short intervals. The people of Britain knew little of the crossing till Monday the 17th, when it was officially announced that it was over. In ten days, by a remarkable feat of transport, more than 150,000 men had been landed at various ports in France.

On 5 August Lord Kitchener, who had been on the eve of returning to Egypt, was appointed, largely by the urgency of Lord Haldane, as Secretary of State for War. He accepted the post with the gravest sense of responsibility. He did not believe in any short and easy contest, or any campaign of limited liability. To the ordinary Briton he was the foremost subject of the King, a man untainted by party politics, aloof from social intrigue, a single- minded servant of the State. He had had a career of brilliant success, and the nation had faith in his star. From the outset he realised that Britain was ill prepared for a great war on land, but he trusted his countrymen and conceived that such preparation could still be achieved. The struggle, as he saw it, would last at least three years, and he laid his plans for an army of seventy divisions, which should reach its maximum strength when the enemy's had begun to decline. Though from his long service abroad he was unfamiliar with European problems, his curious *flair* for essentials made him divine the situation more correctly than the experts of the French Staff. He was convinced that the main German thrust would come through Belgium, and he was anxious that the British army should concentrate about Amiens and not at Maubeuge, for he guessed at the broad sweep of Kluck's envelopment, and he did not wish the *moral* of his troops to be impaired by beginning the campaign with a compulsory retirement. On this point he was overruled, but his instructions to the British Commander-in-Chief showed how little confidence he had in the initial French plan.

The British Expeditionary Force consisted to begin with of two infantry corps and one cavalry division. The Commander-in-Chief, Field-Marshal Sir John French, had long been considered the best field officer on the British active list. His was, perhaps, the chief reputation made by the South African War. He was a personality rather than a mind – a born leader of men, of tried courage, coolness and sagacity. The 1st Corps was under the command of Sir Douglas Haig, a cavalryman like Sir John French, and one of the youngest of British lieutenant-generals. To the 2nd Army Corps had been originally appointed Lieutenant-General Sir James Grierson, but he had died suddenly after the landing of the Expeditionary Force in France. He was succeeded by General Sir Horace Smith-Dorrien, who had done brilliant work in South Africa, and had held the Southern command at home since 1912.

On Saturday the 22nd the British army was a day's march north of the Sambre, getting into position between Condé and Binche. A word must be said of the configuration of this corner of Hainault. West of Mons along the valley of the Haine and the Condé canal lies a country of flat marshy meadows. Mons itself is a mining town, the centre of the Borinage coalfield, an area like any north English colliery district. There was a network of railways, many of them carried on low embankments, and among them the miners' villages, with the headgears of the pits and the tall chimneys of the engine-houses towering above the low-roofed cottages. Around these hamlets the accumulation of shale and waste heaps suggested at first sight ranges of hills, and the illusion was strengthened by the little forests of dwarf firs with which some of the larger heaps had been planted. To the north lay a sandy ridge covered with a wide stretch of woodland, from Saint-Ghislain 6 miles west of Mons to a point some 3 miles east of the town. To the south, after the coalfields were left behind, lay an agricultural region, enclosed on the south by the big wood of Mormal. The place was poor ground for a defensive action, teeming as it was with an industrial population, and endlessly split into enclosures and pockets which gave no observation or free field of fire.

By the evening of the 22nd the British 2nd Corps lay along the Condé canal, while the 1st Corps on its right stretched from Mons to the village of Peissant – a front of about 25 miles, held by a force of some 70,000 men and 300 guns. Sir John French had no general reserve, in the absence of his 3rd Corps, and had to use his cavalry as best he could for the purpose. That day the British horse had been scouting far to the north, and had come into contact with parties of Uhlans, and, driving them in, had discovered behind them large infantry columns on the march – in what force they could not tell, for they could not advance farther, and the thick woodlands about Soignies made the country inscrutable to the British airplanes. Sunday the 23rd brought a hot August morning, and its first hours passed in a Sabbatical calm, while the bells of the village churches rang for Mass. The men in the trenches heard a distant sputter of rifle fire where the German cavalry were, feeling at our outposts. Sir John French met his generals, and explained to them Joffre's plan. His information at the moment was that 'one, or at most two, of the enemy's army corps, with perhaps one cavalry division, were in front of my positions, and I was aware of no outflanking movement by the enemy'. Kluck, though he had not yet half his army in position, did not believe that the main British force was in front of him, and resolved to send his 9th Corps at once into action, and to extend the battle presently with his 3rd Corps. Accordingly, at about 10.30 a.m., he began his artillery preparation, and half an hour later the infantry of the 9th Corps attacked at the angle of the canal north of Mons against Hubert Hamilton's 3rd Division.

The first impression of the British soldier was one of amazement. Instead of the thin and widely extended lines which he had expected he found the enemy coming on in dense masses, which made a wonderful target for his rifle. He found that he could well hold his own, and it was not till the enemy numbers had crossed the canal east of Obourg, and converged upon Mons from north and east, that Hamilton fell back through Mons to a prepared position south of it which linked up with the left of the 1st Corps at Harmignies. But about 5 p.m. the British commander received a message from Joffre which put a new complexion on the affair. He learned of the fall of Namur and the defeat of Charleroi, and that he was not told of these things before shows how feeble was the liaison work between the two commands. He learned, what he had begun to suspect, that Kluck was attacking with two or three times the force originally estimated. He realised that, though his little army might resist for a time against such odds, a prolonged defence of the Mons position would mean that inevitably it would be cut off, enveloped, and destroyed. Already it lay alone in face of an enemy more than twice its strength. The only course was to hold on till nightfall, give his men a brief rest, and begin a fighting retreat southwards at daybreak. Like a prudent commander, he had already reconnoitred and selected a position to be held in the first stage of retirement, should a retirement prove necessary. He issued the order to fall back – to the surprise of his army, which knew nothing of Namur and Charleroi, and was very certain that it had not been beaten.

Joffre, at his headquarters in Champagne, awoke on the morning of Monday the 24th to confront a falling world. The battles of the frontier had one and all ignominiously failed. His three offensives had been met and broken, and the main armies of France hurled back inside their borders. He had used up his only general reserve. In almost every detail of war he had been outwitted by the Germans. Moreover, the fighting had shown the French inferior in many important details – the use of airplanes, heavy artillery, and wired entrenchments – all matters vital to a war of defence. The Germans were pouring through Lorraine. Great armies were flooding over the Ardennes to the Meuse, and the German right wing, far stronger than his wildest imagining, was swinging round the weak Allied left. Rarely has a general been faced with a bleaker prospect. One plan only gave a faint promise of hope. The eastern front must be held at all costs, and the northern armies must by a breakneck retreat slip out of the noose. The whole battle-line of France must fall back and play for time – time to give it a better alignment – time, above all, to create laboriously and feverishly a new reserve, which could be used to restore the war of manoeuvre. Wide regions of France – nay, Paris itself – must be sacrificed, if need be, to keep intact the field strength.

With incomparable courage and patience, and with the mental elasticity of his race, Joffre faced the crisis, jettisoned his cherished preconceptions, and prepared a new plan on the grim facts now at last made plain. We have seen him in his weakness; we are now to see him in his strength.

***

The retreat of the Allied armies of the right and centre was by the left, pivoting on Verdun. Of the three French armies of the north the Fifth had the longest way to go, and the most difficult task, for at Charleroi it had suffered a defeat, and from first to last it was in peril of outflanking.

But the most critical part of the retreat took place on the Allied left. Kluck's intention was to drive Sir John French into Maubeuge, while his right wing should march rapidly on the west side to cut off his retreat. But the movement did not proceed according to plan, for the envelopers were late, and Smith-Dorrien's 2nd Corps, having fallen back from the canal 5 miles to the southward, beat off the attack of the German 3rd and 4th Corps. At 7 a.m., being outnumbered by something like four to one he began his retirement. Haig's 1st Corps had already slipped away, and early in the afternoon the whole British force, intact and in good heart, was assembled on the Maubeuge position. Sir John French, fearing to find himself shut up in Maubeuge, decided to halt for the night but no longer.

On the 25th his aim was to put the forest of Mormal behind him. This woodland, 10 miles long from north to south and 6 miles wide, was rough and tangled with undergrowth, and was believed – wrongly – to have no roads fit for an army to travel. But the roads on the east side were too few and too bad for his whole army to travel; while if he moved by the west side only he would leave a desperate gap between himself and Lanrezac, and moreover would thrust his left wing into the jaws of Kluck's enveloping force. Accordingly, he decided to send Haig by the east roads to Maroilles and Landrecies, while Smith-Dorrien kept the west side in the direction of Le Cateau. It was perhaps the only solution of the problem, but it was a solution with its own risks, for a gap of some 10 miles separated the two corps on the march.

Kluck that day seemed to have the cards in his hand, but he failed to play them. It was a summer's day of intense and glaring heat, and the weary British army found the long march in the dust a trying business. Haig had little trouble on the eastern roads, but it was dusk before the van of the 1st Division reached Maroilles and the 2nd Division the neighbourhood of Landrecies. It had been Sir John French's intention to bring Haig's left more to the west, but the hour was too far advanced and the troops were too exhausted for further movement. It was a dark night with a cloudy sky and a drizzle of rain, which presently changed to a downpour. The advance guards of the German 3rd Corps, which had advanced straight through the forest and so escaped detection by the British airplanes, came into action between 9.30 and 10 p.m. against the 1st Division at Maroilles, and the Guards Brigade of the 2nd Division at Landrecies. The latter assault was gallantly beaten off, and with the assistance of two reserve divisions of the French Fifth Army the situation at Maroilles was saved. When the last shots had died away the men of the 1st Corps lay down where they stood to snatch a brief rest.

But Smith-Dorrien was in worse case. That day he had had no easy march, and his 3rd division had held and beaten off at Solesmes an attack by Marwits's horse and part of the infantry of the 4th Corps. Allenby, too, had been in action south-east of Valenciennes. By dusk, however, Smith-Dorrien had reached a position on the left bank of the Selle west of the town of Le Cateau. In the small hours of the morning of the 26th he had to decide whether he dared to retreat then and there, or must first stand and fight. He had apparently received no explicit orders from Sir John French to retire at once, though he was given the general direction of retirement as the line Ribemont–Saint-Quentin–Vermand, 35 miles away. Clearly instructions as to so distant an objective could not be interpreted by any commander as the immediate orders for his day's work. Smith-Dorrien may well have assumed that the details and the method of retirement were left to his discretion. About 1.30 a.m., having received a cavalry report which warned him of the great strength of Kluck, he learned from Allenby that if a battle was to be avoided the retreat must be begun before daybreak, but that the scattered cavalry could be got together in time to cover it. Presently he realised that battle was already joined. At or just before dawn the advanced guard of the German 3rd Corps was in Le Cateau, and the 4th Corps was attacking his centre at Caudry. In these circumstances it seemed impossible to begin his retreat till he had checked the enemy; and he believed himself competent to do so, remembering the various occasions in the past few days when he had struck back at and crippled the pursuit. Looked at in any way it was a prodigious gamble, but the hazard of retreating from such a position may well have seemed greater than that of fighting in it.

The rain of the night had ceased, and a fine summer morning dawned. Bright sunlight, a pale blue sky, and the thin mists rising from the wet fields gave promise of a sultry day. As the sun rose, the flashes of the German guns tore through the haze, and the first light showed the grey masses of the enemy's infantry pushing forward in dense firing lines. Against Smith-Dorrien's 55,000 Kluck opposed not less than 140,000 men. He was surprised to find the British in position, and hoped at last to have that decisive battle which he had hitherto missed. His tactics were the same as at Mons – a frontal attack mainly by artillery, to be followed by an envelopment on both flanks. At first the British 4th Division, not having its guns up, fell back a little, but presently by its rifle fire it brought the enemy cavalry to a standstill. This, however, was no more than the prologue, and the battle proper began about 7 a.m. with a terrific German bombardment by the artillery of the 4th Corps, gradually reinforced by that of the 3rd and of the 4th Reserve. The ridge which Smith-Dorrien held was studded with villages, the church spires of which gave good targets for the enemy gunners. The British had had little time to entrench their position, though along the front line shelter trenches had been hastily dug and afforded some small cover. Their artillery, though outnumbered by nearly four to one, made a brilliant stand, and for seven hours checked the enemy's infantry rushes. The two points of serious danger were the right wing near Le Cateau, where the Germans managed to work round the flank of the sorely tried 5th Division, and at Caudry, which formed an acute salient, garrisoned by the brigade of the 3rd Division which had been fighting the night before at Solesmes. Nevertheless at 1 p.m. the British front was still intact, and Sordet and Allenby and d'Amade's reserves had for the moment checked the enveloping movements.

About 1 p.m. Smith-Dorrien realised that it was time to leave. His right flank was getting hourly more exposed by Haig's withdrawal, and Kluck's 9th Corps would presently be arriving. He had persuaded the enemy that he was not to be trifled with, and had beaten off his chief corps with heavy losses. If he was to get away, he must issue the orders forthwith, for to break off a battle with a vastly superior opponent is one of the most difficult of the operations of war. The attack of the 3rd Corps about noon broke the 5th Division on the right and precipitated the retreat. Orders could not reach many of the units, who remained in the trenches and so protected the retirement of the rest, but under cover of the devoted artillery most of the infantry quietly withdrew from the field. The batteries left behind had been so knocked to pieces that it was impossible to move them. Before the sun set the 2nd Corps was tramping over the belt of low upland in which the streams of Scheldt and Sambre take their rise, and on the morning of the 27th it halted north of Saint-Quentin where the land begins to fall to the bright valley of the Oise. The chief miracle of the retreat had been effected.

On the 28th the two halves of the British force had been reunited, and that evening the 1st Corps lay south of La Fère between the Saint-Gobain forest and the Oise, while the 2nd Corps was north of the river about Noyon. The British were over the Aisne on the 31st. On 3 September they crossed the Marne, and the long retreat from the Belgian frontier approached its end.

The last days had been hard and critical, the afternoons a blaze of heat, the nights chilly and often wet. There was no rest, for each day's march was continued late, and the incessant retirement might well have broken the spirit of the best of troops. But the men went through it all with fortitude, even with gaiety, and their only anxiety was to know when they would at last be allowed to stand and take order with the enemy. To realise the full achievement of the British force, which in the retreat had the most laborious task, we must remember the temperament of the soldier. He was entering on a war against what public opinion agreed was the most formidable army in the world. Partly, it is true, the legend of German invincibility had been weakened by the stand of Belgium; but, as our soldiers understood that tale, it had been fortress work rather than battles in the field. In such a campaign initial success, however small, works wonders with the spirit of an army. But there had been no success. The men had gone straight from the train, or from a long march, into action, and almost every hour of every day they had been retreating. Often they were given the chance of measuring themselves in close combat against their adversaries, and on these occasions they held their own; but still the retreat went on, and it was difficult to avoid the feeling that, even if their own battalion had stood fast, there must have been a defeat elsewhere in the line to explain this endless retirement. Such conditions are trying to a soldier's nerves. The man who will support cheerfully any fatigue in a forward march will wilt and slacken when he is going backward. Remember, too, that, except for a few members of the Headquarters Staff, the officers and men knew nothing of the general situation. They fell back in complete uncertainty as to what was happening, and could only suspect that the Germans were winning because they were the better army. Under such circumstances to have preserved complete discipline and faithfulness, nay, even to have retained humour and gaiety and unquenchable spirits, was an achievement more remarkable than the most signal victory.

Not less splendid was the performance of the French. Indeed, in many ways they had the more difficult duty. To yield mile after mile was for the French troops of the line, and not less for corps like the Zouaves and Turcos, and almost intolerable discipline. That it was done without grave disaster, and that, after so great a damping of zeal, the fire of attack could be readily rekindled, was an immense tribute to the armies of the Republic.

On the evening of the 4th the van of the retreat saw from the slopes above the Grand Morin a land of coppice and pasture rolling southward to a broad valley, and far off the dusk of many trees. It was the forest of Fontainebleau and the vale of the Seine. The Allies had fallen back behind all but one of the four rivers which from north and east open the way to Paris. That night they were encamped along the very streams towards which a hundred years before Napoleon had retired before Schwarzenberg and Blücher.

2

The War at Sea Begins

Germany's Naval Policy – Sir John Jellicoe's Problem – The Transport of the Armies – Escape of the Goeben *and the* Breslau *– Protection of the Trade Routes – Security of the British Coasts*

Britain declared war on Germany on 4 August 1914, and at 8.30 that morning the British Grand Fleet put out to sea. From that moment it disappeared from English sight. Dwellers on the southern and eastern coasts in the bright weather of early August could see an occasional cruiser or destroyer speeding on some errand, or an escorted mine-sweeper busy at its perilous task. But the great battleships had gone. Somewhere out on the blue waters or hidden in a creek of our northern and western shores lay the vigilant admirals of Britain. But presently came news. On the night of the 4th the German mine-layer *Königin Luise* left Borkum, and about 1l a.m. on the 5th she was sighted, chased, and sunk by two British destroyers. Early on the 6th the British light cruiser *Amphion* struck one of the mines she had laid, and foundered with some loss of life. Battle had been joined at sea.

To the command of the Grand Fleet there had been appointed Admiral Sir John Jellicoe, with Rear-Admiral Charles Madden as Chief of Staff. It consisted at the moment of twenty Dreadnoughts, eight 'King Edwards', four battle-cruisers, two squadrons of cruisers and one of light cruisers. Those who shared Stevenson's view as to the racy nomenclature of British seamen found something reassuring in the name of the new Commander-in-Chief. Admiral Jellicoe had served as a lieutenant in the Egyptian war in 1882. Specialising in gunnery, he had become a commander in 1891 and a captain in 1897; had served on the China station, commanding the Naval Brigade and acting as chief staff officer in the Peking expedition of 1900, where he was severely wounded. Thereafter he became successively Naval Assistant to the Controller of the Navy, Director of Naval Ordnance and Torpedoes, Rear-Admiral in the Atlantic Fleet, a Lord Commissioner of the Admiralty and Controller of the Navy, Vice-Admiral commanding the Atlantic Fleet, Vice-Admiral commanding the Second Division of the Home Fleet, and second Sea Lord of the Admiralty. He brilliantly distinguished himself in the command of the 'Red' Fleet at the naval manoeuvres of 1913. Rear-Admiral Madden, his Chief of Staff, who was also his brother-in-law, had already served with him at the Admiralty. Sir John Jellicoe was one of the officers chiefly responsible for the modern Navy of Britain, and enjoyed not only the admiration and complete confidence of his colleagues, but a peculiar popularity among all grades of British seamen. His nerve and self-possession were not less conspicuous than his professional skill, and in the wearing months ahead of him he had need of all resources of mind and character.

The British fleet had not fought a great battle at sea since Trafalgar. Since those days, only a century removed in time, the conditions of naval warfare had seen greater changes than in the span between Themistocles and Nelson. The old wooden walls, the unrifled guns, the boarders with their cutlasses, belonged to an earlier world. The fleet had no longer to scour the ocean for the enemy's fleet. Wireless telegraphy, aerial reconnaissance, and swift destroyers brought it early news of a foe. The gun power of a modern battleship would have wrecked the Spanish Armada with one broadside, and the enemy could now be engaged at a distance of many miles. Sea fighting was no more the clean and straightforward business of the old days. Destruction dwelt in every element when there was no sign of a hostile pennant. Aircraft dropped bombs from the clouds; unseen submarines, like swordfish, pierced the hull from the depths; and anywhere might lurk those mines which destroyed, like some convulsion of nature, with no human enemy near. Britain had to fight under new conditions, with new strategy and new weapons, with far greater demands on the intellect and a far more deadly strain on the nerves. Most things had changed, but two things remained unaltered – the cool daring of her sailors, and their conviction that the seas were the unquestionable heritage of their race.

Germany's naval policy in the first instance was, as we have seen, to refuse battle and withdraw her fleet behind prepared defences. To this decision various purposes contributed. She needed every soldier she possessed in the battle-line, and wished to avoid the necessity of guarding her Pomeranian coast with an army. Again, she hoped that public opinion in Britain, alarmed at the inactivity of its Navy, would compel an attack on the Elbe position – an attack which, she believed, would end in a British disaster. But her defence was not to be passive. By a mine and submarine offensive, pushed right up to the British coasts, she hoped to wear down Britain's superiority in capital ships and bring it in the end to an equality with her own. Then, and not till then, her High Seas Fleet was willing to sally forth and give battle.

To meet such Fabian tactics was no easy problem for Britain. The ordinary citizen hoped for a theatrical *coup*, a, full dress battle, or at the least a swift series of engagements with enemy warships. When nothing happened he began to think that something was amiss; he could not believe that it was a proof of success that nothing happened – nothing startling, that is to say, for every day had its full record of quiet achievement. As a consequence of this inactivity, false doctrines began to be current, in which, let it be said, the British naval leaders did not share. It was Britain's business to command the sea, and so long as an enemy fleet remained intact, that command was not absolute but qualified. The British fleet might be invincible, but it was not yet victorious. Its numerous minor activities were not undertaken for their own sake, as if in themselves they could give the final victory; they were forms of compulsion conceived in order to force the High Seas Fleet to come out and fight.

But that ultimate battle was not to be induced by measures which spelt suicide for the attacker. There were urgent tasks to be performed on the ocean – in protecting British trade, in cutting off enemy imports, in moving the troops of a world-wide Empire. So long as these were duly performed the practical mastery of the seas was in British hands, and it would have been criminal folly to throw away capital ships in an immediate attack on the fortified retreat of so accommodating an enemy. It was Britain's duty to perform this work of day-to-day sea control, and to be ready at any moment for the grand battle. On land an army fights its way yard by yard to a position from which it can deal a crushing blow. But a fleet needs none of these preliminaries. As soon as the enemy chooses to appear the battle can be joined. Hence Admiral von Ingenohl was right in saving his fleet for what he considered a better chance, and Britain was right in not forcing him unduly. Naval power should be used, not squandered, and the mightiest fleet on earth may be flung away on a fool's errand. It should not be forgotten that the strength of a fleet is a more brittle and less replaceable thing than the strength of an army. New levies can be called for on land, and tolerable infantry trained in a few months. But in the Navy it takes six years to make a junior officer, two years in normal times to build a cruiser, and three years to replace a battleship. A serious loss in fighting units is, for any ordinary naval war, an absolute, not a temporary, calamity. Sir John Jellicoe had to face a problem far more intricate than at the time was commonly believed. Not since the seventeenth century had Britain confronted a great naval Power whose base lay northward of the Straits of Dover. The older British sea strategy had assumed an enemy to southward of the English Channel, and on the southern coasts lay the best and securest of our naval ports. But now the foe lay across the stormy North Sea, 120,000 square miles in extent, into which he possessed two separate entries linked by the Kiel Canal. The east coast of Britain was now the fighting front, and on it lay a dozen vulnerable ports and no first-class fleet base. Before 1914 this situation had been foreseen, but it had not been adequately met. A first-class base was in preparation at Rosyth, but it was not yet ready, and in any case its outer anchorage was exposed to torpedo attack. In 1910 Cromarty had been selected as a fleet base, and Scapa in the Orkneys as a base for minor forces, and by July 1914 the fixed defences of the former were ready. But nothing had been done at Scapa, which from its position and size was selected as the Grand Fleet base on the outbreak of hostilities.

Jellicoe was aware of the German purpose of attrition, and realised that till his base was better secured his fleet was at the mercy of an enemy attack both in harbour and in its North Sea cruises, for he was still very short of mine-sweepers and destroyers to form a protective screen. He saw that Germany's chance lay in the uncertainty of the first month, when Britain had to perform many urgent naval tasks before her sea organisation was complete. He therefore decided to confine his Battle Fleet in ordinary conditions to operations in the more northern waters of the North Sea, and to establish in the southern waters a regular system of cruiser patrols, supported by periodic sweeps of the Battle Fleet. It was his business to avoid losses so far as possible from the casual mine and submarine, and at the same time to protect the British coasts from raids and be ready at any moment to fall upon the High Seas Fleet if it ventured out – a combination of calculated duties and incalculable hazards trying under any circumstances, and doubly trying when the Grand Fleet had not yet found a certain home.

The problems of the Grand Fleet were not the only ones confronting the Admiralty, which had to deal with all the waters of the world. There were three urgent tasks which had to be performed while a wider strategy was in process of shaping – the safe transport of the Expeditionary Force to France; the clearing and safeguarding of the trade routes; and the protection of the British coasts against enemy attacks, whether sporadic raids or a concerted invasion. Let us consider briefly how the three duties were fulfilled before turning to the events in the main battle area of the North Sea. The first, so far as concerned the British army, was brilliantly performed. There were no convoys, but both ends of the Channel were closed against raids, by the Dover Patrol at one end and the Anglo-French cruiser squadron at the other, while the Grand Fleet took up a station from which it could strike at the High Seas Fleet should Ingenohl venture out. During the crossing of the Expeditionary Force there was no sign of the enemy – a piece of supineness which can be explained only on the supposition that Germany considered the British army too trivial a matter to risk ships over. In the Mediterranean France had a similar problem. On 4 August Italy announced her neutrality, and Austria had not yet declared war on Britain or France, though it was clear that the declaration was imminent. The Austrian fleet was in the Northern Adriatic and had to be watched. Germany had in the Mediterranean the fastest armoured ships in her navy: the battle-cruiser *Goeben* and the fast light cruiser *Breslau* – two vessels admirably fitted to act as commerce destroyers. The British squadron consisted of three battle-cruisers, four heavy cruisers, and four light cruisers – a greatly superior force in gun power, but containing no vessel which was the *Goeben*'s equal in speed. It was their business to prevent the German ships making for the Atlantic, and to hunt them down at the earliest possible moment. But the situation was complicated by two factors – one, the necessary co-operation with the French; the other, the difficulty of receiving in time the orders of the British Admiralty, which had the strategic direction of the operations. In such a chase unless the man on the spot can act on his own responsibility the quarry may escape, for from hour to hour the situation changes.

The first orders of Admiral Sir Berkeley Milne, who commanded the British squadron, were to protect the movements of the French transports from Algiers to Toulon. At daybreak on the 4th the *Goeben* and *Breslau* appeared off the Algerian coast and fired a few shots at the coast towns of Bona and Philippeville. Meantime Admiral Souchon, in command of the *Goeben*, had received wireless instructions from Berlin to proceed to Constantinople. Admiral de Lapeyrère, commanding the Toulon fleet, decided on his own initiative to depart from his original instructions (which were to operate to the eastward of the transports) and to form convoys. The decision was sound, for his ships were too slow to hunt down the enemy, and by putting them alongside the transports he was in a better position for both defence and a blow at the Germans if they were shepherded westward.

This decision should have loft Admiral Milne's force to pursue the *Goeben*, but unfortunately his first instructions from the Admiralty were not cancelled, and this was the main cause of the fiasco which followed. Souchon, after feinting to the west, turned eastward and reached Messina on the 5th. Milne took up a position which he believed to be in accordance with his orders, and which would have cut off Souchon had he come westward again. But Souchon passed out of the southern end of the Straits in the evening, and if he could got clear of Admiral Troubridge in the mouth of the Adriatic, the way was open for him to the Dardanelles. Now Troubridge had with him no battle-cruiser, he had instructions from the Admiralty not to risk an action against a superior force, and he considered therefore that he was not entitled to fight unless he could manoeuvre the enemy into a favourable position. Souchon feinted towards the Adriatic, and then turned south-east for Cape Matapan. Troubridge gave up the chase when day broke on the 7th and slowed down, waiting on the British battle-cruisers which did not come. The *Gloucester* (Captain Howard Kelly), a ship scarcely larger than the *Breslau*, clung, however, to the enemy skirts, and fought a running fight till 1.50 p.m. on the 7th. Souchon was not yet out of danger, for when he reached the Ægean he heard that he would not be permitted to enter the Dardanelles, and was compelled for several days to cruise among the islands. Milne, who followed slowly, was soon within a hundred miles of the Germans, but believed that they were making for Alexandria, or about to break to join the Austrians. On the 9th Souchon heard the wireless of the British, and decided at all costs to run for Constantinople. At 8.30 p.m. on the 10th he was allowed to enter the Dardanelles.

The British failure was to have the most malign and far-reaching consequences. Souchon, perplexed by conflicting orders from Berlin, played, largely on his own responsibility, a bold game which succeeded. The British admirals, dutifully following their Admiralty's formal instructions, missed their chance. They were very properly exonerated from blame, for the mistake was the result of the new conditions of war. They received by wireless all the news that reached the Admiralty, and consequently had to keep their eyes turning every way instead of concentrating on the one vital object. In the old days an admiral would have been left to his general instructions, and, had he been a bold man, would have destroyed the enemy.

The second task was the clearing and safeguarding of the world's trade-routes. The first step lay with the Grand Fleet, for, as Sir Julian Corbett has well put it, 'since all the new enemy's home terminals lay within our own home waters, we could close them by the same disposition with which we ensured free access to our own'. But, the earths having been stopped, it was necessary to run down the quarries. All German cables were cut, and, except for wireless, her outlying ships were left without guidance from home. In every quarter of the globe British cruisers spread their net. German merchantmen in the ports of the Empire were detained, and hundreds of ships were made prize of in the high and the narrow seas. Some escaped to the shelter of neutral ports, especially to those of the United States, but none got back to Germany. In a week German seaborne commerce had ceased to exist, and on 14 August the Admiralty could announce that the passage of the Atlantic was safe. It was true that a few German cruisers and armed merchantmen were still at large. Admiral von Spee had in the Pacific the armoured cruisers *Scharnhorst* and *Gneisenau* and the light cruisers *Nürnberg*, *Leipzig*, and *Emden*; the light cruisers *Karlsruhe* and *Dresden* were in the Atlantic. But the number seemed too few and their life too precarious seriously to affect our commerce. The British Government very properly began by guaranteeing part of the risk of maritime insurance; but soon the rates fell of their own accord to a natural level, as it became clear how complete was our security. It was calculated at the outbreak of war that British losses in the first six months would rise to 10 per cent of vessels engaged in foreign trade. A return issued early in October showed that of her mercantile marine Britain had lost up to that date only 1.25 per cent., while Germany and Austria had each lost 10 per cent of their total shipping.

The third problem, the security of the British coast from invasion, loomed large in those early days. The curious inactivity of the enemy during the crossing of the Expeditionary Force seemed to presage a great surprise attack in the near future. The danger was much in Lord Kitchener's mind, and, considering that it was unsafe to leave the country without at least two regular divisions, he postponed the crossing of the 6th Division and brought it to East Anglia. The heavy ships of the Grand Fleet, owing to the risk of submarines, were ordered on 9 August to go north-west of the Orkneys, and since the enemy had located Scapa, a second war anchorage was established on the north-west coast of Scotland at Loch Ewe. They were brought east again on the 15th when the risk of invasion seemed greatest, and took up a midsea position in the latitude of Aberdeen, while Rear-Admiral Christian's Southern Force, which included the Harwich flotilla, and was now an independent command directly under the Admiralty, watched the southern waters. On the 17th, the immediate danger being over, the Grand Fleet returned to Loch Ewe. Against minor raids the protection of the coasts lay with the destroyer flotillas, which were organised in two classes, 'Patrol' and 'Local Defence'. Presently a vast auxiliary service was created from the mercantile marine, from the fishing fleets, from private yachts and motor boats. Britain became a nation in arms on the water as well as on the land, and her merchantmen became part of the Navy as in her ancient wars. Meantime she did not forget the major duty of watching and enticing to battle the German High Seas Fleet. Apart from the regular cruisers of the British fleet and the cruiser squadrons in the North Sea, the Harwich flotilla kept watch to the very edge of the German sanctuary. The German admiral's aim was to send out patrols which would entice the British destroyers inside the Bight of Heligoland and then to cut in behind them with his light cruisers. There was an attempt of this sort on 18 August; another on 21 August, when the German light cruiser *Rostock* had a narrow escape; but both were fruitless thrusts into the void.

A third operation on the night of 25 August laid mines off the Tyne and the Humber. At this time both sides overestimated the danger from submarines and were over-careful with their heavier ships; consequently any action was likely to be fought by only a fraction of the strength of the combatants. But the strategy of two opponents, however cautious, operated on converging lines which were certain sooner or later to meet, and the result was that 28 August, the day when Sir John French's army reached the Oise, saw the first important naval engagement of the war.

3

The War on Commerce

The Commerce Raiders – The Declaration of London

The third method of weakening British sea-power was by the attack upon merchantmen by light cruisers. Germany could send forth no new vessels of this type after the outbreak of war, and her activities were confined to those which were already outside the Narrow Seas, especially those under Admiral von Spee's command at Kiao-chau. So far as the present stage is concerned, we need mention only the *Emden* and the *Königsberg*. The former was to provide the world with a genuine tale of romantic adventure, always welcome among the grave realities of war, and in her short life to emulate the achievements and the fame of the *Alabama*. She appeared in the Bay of Bengal on 10 September, and within a week had captured seven large merchantmen, six of which she sank. Next week she arrived at Rangoon, where her presence cut off all sea communication between India and Burma. On 22 September she was at Madras, and fired a shell or two into the environs of the city, setting an oil tank on fire. On the 29th she was off Pondicherry, and the last day of the month found her running up the Malabar coast. There for the present we leave her, for the tale of her subsequent adventures belongs to another chapter. The *Königsberg* had her beat off the east coast of Africa. Her chief exploit was a dash into Zanzibar harbour, where, on 20 September, she caught the British cruiser *Pegasus* while in the act of repairing her boilers. The *Pegasus* was a seventeen-year-old ship of 2,135 tons, and had no chance against her assailant. She was destroyed by the *Königsberg*'s long-range fire.

The exploits of the two German commerce raiders were magnified because they were the exception, while the British capture of German merchantmen was the rule. We did not destroy our captures, because we had many ports to take them to, and they were duly brought before our prize courts. In addition, we had made havoc of Germany's converted liners. The *Kaiser Wilhelm der Grosse*, which had escaped from Bremerhaven at the beginning of the war, and which had preyed for a fortnight on our South Atlantic commerce, was caught and sunk by the *Highflyer* near the Cape Verde Islands. On 12 September the *Berwick* captured in the North Atlantic the *Spreewald*, of the Hamburg-Amerika line. On 14 September the *Carmania*, Captain Noel Grant, a British converted liner, fell in with a similar German vessel, the *Cap Trafalgar*, off the coast of Brazil. The action began at 9,000 yards, and lasted for an hour and three-quarters. The *Carmania* was skilfully handled, and her excellent gunnery decided the issue. Though the British vessel had to depart prematurely owing to the approach of a German cruiser, she left her antagonist sinking in flames.

These instances will suffice to show how active British vessels were in all the seas. The loss of a few light cruisers and a baker's dozen of merchantmen was a small price to pay for an unimpaired foreign trade and the practical impotence of the enemy. Modern inventions give the weaker Power a better chance for raiding than in the old days; but in spite of that our sufferings at this stage were small compared with those in any other of our great wars. It is instructive to contrast our fortunes during the struggle with Napoleon. Then, even after Trafalgar had been fought, French privateers made almost daily captures of English ships in our home waters. Our coasts were frequently attacked, and the inhabitants of the seaboard went for years in constant expectation of invasion. In the twenty-one years of war we lost 10,248 British ships. Further back in our history our inviolability was even more precarious. In the year after Agincourt the French landed in Portland. Seven years after the defeat of the Armada the Spanish burned Penzance and ravaged the Cornish coasts. In 1667 the Dutch were in the Medway and the Thames. In 1690 the French burned Teignmouth, and landed in Sussex; in 1760 they seized Carrickfergus; in 1797 they landed at Fishguard. In 1775 Paul Jones captured Whitehaven, and was the terror of our home waters. The most prosperous war has its casualties in unexpected places.

The opening stages of the war at sea, though they brought no dramatic *coup*, were of supreme importance in the history of the campaign. A very real crisis had been successfully tided over. Germany had missed a chance which she was never to recover, and her growing difficulties on the Eastern Front compelled her for a time to devote as much attention to the Baltic as to the North Sea. The British Army had safely crossed the Channel, and the French Algerian forces the Mediterranean. The seas of the world had been cleared of German commerce, and, except for a few stragglers, of German warships. The High Seas Fleet was under close observation, and flanking forces at Harwich, in the Humber, and at Rosyth waited on its appearance, while the Grand Fleet closed the northern exits of the North Sea. The Grand Fleet was as yet without a proper base, and the situation was still full of anxiety for its commander. Jellicoe's steadfastness in those difficult days, his caution which never sank into inaction, his boldness which never degenerated into folly, convinced his countrymen that in him they had the naval leader that the times required. The ill-informed might clamour, but the student of history remembered that it had never been an easy task to bring an enemy fleet to book. In the

Revolution Wars, Britain had to wait a year for the first naval battle, Howe's victory of 1 June; while Nelson lay for two years before Toulon, and Cornwallis for longer before Brest. 'They were dull, weary, eventless months' – to quote Admiral Mahan,

> those months of waiting and watching of the big ships before the French arsenals. Purposeless they surely seemed to many, but they saved England. The world has never seen a more impressive demonstration of the influence of sea-power upon its history. Those far-distant, storm-beaten ships, upon which the Grand Army never looked, stood between it and the dominion of the world.

In Nelson's day Britain had one advantage of which she was now deprived. She was not hampered by a code of maritime law framed in the interests of unmaritime nations. The Declaration of Paris of 1856, among other provisions, enacted that a neutral flag covered enemy's merchandise except contraband of war, and that neutral merchandise was not capturable even under the enemy's flag. This Declaration, which was not accepted by the United States, had never received legislative ratification from the British Parliament; but Britain regarded herself as bound by it, though various efforts had been made to get it rescinded in time of peace by those who realised how greatly it weakened the belligerent force of a sea Power. The Declaration of London of 1909 made a further effort to codify maritime law (Parliamentary Paper, Cd. 4554 of 1909. 61). It was signed by the British plenipotentiaries, though Parliament refused to pass the statutes necessary to give effect to certain of its provisions. In some respects it was more favourable to Britain than the Declaration of Paris, but in others it was less favourable, and it was consistently opposed by most good authorities on the subject. Generally speaking, it was more acceptable to a nation like Germany than to one in Britain's case. The following are a few examples of the way in which it impaired our naval power: it was made easy to break a blockade, for the right of a blockading Power to capture a blockade-runner did not cover the whole period of her voyage and was confined to ships of the blockading force (Articles 14, 16, 17, 19, 20); stereotyped lists of contraband and non-contraband were drawn up, instead of the old custom of leaving the question to the discretion of the Prize Court (Articles 22, 23, 24, 25, 28); a ship carrying contraband could only be condemned if the contraband formed more than half its cargo; a belligerent warship could destroy a neutral vessel without taking it to a port for judgement; the transfer of an enemy vessel to a neutral flag was presumed to be valid if effected more than thirty days before the outbreak of war (Article 55); the question of the test of enemy property was left in confusion (Article 58); a neutral vessel, if accompanied by any sort of warship of her own flag, was exempt from search; belligerents in neutral vessels on the high seas were exempt from capture (based on Article 45). With the Declaration of London would go most of the naval findings of the Hague Conference of 1907. The British delegates who assented to the Declaration of London proceeded on the assumption that in any war of the future Britain would be neutral, and so endeavoured to reduce the privileges of maritime belligerents. When war broke out the British Government announced that it accepted the Declaration of London as the basis of its maritime practice. The result was a state of dire confusion, for the consequences of the new law had never been fully realised. Under it, for example, the captain of the *Emden* could justify his sinking of British ships instead of taking them to a port for adjudication. One provision, which seems to have been deduced from it, was so patently ridiculous that it was soon dropped – that belligerents (that is, enemy reservists) in neutral ships were not liable to arrest. Presently successive Orders in Council, instigated by sheer necessity, altered the Declaration of London beyond recognition. The truth is, that Britain was engaged in so novel a war that many of the older rules could not be applied. Germany had become a law unto herself, and the Allies were compelled in self-defence to frame a new code, which should comply not only with the half-dozen great principles of international equity, but with the mandates of common sense.

4

The First Battle of the Marne

The Defence of Paris – Kluck Changes Direction – Eve of the Marne – Battle of the Marne – German Occupation of Belgium

The opening of September brought round the Day of Sedan, that anniversary which for more than forty years has been the national festival of the German Empire. Berlin witnessed a demonstration that was designed to advertise to the Fatherland and to the world that triumphs were being won no less glorious than the victories of 1870. Escorted by brilliant troops, with bands playing patriotic airs, many captured guns were drawn through the gaily decked streets. There one might see Belgian and French cannon and a few British pieces, carefully repaired and remounted to conceal the fact that they had not been taken by a dashing charge but picked up shattered and useless on some Picardy battlefield. The momentary depression caused by the entry of Britain into the war had passed. In their chief newspapers they read that words were too weak to describe the magnitude of the German triumph.

On 26 August Galliéni had been appointed Governor of Paris, and his predecessor, Michel, had volunteered to serve under him. The defences of the French capital had been widely extended since the siege of 1870, when the circuit of the outlying forts was about 32 miles. The drawback of such a vast entrenched camp was that it required a huge army for its garrison, and though its extent made investment almost impossible, no such operation was required for the attack. Further, it was an open secret that even the outer and newer defences were not of any great strength. They were armed with old guns, and there was a deficiency of stores for completing the defences between the forts.

Paris had refused to be alarmed by the exploits of German airmen who made daring flights over the city and dropped bombs into the streets. Curiosity seemed to banish fear. Instead of taking refuge under cover, men, women, and children stood gazing up at the enemy's war-hawks. When in the last days of August, however, the official news at last admitted that the Allied armies were everywhere in retreat, when numbers of strayed and wounded soldiers appeared in the streets, and the distant growling of cannon and the blowing up of bridges could be heard from the north-eastern suburbs, there came a wave of anxiety and alarm. A considerable exodus began of the well-to-do classes, who dreaded a siege and could afford to make a long journey. Those who were in the secrets of the Government had most cause for alarm. On the 28th it was resolved to declare Paris an open town and abandon it, but on the 30th this decision was cancelled, and Galliéni announced that he had received Joffre's orders to defend the capital against all invaders and would fulfil the mandate to the end – '*jusqu'au bout*', a phrase soon to become a national watchword. On the night of the 31st it was known that the Government meant to leave the city, and two days later the President and the Ministers departed for Bordeaux. The step awoke disquieting memories of 1870. Already the enemy was as near to the towers of Notre Dame as is Windsor to the dome of St Paul's.

But in truth there was no parallel. The Allied armies had, indeed, suffered defeat in a gigantic clash of arms, compared to which the battles of 1870 were small engagements; but they had not been destroyed. They were still intact, and ready to measure themselves once more against the invader. They had trained men ready to make good their losses. The Germans had failed in their main object – to put masses of their opponents permanently out of action in a decisive battle, so that the subsequent operations would be merely a gathering up of the fruits of victory. Apart from the military position, the *moral* of the nation was wholly different from 1870. There had been no easy confidence of victory, no boasting, no singing of music-hall catches, when the French armies marched north and east. War had come to France as a solemn duty, long foreseen – a national sacrifice of which the cost had been counted. In 1914 France had forgotten all lesser rivalries, and was united in one grave and inflexible purpose. In M. Poincaré she had as President a man whose brilliant attainments and sober good sense carried on the best traditions of Republican statesmanship.

In every campaign there comes a moment of high tide, when the strength of one of the combatants is stretched taut, and on the fighting of the next day or two depends the success or failure of a great strategical plan. That moment was now approaching in the Western theatre. By one of the mysterious anticlimaxes so common in war, a complete change was coming over the scene. The time had arrived for the Allies to strike back and go forward. With the battles on the Marne – battles to be fought on a front of more than a hundred miles – began a new act in the drama.

We must first consider the plan of German Great Headquarters. There is no evidence that at any time they regarded Paris as the main object of attack, though all their armies were cheered by the promise of a speedy entry into the French capital. For investment they simply had not the men. By the end of August, when the resolution of the French Government and of Galliéni was apparent, they may well have been convinced that even the capture of Paris would not mean the demoralisation of France. On the night of 2 September Kluck was informed that the intention was to drive the French in a south-easterly direction away from the capital, and was ordered to follow in echelon behind Bülow and make himself responsible for the flank protection of the German front. That he chose to disregard this order was not the fault of Great Headquarters.

But in a sense he was justified in his disobedience. Great Headquarters wished to have both success and security, and the two were incompatible. Their urgent need was a decisive victory. Things were in a perilous state in the East. Austria was stumbling from failure to failure, and would presently need help. Already corps had had to be sent eastward from France, and large bodies of troops were detained at Antwerp, at Brussels, at Maubeuge, and along the ever lengthening communications. Kluck and Bülow, the marching wing of the advance, had been compelled to shed brigades as if there were no armies of France before them. By this time the German forces had lost any chance of superiority in numbers. Their men, who had broken every record for their speed of advance, were, as the daily reports of the army commanders told them, very weary. The German people might be confident and hilarious, but Great Headquarters knew that their fortunes were on a razor edge. At all costs they must bring the enemy to action at once and secure a decision.

The true criticism of Germany is not that out of pedantry she forewent her chance of demoralising the enemy by the seizure of his capital. Where she failed was far back in her whole conception of enveloping strategy. To envelop great armies without a colossal superiority in numbers was from the start a forlorn hope. It was a plan born of over-confidence and one contrary to the doctrine of Clausewitz, who had always taught that the manoeuvre was impossible unless the enemy force was wholly engaged with the attackers' centre. Kluck, on whom the main duty of envelopment lay, fulfilled what he believed to be the spirit of the orders of Great

Headquarters, but disobeyed them in detail. He saw Germany's need for a decisive battle, and he was resolved to give it her. For this reason he refused to obey the order of 28 August to march to the south-west, and on the 30th began to turn south and south-east to close in on the II Army. His object was to find the operative flank of the enemy, which he conceived to be the French Fifth Army. Such we may assume to have been the reasoning of the commander of the I Army. His whole thoughts were directed to forcing battle, and with this in mind he deliberately neglected the orders of 2 September to echelon himself behind Bülow. He pressed on till on 5 September he was south of the Grand Morin. In about thirty days his army had covered 312 miles without a rest – an achievement of which much of the renown must rest with its dogged commanding officer.

The last stage, presenting as it did a flank to the enemy, has been and must continue to be among the most sharply criticised movements of the campaign. But the failure in which it resulted does not necessarily involve an extreme reprobation of the responsible general. Kluck was left with no other choice. If an enveloping battle was required, it was the only means to force it. He did not hear till the evening of 5 September that the German left wing, which he had believed to be triumphantly advancing, was checked before the eastern fortresses. He thought that the French armies of the centre and right were so closely engaged that they could not spare troops to move to the left behind the French front. He erred, too, in underestimating the British army. He thought that it was broken, demoralised, and out of action.

About midnight on 31 August, Maunoury telegraphed to Galliéni that Kluck seemed to be sheering off from Paris. But it was not until the 3rd that indisputable evidence came. Gallon issued a note to the garrison warning them of the apparent change in the German march, and at once communicated with Joffre. He received no reply that day, and indeed seems not to have been aware of the orders for the further retreat issued on 1 September. Next morning he took the matter into his own hands. At 9 a.m. on the 4th he warned the Sixth Army that he intended to use it for an attack on Kluck's flank, and ordered it to be ready to march that afternoon and begin the general movement next day. Then he proceeded to telephone to Joffre, who from captured maps had learned about Kluck on the evening of the 2nd, but who had to wait till the Sixth Army was disengaged, which did not happen till the 4th. At 2 50 p.m. the Commander-in-Chief authorised the advance of Maunoury's army for the next day. Meantime Galliéni had received orders, issued two days before, directing the British army to go behind the Seine. Such a move would wreck his plans, so he hastened with Maunoury to the British Headquarters, from which, unfortunately, Sir John French was absent. The British retirement, therefore, could not be stayed on that day. At this most critical juncture it is obvious that the machinery of direction was difficult owing to the several semi-independent commands. But Joffre showed no indecision. His mind was made up when the news about Kluck's march was verified, and he struck as soon as the Sixth Army was ready. During the evening of 4 September he issued his first orders for battle.

***

The main German forces lay in a semicircle 200 miles wide and 30 miles deep, from Verdun to the skirts of Paris. Against this array the Allied front lay in concave form, from Maunoury west of the Ourcq to Sarrail bent in a coil round Verdun.

It will be observed that the concave arc of the Allied main front rested on 5 September on two fortified areas, Paris and Verdun; that there intervened a tract of difficult hilly country between the Meuse and Nancy; and that its detached right wing held the gateway to Lorraine. It was a situation to cause acute anxiety, for if Castelnau failed to bar the door, the whole line would be turned. But, assuming his success, the position had obvious advantages. Its hinterland was magnificently served by roads and railways, so that troops could be moved easily behind the front. The mass of the Argonne would impede the enemy's lateral communications, while his main line of supply was already desperately long and seriously congested by the resistance of Maubeuge. The chances of outflanking were declining for him – except in Lorraine – since the 60 miles of upland between Verdun and Nancy made a large operation difficult, while Kluck at the other end was himself outflanked. Moreover, the numerical advantage was clearly with the Allies. Between Verdun and Paris the latter had now a superiority in manpower equivalent to at least two first-line corps. Yet, when all has been said, the decision to give battle involved many hazards. The enemy had reserves detained at Maubeuge and in Belgium which might at any moment arrive, and Joffre had none. Could Castelnau hold in Lorraine? Could Sarrail prevent a break into Burgundy? Above all, could Langle and Foch stand against the united assault of the Duke of Würtenberg, Hausen, and Bülow? To these questions a less bold man than the French Commander-in-Chief might well have returned a desponding answer. It is not the least of Joffre's titles to admiration that, having failed once, he had the courage a second time to stake everything on a plan where failure could not be retrieved.

In telling the tale of the Marne it is simplest to group the action under three heads: the fight of the Allied left – Maunoury, the British, and Franchet d'Esperey – in their effort to envelop the enveloper, the resistance of the Allied centre and right centre – Foch, Langle, and Sarrail – against the German attempt to pierce their front; and the stand of the Allied right – Castelnau and Dubail against the Bavarians at Nancy. Both sides recognised the gravity of the coming battle. On the morning of 6 September the French Generalissimo issued from the old château of Marshal Marmont at Châtillon-sur-Seine the following order to his men:

At the moment when a battle is about to begin on which the salvation of the country depends, it is my duty to remind you that the time has gone for looking back. We have but one business on hand – to attack and repel the enemy. Any troops which can no longer advance will at all costs hold the ground they have won, and allow themselves to be slain where they stand rather than give way. This is no time for faltering, and it will not be tolerated.

We possess an order issued to the German 8th Corps at Vitry: 'The object of our long and arduous marches has been achieved. The principal French troops have been forced to accept battle after having been continually driven back. The great decision is without doubt at hand.'

Upon the 6th, the great day, Maunoury's Sixth Army advanced with hope and resolution. At first it seemed to be succeeding, but suddenly it found the enemy resistance stiffen and the advance came to a standstill. Kluck had been fully warned of the surprise envelopment and had taken steps to meet it. The whole German plan was in process of revision. The old enveloping scheme was now impossible, but another had revealed itself. Kluck would turn and deal with Maunoury, outflank him on the right and drive him back on Pans. If the Allied centre could be routed, the decisive battle would have been won, for French and Franchet d'Esperey would be penned between Pans and the victorious Germans wheeling to the right. The plan involved one immense hazard. Bülow and Kluck would be operating in different directions, one to the south-east and the other to the north-west, and every hour they would feel the '*effet de ventouse*', and tend to draw farther apart. Could the void be filled sufficiently to keep French and Franchet d'Esperey at arm's length?

The day of the 7th was one of long and desperate battle. All possible reserves were brought in, and it became a race who should grow faster. Kluck extended his right with a view to envelopment, and Maunoury duly extended his left, but he was desperately short of reserves. That evening the French Sixth Army, as it clung to the skirts of the blazing hills, might well have viewed the future with dismay. It was the anvil for the hammer, and it could not see the thrust which was to cripple the hammer arm. Reinforcements were sent from Paris, and since the need was urgent many of them covered the 40 miles in Paris taxi-cabs. Maunoury attacked on his wing, but in spite of desperate efforts failed to make way. The old game had been played, and once again the enveloper had become the enveloped. Maunoury and his men were at the very limit of their strength. But French and Franchet d'Esperey were moving fast, and the gap between Kluck and Bülow was widening. A rent of 30 miles stretched between them. If Maunoury could endure for twelve hours more his opponent must retire or be destroyed.

Wednesday 9 September, a day of rain and high winds, was everywhere the crisis of the battle. For Maunoury it seemed that the crisis had passed, and he was beaten. He was heavily outnumbered; his troops were hungry, ragged, parched with thirst, and bone-weary. For a moment it looked as though all were over and Kluck would soon be hammering at the gates of Paris. Suddenly there came strange news from the front line. The enemy had evacuated their positions! This eleventh-hour salvation of the Sixth Army was due to the doings on the 9th of the Fifth Army and the British. Straight through the ever-widening gap, and against Kluck's flank and rear, the British were marching, while Franchet d'Esperey was driving Bülow's right before him like a flock before a shepherd.

By midday on the 9th the left wing of the Allies had won an indisputable victory. But their centre was still hard pressed and on the verge of breaking. But Foch, who had against him Bülow's VI Army, held firm. The 'last ounce of resolution' won. Beyond doubt, Foch's stubborn defence was one of the main causes of the Allied victory. Farther eastward in the battle line the actions of the French Third and Fourth Armies were stubborn pieces of stonewalling against an antagonist slightly superior in numbers. In Lorraine, Dubail and Castelnau held firm against the Bavarians.

On the evening of 9 September, in a gale of wind and rain, the right wing of the German armies was in full retreat before Maunoury and French, Foch and Franchet d'Esperey. On the 11th the Fifth Army was in Épernay; on the 12th it was in Rheims, while Foch entered Châlons. That same day Langle had recovered Vitry-le-François and Revigny, and on the 13th the Imperial Crown Prince had fallen back to Montfaucon before Sarrail, who had now recovered his direct communications with the capital. The Battle of the Marne was over, and a new battle was beginning.

The First Battle of the Marne ranks by common consent as the greatest, because the most significant, contest of the war. In one sense it was not decisive; it did not destroy one of the combatant forces like Jena, or make peace inevitable like Sadowa and Solferino. The German losses were not overwhelming; they kept their armies in being, and were able to make a masterly retirement. But it was decisive in another sense; for it meant the defeat of the first German plan of campaign, and it utterly transformed the strategical situation. The avalanche designed to crush French resistance in a month had failed of its purpose. The 'battle without a morrow' had gone beyond hope; the battle had been fought and the morrow was come. Thereafter Germany was compelled

Vosges glens. It was a tale of horrors which revealed a new thing in war, and to read the full text of it we must return to Belgium.

The terrorisation of Belgium was no part of the original German plan. The Emperor and his advisers had sincerely hoped that she would for due consideration sell Germany the right of passage. Had she done that, we may be certain that the march through Belgium would have been a miracle of decorum. Failing the right of entry, the German leaders believed that the complete repulse of the Belgian forces, the occupation of her capital, and the sight of the omnipotent German armies, would awe her into an abject, if sullen, submission. If, on the other hand, the nation should prove refractory, the position might be serious, and would demand stringent measures. For through the plain of Belgium and the hilly Ardennes ran the communications of the great armies now sweeping towards Paris. No first-line troops could be spared to guard them; only reserves, and a limited number of these. The process of Germanisation was at once set going. Marshal von der Goltz had been nominated military governor of Belgium; governors were appointed for districts and cities; fines were levied on the different localities; the clocks were changed to German time; German currency was introduced, and German nomenclature adopted. Everything was done to convince the Belgian people that the conquest of Belgium was an accomplished fact.

But the Belgian people obstinately refused to be convinced. The field army was not content with the security of Antwerp. On 24 August it made a sortie and took Malines, which commanded the best railway connection between Germany and West Flanders. On 27 August three battalions of British Marines occupied Ostend. With the British at Ostend, and the Belgians at Malines, the German forces in West Flanders might be caught in a trap and the communications on which the great armies depended seriously imperilled. The Belgian sortie had the valuable result of depriving Kluck of reinforcements. A second sortie on 9 September gave the Belgians Termonde and

Aerschot, but by the 13th they had retired, when the Germans brought up a fresh division of the 3rd Reserve Corps. Thereafter there was nothing before them but a slow falling back upon Antwerp, and the enemy began to close in on that devoted city.

After this gallant diversion the misery which is inseparable from war increased to something like a reign of terror. Belgium was a most vulnerable land. The long-descended habits of its people made of it a hive of industry; its fields were tilled like gardens, its little cities were history embodied and visible, full of precious tokens of their stormy past and industrious present. Everywhere was a civilisation rich, warm, compact, and continuous. In this most habitable land was to be seen some of the finest stone- and brickwork of the Flemish Renaissance, and whole streets and towns might have come intact from the fifteenth century. Everywhere were ancient church spires, rising far over the flats, and sweetening the air with their carillons; and in town and hamlet alike were masterpieces of Flemish tapestry and painting – the handiwork of Rubens and Vandyck, and Bouts and Matsys. A bull on a common is a harmless creature, but he will play havoc in the cabinet of the virtuoso.

The unhappy consequence of those deeds in France and Belgium was to destroy among the Allies the chivalrous respect for their opponents which is one of the antiseptics of war – that feeling which found expression in Whitman's cry, 'My enemy is dead, a man divine as myself is dead.' The impression left by the spectacle of the wonderful machine, the proudest achievement of the modern German spirit, with its astonishing efficiency up to a point, its evidence of unwearied care and endless industry, remained oddly childish, like a toy on the making of which a passion of affection has been lavished. It was a perversion, an aberration, not a healthy development from the great Germany of the past. And the profession of a morality above all humble conventions, so far from impressing the world as godlike, seemed nothing but the swagger of a hobbledehoy. It was not barbarism, which is an honest and respectable thing; it was decivilisation, which stands to civilisation as a man's decay stands to his prime.

What of the little people who bore the brunt of this savagery? Britain, the old ally and protector of Belgium, did the little in her power to mitigate this suffering. Did the crowds that stared curiously at the haggard grey-faced people who arrived by every boat at Folkestone, and soon began to throng the London streets – all classes of society – all forms of raiment – realise that they were looking upon the results of the most heroic sacrifice in modern history? The miracle was the more wonderful from its unexpectedness. We are ready to cheer Mr Greatheart when he advances to meet the giant; it is splendid, but we knew it would happen, for after all giant-killing is his profession. But when some homely pilgrim, without shining armour or great sword, seizes his staff and marches stoutly to a more desperate conflict we do not cheer. It is a marvel which dims the eyes and catches at the heart-strings.

Much was due to her King, the most purely heroic figure of the day. No monarch of the great ages more nobly fulfilled the ideal of kingship. He raised Belgium to the position of a Great Power, if moral dignity has any meaning in the world. There can be no finer tribute to him than some words spoken by a refugee, a quiet little man who had lost family and livelihood, and seemed to peer out upon a new world like a dazed child:

> Frankly, we did not think we could have behaved so well. You will understand that we are a small people, a people of traders, not greatly interested in high politics or war. We needed a leader, and God sent that leader. We owe everything to our King. He has made of our farmers and tradesmen a nation of heroes. When the war is over he will rule over a broken land and a very poor people, but for all that he will be one of the greatest kings in the world.

5

From the Aisne to the First Battle of Ypres

Battle of the Aisne – The Race to the Sea – Fall of Antwerp – Fight of the 2nd and 3rd Corps – Battle of the Yser – The First Battle of Ypres – Death of Lord Roberts

The place chosen by the German armies for their stand at the end of their retreat from the Marne was upon the Aisne – not upon the line of the river itself, but the crest of the plateau beyond it, at an average of 2 miles from the stream's side. A more perfect position could not be found. It commanded all the crossings of the river and most of the roads on the south bank, and even if the Allies reached the north side, the outjutting spurs gave excellent opportunities for an enfilading fire. The blindness of the crests made it almost impossible for the German trenches to be detected. Eastward towards Neufchâtel the position was still stronger. Before them they had a natural glacis, and across the river they could command the bare swelling downs for miles. The fine crossed the Champagne-Pouilleuse, with the Bazancourt–Grand-Pré railway behind it, and rested on the Argonne, to the east of which the army of the Imperial Crown Prince was ringing Verdun on north and east from Montfaucon to the shaggy folds of the Woëvre. Germany in retreat had lost the offensive, but had snatched again the initiative; she was about to dictate to her enemies the form of the struggle – to compel them to accept a trench battle, well suited to her own stubborn and mechanical genius.

When the Allied troops on 13 and 14 September first became dimly cognisant of the nature of the German position they did not realise its full meaning. They could not know that they were on the glacis of the new type of fortress which Germany had built for herself, and which was presently to embrace about a fifth of Europe. On the 11th and the 12th they had believed the enemy to be in full retreat, and when they felt his strength their generals were puzzled to decide whether he meant to make a serious stand, or was only fighting delaying actions preparatory to a further retirement to the Sambre or beyond. Had Joffre known the strength of the Aisne positions, he would probably from the beginning have endeavoured to turn them on the west, or what would give far more decisive results – to break through the Crown Prince's army in the east, and so get between them and their own country. As it was, he decided to make a frontal attack, which would be the natural course against an enemy in retreat who had merely halted to show his fangs. The fighting on the Aisne was to continue for many weary months, and to show a slow and confusing series of trench attacks sandwiched between long periods of stagnant cannonades. But the First Battle of the Aisne in the strict sense of the word – the battle during which the Allied plan was a frontal assault – lasted for six days only, and on the widest interpretation for no more than a fortnight. It represented a delaying action, while Germany changed from her first to her second plan of campaign.

Sunday the 13th was the beginning of the passage of the Aisne. The French Sixth Army constructed pontoons at various places under a heavy fire, and several divisions were got over. To the east the British operations during the day were full of interest. The 3rd Corps attempted the section between Soissons and Venizel. The Aisne was in high flood, and the heavy rain made every movement difficult. Its bridging train attempted to build a heavy pontoon bridge on the French right, but this failed, like the similar French attempt, owing to the fire of the German howitzers. At Venizel there was a road bridge, not completely destroyed, which was mended sufficiently to allow of the passage of field guns. A pontoon bridge was built beside it, and early in the afternoon the whole of the 4th Division were across, and cooperating with the left of the 2nd Corps against the German positions at Chivres and Vregny. Farther east the 2nd Corps had been in difficulties. The open space between the river and the heights opposite Missy were a death-trap from German guns. But crossings were made by means of rafts, boats, and the broken girders of a bridge, with the flooded river rushing over this precarious foothold. On the evening of that difficult Sunday we may summarise the situation by saying that, on the 15 miles of front allotted to the British, they had crossed the river at most points, and had entrenched themselves well up the farther slopes. High honour was won by our artillery, working under desperate conditions, and most notably by the Royal Engineers, who wrought with all the coolness they had once shown at the Delhi Gate, and went on calmly with their work of flinging across pontoon bridges and repairing damaged girders in places where it seemed that no human being could live.

During the night of the 13th, while the German searchlights played upon the sodden riverside fields, Joffre decided that the following day must be made to reveal the nature of the German plans. Accordingly on the 14th, while the engineers were busy strengthening the new bridges and repairing some of the old for heavy traffic, a general advance was begun along the whole western section of the front. It was not long before the Allied commanders realised the nature of the trenches which the enemy had prepared. This was no halting-place for a rearguard action, but the long-thought-out defences of an army ready and willing for battle. Everywhere as soon as they felt the enemy they began to dig themselves in on the slopes – their first real experience of a task which was soon to become their staple military duty. By the 18th they had got ready their trenches, and were settling down to this novel warfare. The battle of the Aisne, so far as Maunoury and French were concerned, degenerated into a sullen trench warfare, with no possibility of any great movement.

But if the gravest peril had gone, the discomfort remained. The first two weeks at the Aisne were one long downpour. To them succeeded a week of St Martin's summer, and then came autumn damp and mist. On the sides of the plateau the chalky mud seemed bottomless. It filled the ears and eyes and throats of the men, it plastered their clothing, and mingled generously with their diet.

The situation demanded a counter-offensive which should promise more speedy results than a frontal assault upon the Aisne plateau. Accordingly, as early as 16 September, Joffre changed his strategy. He resolved to play the German game, fling out his line to the West, and attempt to envelop Kluck's right. The true offensive of the Allies was now on the extreme left, where Maunoury had extended his flank up the Oise, and the armies of Castelnau and Maud'huy were lengthening the line towards the north. In the last week of September, Maud'huy's Tenth Army was engaged in a struggle for the Albert plateau. He never attained it, and when the fighting ceased his line lay well to the west of Bapaume, and behind the upper Ancre – a situation which was to be of vital importance two years later. But, as his divisions came up, his left went on extending till presently it covered Arras and Lens, and on 3 October his left corps, the 21st, was 3 miles west of Lille. The French left now ran for 70 miles north of Compiègne, almost to the Belgian frontier. It was a comprehensive piece of outflanking, and it bent back the German right from its apex on the heights above the forest of Laigue in the shape of a gigantic

L. A little more pressure, and it looked as if the angle might be made so acute that the great Oise railway would be uncovered and the main line of German communications on the west made untenable. If that happened there must be a general retirement; for, though the Germans had other lines of supply, they had none which could keep their right and right-centre rapidly fed with the vast quantities of heavy ammunition on which the holding of their Aisne position depended.

But presently it appeared that this flanking strategy was being met by another. The Germans were themselves taking the offensive, and stretching out their right, not to conform with, but to outstrip our movement. It was becoming a race for the northern sea.

As early as 16 September, Sir John French had become anxious about his position, and had reached the conclusion that the British army was in the wrong place. At Mons it had been the extreme left, now it was almost the centre of the Allied line. This meant constant difficulties with supplies and communications, for these now ran through Paris to the Atlantic coast, and so crossed those of Maunoury, Castelnau, and Maud'huy. If, on the other hand, the British were transferred once more to the left wing, they could draw upon the Channel ports, and would be within easy reach of home. Above all, the British Commander-in-Chief saw the dawning of a dangerous German offensive, directed especially against Britain, and aiming at the possession of Calais and the Channel ports. News was arriving that the great fortress of Antwerp was in extremity, and once it fell a fresh army could be hurled at the gap between Lille and the sea. A campaign is full of surprises, and this one had by now taken on the character of a siege. Germany had been forced to accept the position, and was penned behind a line of entrenchments running in the West from Lille to Switzerland. The one sally-port was West Flanders, and without delay that bolt-hole must be stopped. On 29 September he formally approached Joffre, and on 1 October the French Commander-in-Chief accepted the plan.

The French and British Staffs worked in perfect concord, and the result was a brilliant piece of transport. We won the race to the sea, but only by the narrowest margin. The Germans' sally was stronger than we had dreamed, and a host of new corps, of which the investing force from Antwerp was only a small part, was about to pour westward over the Flanders flats. How the pass was held will be the subject of a later chapter. The movement of the British northward marked the end of the second phase of the war. In the first, which ended before the Marne, the Allies were on the defensive before the great German 'out-march'. In the second, which included the Battles of the Marne and the Aisne, they had the offensive; but after the defeat of the Marne the Germans regained the initiative, and compelled the Allies to accept the kind of battle they had chosen. Presently the Allies changed their plans, and endeavoured to hoist the enemy with his own petard, the enveloping movement; but, while seeking to envelop him, they found themselves in danger of envelopment. He was soon to possess himself of both the initiative and the offensive, and in the dark winter months his opponents replied with the very strategy he had practised on the Aisne, and dug themselves into trenches from which he could not oust them.

Sir John French, when he began the march to the sea, thought less of defence than attack. He expected that in a few weeks he would have under him a force of ten infantry and four cavalry divisions with which to turn the German right and swing eastward along the coast. But on 2 October he heard from Kitchener that Antwerp was in imminent danger, and on the 9th came the news of its fall.

* * *

With the news of the fall of Antwerp the original Allied plan was replaced by a second. The Belgian army would retire by Bruges and Ghent to the line of the Yser to protect the Allied left. Lille and La Bassée must be held by the Allies, and the British, pivoting on the latter place, would swing south-eastward and threaten the north-western communications of the vast German front, which now ran from somewhere near Toumai southward to the Aisne Heights. In the last resort, if the Allies were forestalled in La Bassée and Lille, the strategy of Marlborough might be used, and, instead of a frontal attack, an enveloping movement could be attempted from the line of the Lys against the right flank of the main German armies. The Germans were from the start well-informed as to the Allied movements, and divined Joffre's intention. By the end of September they had begun the transference of first-line corps from the southern part of their front. For them, not less than for the Allies, it was a race to the salt water. To the Allies' scheme they sought to oppose a counter offensive which would give them Calais and the Channel ports, and ultimately the Seine valley for an advance to Paris. To succeed they must be first through the sally-port between La Bassée and the sea. The 40 miles between Lille and Nieuport became suddenly the critical terrain of the war.

On 8 October Foch, who had been appointed to the general command over all the Allied troops north of Maunoury, was at Doullens, some 20 miles north of Amiens. There he was visited by Sir John French, who arranged with him a plan of operations. In all likelihood the Germans would attack the points of junction of the Allied armies – always the weak spots in a front – and it was necessary to determine these points with some care. The road between Béthune and Lille was fixed as the dividing line between the British command and Maud'huy. If an advance were possible it would be eastward, when the British right and the French left would be directed upon Lille.

During the first three weeks of October the British army was coming into line north of Maud'huy. On 11 October Smith-Dorrien, with the British 2nd Corps, had marched from Abbeville to the line of the canal between Aire and Béthune. Sir John French's plan at this time for the 2nd Corps was a rapid dash upon La Bassée and Lille. Smith-Dorrien, however, found that the enemy were in great strength – four cavalry divisions and several Jäger battalions holding the road to Lille. He resolved to try to isolate La Bassée. His object was to wheel to his right pivoting on Givenchy, and get astride the La Bassée–Lille road, so as to threaten the right flank and rear of the enemy's position on the high ground south of La Bassée. On the 13th the wheel commenced, but it met with strong resistance. On the 15th a brilliant advance drove the enemy off the Estaires–La Bassée road. On the 17th Aubers was taken, and late that evening Herlies was carried at the point of the bayonet. This was the end of the movement of the 2nd Corps. They were now up against the wall of the main German line, the centre of the Sixth Army, and no further progress was made.

The 3rd Corps, under Pulteney, destined for the position on the left of the 2nd Corps, had completed its detrainment at Saint-Omer on the night of the 11th. It marched to Hazebrouck, where it remained during the 12th, and the next day moved generally eastward. Pulteney's aim was to get east of Armentières, astride the Lys, and join up the Ypres and La Bassée sections of the front. By the evening of the 15th he was on the Lys. Next day he entered Armentières, and on the 17th had pushed beyond it. It was now ascertained that the Germans were holding in some strength a line running from Radinghem in the south, through Pérenchies, to Frelinghien on the Lys, while the right bank of the river below Frelinghien was held as far as Wervicq. As a matter of fact the 3rd Corps was now approaching the main German position as the 2nd Corps about the same time was finding it at Aubers and

Herlies. They found themselves firmly held at all points, and their position on the night of the 18th and on the 19th represented the farthest line held by this section of our front. One link was still necessary to connect the 3rd Corps with the infantry farther north. This was provided by the two divisions of Allenby's cavalry corps. By this time the 4th Corps was in Flanders, and the Belgian army, very weary and broken, was in the forest of Houthulst, north-east of Ypres, and had begun to extend along the line of the Yser by Dixmude to Nieuport.

Sir John French was still uncertain about the forces opposing him. He knew of an army on the coast route, and was naturally anxious as to the stand which the wearied Belgians could make on the Yser. But he did not know that the movement on the coast was no more than the outer rim of a huge serried line wheeling against the Allies from the north-east, and that four new reserve corps had been rushed through from Germany and were on their way westward. On the night of the 17th he decided to put into effect an alternative strategical plan. If La Bassée and Lille had proved too strong for the 2nd Corps, then Marlborough's strategy might be employed against the German right. With Menin as a pivot, commanding an important railway and the line of the Lys, a flanking movement might be instituted against Courtrai and the line of the Scheldt. Accordingly he instructed Rawlinson to advance next morning, seize Menin, and await the support of the 1st Corps, which was due in two days.

Rawlinson had an impossible task. He had to operate on a front at least 20 miles wide, and he could look for no supports till Haig arrived. Moreover, he knew of the four new German corps, which were still hardly credited at headquarters. On the morning of the 19th he moved out towards Menin. The cavalry to the left presently came in touch with large enemy forces advancing from Roulers, while the progress of the infantry was summarily stopped by the advance of enormous masses from the direction of Courtrai. It had to fall back at once to avoid utter disaster, and entrenched itself on a line of 8 miles just east of the Gheluvelt crossroads, a name soon to be famous in the annals of the war. The great struggle for Ypres was on the eve of beginning.

On that day, 19 October, the 1st Corps, under Sir Douglas Haig, detrained at Saint-Omer and marched to Hazebrouck. That evening Haig was instructed to move through Ypres to Thourout with the intention of advancing on Bruges and Ghent. The 1st Corps, however, never approached Thourout but was detained in front of Ypres, where it formed the left wing of the British in the great struggle.

By the 19th – to continue our course to the sea – the Belgians had fallen back nearly to the line of the Yser from Dixmude to Nieuport. The Belgians were nominally six divisions, but three had been reduced to the strength of brigades, and were in the last stages of exhaustion. For ten weeks they had scarcely been out of action, but their spirit was unconquered, and the gaps in their line – they were no more than 48,000 strong – were filled up by French Marines, while the British and French fleets were waiting to give them support from the sea. But the front was still dangerously weak, and on 18 October Joffre placed at the disposal of Foch the reinforcements which were to complete the French Eighth Army.

20 October saw the whole Allied line from Albert to the sea in the position in which it had to meet the desperate effort of the Germans to regain the initiative and the offensive. Upon this line, little short of a hundred miles long, they awaited the attack of the enemy, as they had done two months before on the Sambre and the Meuse. Now, as then, they were outnumbered; now, as then, they did not know the enemy's strength; now, as then, their initial strategy had failed. The fall of Antwerp had destroyed the hope of holding the line of the Scheldt; the German occupation

public opinion in Britain, and interfere with the sending of the new levies. In the second place, with the coast in their possession, they hoped to mount big guns which would command the narrows of the Channel, to lay under their cover a mine-field, and to prepare a base for a future invasion of England. Now, with this purpose, the best road was clearly not the shortest. If the Allied front could be pierced at La Bassée, or, still better, at Arras, and a gate were forced for the passage of the German legions, then two of the Allied armies would be cut off and penned between the enemy and the sea. Further, a magnificent line of communications to the coast would be opened up – communications which could not be cut, for all the Channel littoral and hinterland east of Antwerp would be in German hands. If, on the other hand, a way were won along the shore by Nieuport, all that would happen would be that the Allies' left would fall back to the line of heights which ends in Cape Grisnez, and their front, instead of running due north from Albert, would bend to the north-west in an easy angle. Further, the coast road would be a poor line of communications at the best, and most open to attack by a movement from Ypres or La Bassée.

It is a sound rule in war that strength should not be dissipated. On this principle it is at first sight hard to discover an explanation for the course which the Germans actually followed. For they attacked almost simultaneously at all four points, and for three desperate weeks persisted in the attack. The explanation seems to be that Falkenhayn was imperfectly informed of the position of the Allies. As it happened, their front was more stable than he anticipated, and what were meant for holding attacks developed by the odd logic of circumstance into full-dress battles, so that the action instead of concentrating in the coast terrain became a series of alternating efforts to break the front at presumably weak points. This in turn was an intelligible plan – it was Foch's in 1918 – but Falkenhayn had leaned so heavily on the first scheme that his balance was shaken before he essayed the second.

Our first task is to consider the assault on the Yser, and the subsidiary attacks at La Bassée and Arras, before dealing with the supreme effort against Ypres, but it must be understood that all four attacks were to a large extent contemporaneous and merged one into the other.

We turn first to the fighting along the canal, usually dignified by the name of the Yser, where the country is blind and sodden, as ill-fitted for the passage of troops and heavy guns as the creeks and salt marshes of the Essex coast. On 16 October the right wing of the retreating Belgian army had reached the forest of Houthulst, north-east of Ypres, and had been driven out of it by the German movement from Roulers. They now drew in that wing, and by the following day were aligned on the east bank of the Yser, with French cavalry and Territorials connecting them with the British army to the south. King Albert had under 50,000 in his command, and to a man they were battle-weary. But the presence of their King, and the consciousness that they were waging no longer a solitary war, but were arrayed with their Allies, spurred them to a great effort. The Yser was the natural line for them to hold, for, more than French or British, they were accustomed to war among devious water-courses. The plan was to hold strong bridgeheads at Nieuport and Dixmude, and an advance line covering them on the east bank of the river. Behind this lay the line of the Yser itself, and, should that be lost, the Nieuport–Dixmude railway embankment for a last stand.

By the evening of the 17th, Beseler, to whom the first coast attack had been entrusted, was in position just east of Nieuport. Early on the morning of the 18th he attacked with the object of seizing the Nieuport bridge. The sudden and violent assault of a superior force upon the left wing of a much-enduring army would in all likelihood have succeeded, and if at this date King Albert had been pushed well back from the Yser towards Furnes, Beseler would have been in Dunkirk in two days and in Calais the day after. But at this most critical moment help arrived from an unexpected quarter. Suddenly the German right resting on the sand-dunes found itself enfiladed. Shells fell in their trenches from the direction of the sea, and looking towards the Channel they saw the ominous grey shapes of British warships.

Germany had never dreamed of any serious danger from the sea. She believed from the charts that off that shelving shore, with its yeasty coastal waters, there was no room for even a small gunboat to get within range, and she did not imagine that Britain would venture her ships in such perilous seas. But at the outbreak of war three strange vessels lay at Barrow, built to the order of the Brazilian Government. Broad in the beam, and shallow of draught, they had been intended as patrol ships for the River Amazon. In August the Admiralty, with fortunate prescience, purchased these odd craft, which were heavily armoured, and carried each two 6-inch guns mounted forward in an armoured barbette, and two 4-foot-7-inch howitzers aft, while four 3-pounder guns were placed amidships. Their draught was only 4 feet 7 inches, so that they could move in shoal water where an ordinary warship would run aground. These monitors were presently joined by other craft, chiefly old ships of little value. French warships co-operated, and the bombardment extended east to Ostend. The Germans, unable to retaliate, were pushed away from the coast. Nieuport was saved.

But the battle for the coast route was only beginning. During the previous days, out of range of the British fleet, the Germans had been struggling desperately for the Yser passage. The Duke of Würtemberg was now in command, and with him were the four new reserve corps. On Sunday the 25th there was a crossing in great force, and for a moment it looked as if the line of the

Yser had been lost. But in that country it is one thing to gain a position on the west bank and quite another to be able to advance from it through the miry fields, intersected with countless sluggish rivulets. As the Germans tried to deploy from each bridge-head they were met with stubborn resistance from the Belgian and French entrenched among the dykes. For three days those ragged battalions fought a desperate action in the meadows. But even in country where the defence has a natural advantage numbers are bound to tell, and the steady stream of German reinforcements was pressing back the French and Belgians. By the 28th they had retired almost to the Dixmude–Nieuport railway, which ran on an embankment above the level of the fields. The Emperor was with the Duke of Würtemberg, and under his eye the German attack grew hourly in impetus. Another day, and the Allied left might have been broken.

In that moment of crisis the Belgians played their last card. Once more they sought aid from the water, and, after the fashion of their ancestors, broke down the dykes. The Yser lipped over its brim, and spread in great lagoons over the flat meadows. The German forces on the west bank found themselves floundering in a foot of water, while their guns were water-logged and deep in mud. Presently the Belgians prepared a greater destruction. Far and wide, in all the drainage area of the Yser, they had succeeded by now in opening the sluices of the canals. Suddenly on all sides the water rose. Dammed at its mouth, and fed by a thousand little floods, the Yser spread itself in seething brown waves over the whole country up to the railway line. The depth now was not of inches but of feet. The Germans, caught in the tide, were drowned in scores. A black nozzle of a field gun would show for a moment above the current, and presently disappear. The attack had failed finally and disastrously. The Emperor, who had watched the operations through his glasses, shut them up and turned away.

The coast road was barred, and he must look for success farther south, at Ypres or La Bassée.

The flooding of the Yser marked the end of the main struggle for the shortest route to Calais. In this section the Germans' main efforts wore now directed against Dixmude, which was the only point where a bridgehead, if won, could be maintained. The defence of this town by Ronarc'h's marines and the Belgian 5th Division was one of the conspicuous feats of the war. It was a vital position, for its capture by the Germans at any time before 1 November would have meant the turning of the Belgian right. Desperate fighting took place, but the defence held firm until 10 November, when its fall gave the Germans no advantage. There was still half a mile of floods between them and the Belgians, and by that date the first fury of their attack had been gravely weakened. For in the great battle of the south, after three weeks of constant struggle, the flower of their armies had been repelled everywhere from the Allied line.

We pass over the 20 miles which separate Dixmude from the Lys, and which constituted the terrain of the Battle of Ypres. For the present we will consider only the work of Smith-Dorrien's 2nd Corps, which was engaged in repelling the German advance from Lille against La Bassée and Béthune.

On 19 October the 2nd Corps held a line pivoting on Givenchy in the south, and then running east in a salient north of the La Bassée–Lille road to the village of Herlies, where it bent westward to Aubers, and connected with Conneau's cavalry in the neighbourhood of the La Bassée–Armentières highway. But from the 20th onward, as he felt the surge of the great German advance, Smith-Dorrien's whole energies were devoted to maintaining his ground and blocking the passage to Béthune and the west. The main attack at La Bassée lasted for ten days – from 22 October to 2 November. The fighting was confused and desperate. On the 27th the Germans got into Neuve Chapelle, and the task of retaking it was given to the newly arrived Indian troops. Gradually during the next three weeks the fighting slackened off, owing to the concentration against Ypres. Ypres was a merciful intervention, for it is difficult to believe that if the attacks had been continued with the violence of that of 22 October our line could have held its position. As it was, it was slowly forced back till it ran from Givenchy, to which we stubbornly clung, north by Festubert towards Estaires.

The last stroke against Arras, which, properly dealt, would have been the greatest menace of all, was delivered from 20 October to 26 October. Happily for Maud'huy's slender army the attack was not made one of the major operations. It was vigorously pressed, but advantage could not be followed up, because of the growing demands of the northern battles. The German guns were now near enough to bombard the city a second time, and for a week shells rained in its ancient streets. But the destruction of Arras did not give the enemy possession. All attempts to break the French line failed, and by the 26th Maud'huy had begun to retaliate in many places, pushed the Germans out of their advanced trenches, and restored to the French some of the little villages in the flats of the Scheldt. Bit by bit the circle was widened, till Arras was beyond the reach of the German howitzers, and the inhabitants began to return to their ruined dwellings. The enemy held the Vimy Ridge, and his lines lay in a loop round the city, but he was never fated to enter its streets.

* * *

The little city of Ypres, now only the shade of its former grandeur, stood midway between the smoky industrial beehive of the Lys and the well-tilled flats of the Yser. Once it had been the centre of the wool trade of Flanders, and its noble Cloth Hall, dating from the twelfth century, testified to its vanished mercantile pre-eminence. No Flemish town could boast a prouder history.

The town stood on a tiny stream, the Yperlée, a tributary of the Yser, which had long ago been canalised. A single-line railway passed through it from Roulers to the main Lille–Saint-Omer line at Hazebrouck. An important canal ran from Yser in the north to the River Lys at Comines, and 2 miles south of the town, at the village of Saint-Eloi, turned eastward, bending south again in a broad angle between Hollebeke and Zandvoorde. To the east there were considerable patches of forest between Bixschoote and the Lys valley. A series of slight ridges rose towards the south and east in a curve just inside the Belgian frontier from west of Messines to the neighbourhood of Zonnebeke. For the rest, the country was dead flat, so that the spires of Ypres made a landmark for many miles. On all sides from the town radiated the cobbled Flemish roads, the two main highways on the east being those to Roulers and to Menin, with an important connecting road cutting the latter 5 miles from Ypres at the village of Gheluvelt.

On the evening of the 19th the Allied offensive had virtually ceased. We were aware that at last we had reached the main German front in position everywhere from Lille to the sea, and daily growing in numbers which threatened to fall in a tidal wave upon the thin and far-stretched Allied line. But Sir John French, though cognisant of the enemy's strength, was not yet fully informed about its details, and he made one more effort to break through with a counterstroke. Haig with the 1st Corps had, as we have seen, arrived behind the front on the 19th, and had been directed to move to the north of Ypres in the direction of Thourout. 'The object he was to have in view,' Sir John wrote, 'was to be the capture of Bruges, and subsequently, if possible, to drive the enemy towards Ghent.' But Sir John had his doubts about its possibility, and Haig was instructed after passing Ypres to use his own judgment. He advanced successfully till about two o'clock in the afternoon, when news came of trouble on his flanks. The French Territorials on the left were driven out of the forest of Houthulst, and they and their supports of the 1st French Cavalry Corps retired across the Yser Canal. At the same time he was informed that the 7th Division and Allenby's 2nd Cavalry Division beyond it were heavily attacked, and it became necessary to halt on the line Bixschoote–Langemarck–Saint-Julien–Zonnebeke. That line marked the limits of the last British offensive. Thourout and Bruges were now as inaccessible as the moon.

That evening Sir John French in Ypres had an anxious consultation with Haig and Rawlinson, Mitry and Bidon. It was now abundantly clear that the most they could do was to hold the Ypres Salient from the Lys to Dixmude till Joffre could send help – a length of fully 30 miles. This help could not arrive before the 24th, and for three days the present line must maintain its precarious and extended front.

So began the First Battle of Ypres, on the rim of upland east of the old Flemish city. The great battles of the world have not uncommonly been fought in places worthy of so fierce a drama. The mountains looked upon Marathon and Thermopylae, Marengo, Solferino, and Plevna; mighty plains gave dignity to Châlons and Borodino; the magic of the desert encompassed Arbela and Omdurman; or some fantasy of weather lent strangeness to death, like the snow at Austerlitz or the harvest moon at Chattanooga, against which was silhouetted Sheridan's charge. Ypres was stark carnage and grim endurance, without glamour of earth or sky. The sullen heavens hung low over the dank fields, the dripping woods, the mean houses, and all the sour and unsightly land. It was such a struggle as Lee's Wilderness stand, where, amid tattered scrub and dismal swamps, the ragged soldiers of the Confederacy fought their last battles. There was no general plan and no central leading. Foch and French rarely understood what was happening, and contributed little beyond an ill-founded optimism; the brunt fell upon Haig, his divisional and brigade commanders, and above all on the regimental officers. There were moments, as on 29, 30, and 31 October, and 11 November, when only a miracle seemed to save our thin front from destruction.

Very early on Thursday the 29th, in a sudden spell of clear weather, the first wave broke against the centre of the 1st Corps at the point of the Salient on the Gheluvelt cross-roads. The 1st Division was driven back from its trenches, and all morning the line swayed backwards and forwards. The 30th was the day fixed for the main German attack. The Duke of Würtemberg was to press hard on his left against Bixschoote and Langemarck, while attacks were also directed against Gheluvelt and the southern side of the Salient. Daylight had scarcely come when the battle began. Würtemberg took the ruins of Bixschoote but failed to drive the French from Langemarck. Farther south the Germans, who had great weight of heavy artillery, simply blew the British trenches to pieces. The cavalry who held that part of the line were compelled to fall back a mile. The situation was desperately critical. If the Germans got to the Ypres–Comines canal at any point north of Hollebeke they would speedily cut the communications of the 1st Corps holding the Salient and nothing would lie between them and Ypres itself. The Emperor was with his men and had told the Bavarians that the winning of the town would determine the issue of the war. Farther south the 2nd Cavalry Division had been driven out of Hollebeke, while the 1st Cavalry Division were in heavy conflict round Messine. Pulteney, too, in the south, had his line broken at Saint-Yves, but the situation was saved by a spirited counter-attack.

Next day came the crisis. The attack developed in great force against Gheluvelt village. The 1st Division was driven back from Gheluvelt to the woods between Hooge and Veldhoek This menaced the flank of the 7th Division. On the right of that Division the force known as Bulfin's detachment was exposed by its attack on its left-hand neighbours but managed to cling to its trenches till the evening. On Bulfin's right, Mussy, with the 9th French Corps, was struggling hard to keep the line intact towards Klein Zillebeke. At one moment it looked as if he might have to yield, hut he saved himself by novel reinforcements. He bade the corporal commanding his escort collect every available man from cooks to cuirassiers. The bold adventure prospered, and Mussy was able to hold his ground.

Between two and three o'clock on Saturday the 31st was the most critical hour in the whole battle. It seemed as if the slightest forward pressure would crumble the Ypres defence. French sent an urgent message to Foch for reinforcements, but Foch had none to send, for his own losses had been greater than ours. It seemed impossible to stop the gap. Between two and two-thirty Haig gave orders to retire to a line a little west of Hooge and stand there, though he well knew that no stand, however heroic, could save the town. And then suddenly out of the void came a strange story. A white-faced staff officer reported that something odd was happening north of the Menin road. The enemy advance had halted! Then came the word that the 1st Division was re-forming. The anxious generals could scarcely believe their ears, for it sounded a sheer miracle. But presently came the proof, though it was not for months that the full tale was known. Brigadier-General FitzClarence, commanding the 1st (Guards) Brigade in the 1st Division, had sent in his last reserves and failed to stop the gap. He then rode off to the headquarters of the division to explain how desperate was the position. But on the way, at the south-west corner of the Polygon Wood, he stumbled upon a battalion waiting in support. It was the 2nd Worcesters, who were part of the right brigade of the 2nd Division. FitzClarence saw in them his last chance. They belonged to another division, but it was no time to stand on ceremony, and the officer in command at once put them at his disposal. The Worcesters, under very heavy artillery fire, advanced in a series of rushes for about a thousand yards between the right of the South Wales Borderers and the northern edge of Gheluvelt. Like Cole's fusiliers at Albuera, they came suddenly and unexpectedly upon the foe. There they dug themselves in, broke up the German advance into bunches, enfiladed it heavily, and brought it to a standstill. Before night fell the German advance west of Gheluvelt was stayed, and the British front was out of immediate danger.

On Wednesday the 11th came the supreme effort. As Napoleon had used his Guards for the final attack at Waterloo so the Emperor used his for the culminating stroke at Ypres. At first they used their parade march, and our men, rubbing their eyes in the darkness, could scarcely credit the portent. Long before they reached the shock our fire had taken toll of them, but so mighty is discipline that their impact told and at several points they pierced our front, though they were presently driven out with heavy losses. With the failure of the Prussian Guard the enemy seemed to have exhausted his vitality. His tide of men had failed to swamp the thin Allied lines, and wearied out, and with terrible losses, he slackened his efforts and fell back upon the routine of trench warfare.

* * *

First Ypres must rank as one of the most remarkable contests of the war; it is certainly one of the most remarkable in the record of the British army. Let us put the achievement in the simplest terms. Between Armentières and the sea the Germans had, apart from their cavalry, which was double that of the Allies, thirty-one divisions and thirty-two battalions, a total of 402 battalions, as against 267 Allied battalions. The greater part of their troops were of the first line, and even the new formations were terrible in assault – more terrible than the veterans, perhaps, for they were still unwearied, and the edge of their keenness was undulled. The immature boys and elderly men, who often fell to pieces before our counter-attacks, came on with incredible valour in their early charges. They were like the soldiers of the Revolution – the more dangerous at times because they did not fight by rule. Against the part of this force which faced them the British opposed five infantry divisions, three of them very weak. In the actual Salient of Ypres they had three divisions and some cavalry. For the better part of two days one division held a front of 8 miles against two army corps. At all stages the Germans had an immense superiority in guns. In this mad mêlée strange things happened. Units became hopelessly mixed, and officers had to fling into the breach whatever men they could collect. A subaltern often found himself in command of a battalion; a brigadier commanded one or two companies, or a division, as the fates ordered.

Ypres was a victory, a decisive victory, for it achieved its purpose. The Allied line stood secure from the Oise to the sea; turning movement and piercing movement had alike been foiled, and the enemy's short-lived initiative was over. He was now compelled to conform to the battle which the Allies had set, with the edge taken from his ardour, and everywhere gaps in his ranks. Had they failed, he would have won the Channel ports and destroyed the Allied left, and the war would have taken on a new character. Ypres, like Le Cateau, was in a special sense a British achievement. Without the splendid support of d'Urbal's corps, without the Belgians on the Yser and Mand'huy at Arras, the case would have indeed been hopeless, and no allies ever fought in more gallant accord. But the most critical task fell to the British troops, and not the least of the gain was the complete assurance it gave of their quality. They opposed the blood and iron of the German onslaught with a stronger blood and a finer steel.

Within hearing of the guns at Ypres roaring their last challenge, the greatest British soldier passed away. Lord Roberts landed at Boulogne on 11 November on a visit to his beloved Indian troops. On the 12th he was at the headquarters of the corps, and went about among his old friends, speaking their own tongue, and greeting many who had fought with him in the frontier wars. The strain proved too great for the veteran; he caught a chill in the bitter weather; and while the Indian wounded waited in hospital on his coming, the news arrived that he was seriously ill. Pleurisy followed and at eight o'clock on the night of Saturday the 14th the end came. Lord Roberts's death synchronised with the passing of the army which he had commanded and done much to create. First Ypres saw the apotheosis of the British regulars, but also their end. That army was now to change its character in welcoming all classes and conditions within its ranks, and growing from a small professional force to the armed strength of a nation.

6

The Battle of Coronel

The Position in Home Waters – Cradock and von Spee – Battle of Coronel

On 29 October, Prince Louis of Battenberg, who as First Sea Lord had done good service to his adopted country, retired from office, and Lord Fisher returned to the post which he had held four years before. Lord Fisher was beyond doubt the greatest living sailor, and the modern British Navy was largely his creation. Explosive, erratic, a dangerous enemy, a difficult friend, this 'proud and rebellious creature of God' had the width of imagination and the sudden lightning flashes of insight which entitle him to rank as a man of genius. Behind a smoke-screen of vulgar rhodomontade, his powerful mind worked on the data of a vast experience. Moreover, he had that rarest of gifts – courage, as the French say of the head as well as of the heart. His policy in war might be too bold or too whimsical, but it would never be timorous or supine.

The situation which he had to face in October did not differ greatly from that of the preceding months. Jellicoe, without adequate bases, was engaged in the difficult task of performing a multitude of duties while keeping intact his capital ships. He had to arrange for the convoying of the first contingent of Canadian troops, and to meet and defeat the German campaign of submarines and mines around the British coasts. On 16 October an alarm of enemy submarines at Scapa compelled him to leave that anchorage till its defences were complete, and, after moving his whole cruiser system farther north, he chose as his battleship bases the natural harbours of Skye and Mull, and Lough Swilly in Ireland. The German liner *Berlin*, which had managed to slip through our North Sea patrols at the end of September, had sown mines in the north Irish waters, and one of them was struck on 27 October by the *Audacious* of the Second Battle Squadron, which sank after a twelve-hour struggle to get to port. As a protest and a protection against indiscriminate mine-laying in the great highways of ocean trade the British Admiralty on 2 November notified to the world that the whole of the North Sea would thenceforth be regarded as a military area, and that neutral ships could only pass through it by conforming to Admiralty instructions and keeping to certain predetermined routes. Presently the situation improved, the defences of Scapa were completed, and the German submarine attack languished, as if its promoters were disappointed with its results and were casting about for a new policy.

It was well that the Admiralty had an easier mind in home waters, for they were faced with an urgent and intricate problem in more distant seas. The existence of Admiral von Spee's squadron left our overseas possessions and our great trade routes at the mercy of enemy raids. Till it was hunted down no overseas port could feel security, and the Australian and New Zealand Governments, busy with sending contingents to the fighting fronts, demanded not unnaturally that this should be made the first duty of the British Navy. Whether the squadron kept together or split into raiding units it was no light task to bring it to book when it had the oceans of the world for its hunting ground. Sooner or later it was doomed, and von Spee, hampered with difficulties of coaling and supplies, could only hope for a brief career. But during that career a bold man might do incalculable damage to the Allies and deflect and cripple all their strategic plans, and the German admiral was a most bold and gallant commander.

About the middle of August two of his light cruisers, the *Dresden* and the *Karlsruhe*, appeared in the mid-Atlantic, while the *Emden*, as we have seen, harried the Indian Ocean. Rear-Admiral Sir Christopher Cradock, in command of the North American station, took up the chase of the first two throughout the West Indian islands and down the east coast of South America. Meantime von Spee was somewhere in the Central Pacific, where at the end of September he bombarded Tahiti, and presently it became clear that the *Dresden* had joined him. His squadron now comprised two armoured cruisers – the *Gneisenau* and the *Scharnhorst*; and three light cruisers – the *Dresden*, *Leipzig*, and *Nürnberg*. The first two were sister ships, both launched in 1906, with a tonnage of 11,400 and a speed of at least 23 knots. They carried 6-inch armour, and mounted eight 8.2-inch, six 5.9-inch, and eighteen 21-pounder guns. The *Dresden* was a sister ship of the *Emden* – 3,592 tons, 24½ knots, and ten 4.1-inch guns. The *Nürnberg* was slightly smaller – 3,400 tons – her armament was the same, and her speed was about half a knot quicker. Smaller still was the *Leipzig* – 3,200 tons – with the same armament as the other two, and a speed of over 22 knots. This squadron set itself to prey upon our commerce routes, remembering that the British Navy was short in cruisers of the class best fitted to patrol and guard the great trade highways. Von Spee moved nearer the western coast of South America, and found coaling and provisioning bases on the coast of Ecuador and Colombia, and in the Galapagos Islands. The duties of neutrals were either imperfectly understood or slackly observed by some of the South American states at this stage, and the German admiral seems to have been permitted the use of wireless stations, which gave him valuable information as to his enemy's movements.

So soon as definite news came of von Spee's whereabouts, Cradock sailed south to the Horn. He had in his squadron, when formed, the twelve-year-old battleship *Canopus*, two armoured cruisers, the *Good Hope* and the *Monmouth*, the light cruiser *Glasgow*, and an armed liner, the *Otranto*, belonging to the Orient Steam Navigation Company. None of his vessels was strong either in speed or armament. The *Canopus* belonged to a class which had been long obsolete; her tonnage was 12,950, her speed under 19 knots, and her armament four 12-inch, twelve 6-inch, and ten 12-pounder guns, all of an old-fashioned pattern. Her armour belt was only 6 inches thick. The *Good Hope* was also twelve years old; her tonnage was 14,100, her speed 23 knots, and her armament two 9.2-inch, sixteen 6-inch, and twelve 12-pounder guns. The *Monmouth* was a smaller vessel of 9,800 tons, with the same speed, and mounting fourteen 6-inch and eight 12-pounder guns. The *Glasgow* was a much newer vessel, and had a speed of 25 knots. Her tonnage was 4,800, and her armament two 6-inch and ten 4-inch guns.

Cradock's instructions, received on 14 September, were to make the Falkland Islands his base and to concentrate there a squadron strong enough to meet von Spee. A week later it appeared as if von Spee had gone off north-west from Samoa to his original station in the North Pacific, where the Japanese could deal with him. It looked therefore as if Cradock were safe; so he was ordered not to concentrate all his cruisers, but to attack German trade west of the Magellan Straits, for which task two cruisers and an armed liner would be sufficient. The news of the arrival of the *Dresden* did not seem to alter the situation. But on 5 October the Admiralty had information which suggested that von Spee was making for Easter Island, and Cradock was warned that he might have to meet the *Scharnhorst* and the *Gneisenau*, and consequently was ordered to take the *Canopus* with him. Cradock asked for reinforcements, and protested that his instructions were impossible, for with his small squadron he could not watch both coasts of South America. For some days, owing to bad weather and the pressure of other duties, there came no reply from the Admiralty. If von Spee escaped he might cripple our operations in the Cameroons, and might work untold harm in the troubled waters of South Africa. On 14 October Cradock was told to concentrate the *Good Hope*, *Canopus*, *Monmouth*, *Glasgow*, and *Otranto* for a combined operation on the west coast of South America, and informed that a second squadron was being formed for the Plate area. Cradock assumed that his former orders also held good, and that he was expected to bring the enemy to action. His difficulty was with the *Canopus*, which was hopelessly slow. On 22 October he left the Falklands to make a sweep round the Horn, leaving the *Canopus* to join him by way of the Magellan Straits.

He had no illusions about the dangers of his task for he knew that if he met von Spee he would meet an enemy more than his match. During these weeks weather conditions made communication with the Admiralty exceptionally difficult; he was not aware that an Anglo-Japanese squadron was operating in the North Pacific; and he seems to have regarded the charge of all the western coasts as resting on himself alone. In this spirit of devotion to a desperate duty he left the slow *Canopus* behind him, and with his two chief ships but newly commissioned and poor in gunnery, set out on a task which might engage him with two of the best cruisers in the German fleet. He may have argued further – for no height of gallantry was impossible to such a man – that even if he perished the special circumstances of the conqueror might turn his victory into defeat. For, in Mr Balfour's words,

the German admiral in the Pacific was far from any front where he could have refitted. No friendly bases were open to him. If, therefore, he suffered damage, even though in suffering damage he inflicted apparently greater damage than he received, yet his power, great for evil while he remained untouched, might suddenly, as by a stroke of an enchanter's wand, be utterly destroyed. (Speech at the unveiling of Cradock's memorial in York Minster.)

The opponents, Cradock from the south and von Spee from the north, were moving towards a conflict like one of the historic naval battles, a fight without mines, submarines, or destroyers, where the two squadrons were to draw into line ahead and each ship select its antagonist as in the ancient days. The *Glasgow*, which had been sent forward to scout, a little after 4 o'clock in the afternoon of 1 November sighted the enemy. She made out the two big armoured cruisers leading, and the light cruisers following in open order, and at once sent a wireless signal to the flagship. By 5 o'clock the *Good Hope* came up, and the *Monmouth* had already joined the *Glasgow* and the *Otranto*. Both squadrons were now moving southwards, the Germans having the in-shore course. The British were led by the *Good Hope*, with the *Monmouth*, *Glasgow*, and *Otranto* following in order; the Germans by the *Scharnhorst*, with the *Gneisenau*, *Dresden*, and *Nürnberg* behind.

We can reconstruct something of the picture. To the east was the land, with the snowy heights of the southern Andes fired by the evening glow. To the west burned one of those flaming sunsets which the Pacific knows, and silhouetted against its crimson and orange were the British ships, like woodcuts in a naval handbook. A high sea was running from the south, and half a gale was blowing. At first some 12 miles separated the two squadrons, but the distance rapidly shrank till it was 8 miles at 6.18 p.m. About 7 o'clock the squadrons were converging, and the enemy's leading cruiser opened fire at 7 miles. By this time the sun had gone down behind the horizon, but the lemon afterglow showed up the British ships, while the German were shrouded in the in-shore twilight. Presently the enemy got the range, and shell after shell hit the *Good Hope* and the *Monmouth*, while the bad light and the spray from the head seas made good gunnery for them almost impossible. At 7.50 there was a great explosion on the *Good Hope*, which had already been set on fire. The flames leaped to an enormous height in the air, and the doomed vessel, which had been drifting towards the enemy's lines, soon disappeared below the water. The *Monmouth* was also on fire and down by the head, and turned away seaward in her distress. Meantime the *Glasgow* had received only stray shots, for the battle so far had been waged between the four armoured cruisers. But as the *Good Hope* sank and the *Monmouth* was obviously near her end, the enemy cruisers fell back and began to shell the *Glasgow* at a range of 2½ miles. That the *Glasgow* escaped was something of a miracle. She was scarcely armoured at all, and was struck by five shells at the water line, but her coal seems to have saved her.

The moon was now rising, and the *Glasgow*, which had been trying to stand by the *Monmouth*, saw the whole German squadron bearing down upon her. The *Monmouth*, refusing to surrender, was past hope, so she did the proper thing and fled. By ten minutes to nine she was out of sight of the enemy, though she occasionally saw flashes of gun-fire and the play of searchlights, for fortunately a flurry of rain had hidden the unwelcome moon. She steered at first WNW, but gradually worked round to south, for she desired to warn the *Canopus*, which was coming up from the direction of Cape Horn. Next day she found that battleship 200 miles off, and the two proceeded towards the Straits of Magellan.

Cradock, out of touch with the Admiralty and perplexed by contradictory telegrams, could only 'take counsel from the valour of his heart'. He chose the heroic course, and he and his 1,650 officers and men went to their death in the spirit of Drake and Grenville. The Germans had two light cruisers to his one, for the *Otranto* was negligible; but these vessels were never seriously in action, and the battle was decided in the duel between the armoured cruisers. The *Good Hope* mounted two 9.2-inch guns, but these were old-fashioned, and were put out of action at the start. The 6-inch guns which she and the *Monmouth* possessed were no match for the broadsides of twelve 8.2-inch guns fired by the *Scharnhorst* and the *Gneisenau*. The German vessels were also far more heavily armoured, and they had the inestimable advantage of speed. They were able to get the requisite range first and to cripple Cradock before he could reply, and they had a superb target in his hulls silhouetted against the afterglow of sunset. The Battle of Coronel was fought with all conceivable odds against us.

7

The Battle of
the Falkland Islands

Sturdee Leaves England with the Battle-Cruisers – Battle of the Falkland Islands – Its Results

The defeat of Coronel played havoc with the British Admiralty's plans and dispositions, and left a hundred vulnerable spots throughout the Empire open to von Spee. Mr Churchill and Lord Fisher did not hesitate; a blow must be struck and at once, and that blow must be decisive. The *Defence*, *Carnarvon*, and *Cornwall* were ordered to concentrate at Montevideo, where the remnant of Cradock's squadron was instructed to join them. Jellicoe was summoned to lend his two battle-cruisers the *Invincible* and the *Inflexible*, each with a tonnage of 17,250, a speed of from 25 to 28 knots, and eight 12-inch guns so placed that all eight could be fired on either broadside. Sir Frederick Doveton Sturdee, the Chief of the War Staff at the Admiralty, was put in charge of the expedition, with the post of Commander-in-Chief of the South Atlantic and Pacific. His business was to take over the ships at Montevideo and seek out von Spee should he attempt to break into the Atlantic by the Horn. If, on the other hand, the German admiral was aiming at the Panama Canal or the Canadian coasts, he would be dealt with by the Anglo-Japanese squadron in the North Pacific.

On 11 November Sturdee sailed, and on the 26th reached the rendezvous, where he found the *Carnarvon*, *Cornwall*, *Kent*, and

Bristol. Von Spee after Coronel lingered for some time on the coast of Chile, waiting on colliers, and apparently also in the hope that the German battle-cruisers might break out of the North Sea and join him. Then, finding that the Anglo-Japanese squadron was becoming troublesome in the Pacific, he steered for the Horn, which he rounded at midnight on 1 December. He was aiming at the Falklands, where he expected to find a weak British squadron coaling; he meant to draw it out to sea and destroy it, and then occupy the islands and demolish the wireless installation. As a matter of fact only the *Canopus* was there, and the little colony expected that at any moment the blow would fall. But on the afternoon of 7 December, Sturdee appeared with his squadron, intending to coal, and then go round the Horn in search of the enemy. The Falklands with their bare brown moors shining with quartz, their innumerable lochans, their prevailing mists, their grey stone houses, and their population of Scots shepherds, look like a group of the Orkneys or Outer Hebrides set down in the southern seas. Port Stanley lies at the eastern corner of East Island. There is a deeply cut gulf leading to an inner harbour, on the shores of which stands the little capital. The low shores on the south side almost give a vessel in port a sight of the outer sea. The night of 7 December was spent by the British squadron in coaling. The *Canopus*, the *Glasgow*, and the *Bristol* were in the inner harbour; while the *Invincible*, *Inflexible*, *Carnarvon*, *Kent*, and *Cornwall* lay in the outer gulf.

About daybreak on the morning of the 8th, von Spee arrived from the direction of Cape Horn. The *Gneisenau* and the *Nürnberg* were ahead, and reported the presence of two British ships, probably the *Macedonia* and the *Kent*, which would be the first vessels visible to a ship rounding the islands. Upon this von Spee gave the order to prepare for battle, expecting to find only the remnants of Cradock's squadron. At 8 o'clock the signal station announced to Sturdee the presence of the enemy. It was a clear, fresh morning, with a bright sun, and light breezes from the north-west. All our vessels had finished coaling, except the battle-cruisers, which had begun only half an hour before. Orders were at once given to get up steam for full speed. The battle-cruisers raised steam with oil fuel, and made so dense a smoke that the German look-outs did not detect them. About 9 the *Canopus* had a shot at the *Gneisenau* over the neck of land, directed by signal officers on shore. At 9.30 von Spee came abreast the harbour mouth, and saw the ominous tripod masts which revealed the strength of the British squadron. He at once signalled to the *Gneisenau* and the *Nürnberg* not to accept action, and altered his course to east, while Sturdee's command streamed out in pursuit.

First went the *Kent* and then the *Glasgow*, followed by the *Carnarvon*, the battle-cruisers, and the *Cornwall*. The Germans had transports with them, the *Baden* and the *Santa Isabel*, and these fell back to the south of the island, with the *Bristol* and the *Macedonia* in pursuit. The *Canopus* remained in the harbour, where she had been moored in the mud as a fort. At about 10 o'clock the two forces were some 12 miles apart, von Spee steering almost due east. The *Invincible* and the *Inflexible* quickly drew ahead, but had to slacken speed to 20 knots to allow the cruisers to keep up with them. At 11 o'clock about 11 miles separated the two forces. At five minutes to one we had drawn closer, and opened fire upon the *Leipzig*, which was last of the German line.

Von Spee, seeing that flight was impossible, prepared to give battle. So far as the battle-cruisers were concerned, it was a foregone conclusion, for the British had the greater speed and the longer range. Ever since Coronel he had had a sense of impending doom, and had known that the time left to him was short. He saw, like the great sailor he was, that while his flagship and her consort were in any case doomed their loss might enable his light cruisers to escape, and that these could still do work for his country by harrying British trade. About 1 o'clock he signalled to the latter to disperse and make for the South American coast, while he accepted battle with his armoured ships. His three light cruisers turned therefore and made off to the south, followed by the *Kent*, the *Glasgow*, and the *Cornwall*, while the *Invincible*, the *Inflexible*, and the *Carnarvon* engaged the *Scharnhorst* and the *Gneisenau*.

About 2 o'clock our battle-cruisers had the range of the German flagship, and a terrific artillery duel began. The British armour-piercing shells from some defect in construction burst on impact, and this explained the long-drawn agony of the German ships, which remained afloat when their decks had become places of torment. The smoke was getting in our way, and Sturdee used his superior speed to reach the other side of the enemy. He simply pounded the *Scharnhorst* to pieces, and just after 4 o'clock she listed to port and then turned bottom upwards with her propeller still going round. The battle-cruisers and the *Carnarvon* then concentrated on the *Gneisenau*, which was sheering off to the south-east, and at 6 o'clock she too listed and went under.

Meanwhile the *Kent*, *Glasgow*, and *Cornwall* were hot in pursuit of the three light cruisers, and here was a more equally matched battle. The *Dresden*, which was farthest to the east, had, with her pace and her long start, no difficulty in escaping. The other two had slightly the advantage of speed of the British ships, but our engineers and stokers worked magnificently, and managed to get 25 knots out of the *Kent*. It was now a thick misty afternoon, with a drizzle of rain, and each duel had consequently the form of a separate battle. The news of the sinking of the *Scharnhorst* and the *Gneisenau* put new spirit into our men, and at 7.30 p.m. the *Nürnberg*, which had been set on fire by the *Kent*, went down with her guns still firing. The *Leipzig*, which had to face the *Glasgow* and the *Cornwall*, kept afloat, fighting most gallantly, till close upon 8 p.m., when she too heeled over and sank.

As the wet night closed in the battle died away. Only the *Dresden*, battered and fleeing far out in the southern waters, remained of the proud squadron which at dawn had sailed to what it believed to be an easy victory. The defeat of Cradock in the murky sunset off Coronel had been amply avenged.

The Battle of the Falkland Islands was a brilliant piece of strategy, for a plan, initiated more than a month before, and involving a journey across the world, was executed with complete secrecy and precision. Tactically it was an easy victory owing to Sturdee's huge preponderance in strength. The British gunnery was good, and the battle might have been won in half the time but for the British admiral's very proper desire to win without loss and return the battle-cruisers intact to Jellicoe. Yet, when this has been said, it was a workmanlike performance, doing honour to all concerned. Technically, the sole blemish was the escape of the *Dresden*, which could not, however, have been prevented; for the speediest of the available ships, the *Glasgow*, had only 25 knots against the 27 which the German cruiser managed to achieve. The result had a vital bearing on the position of Germany. It annihilated the one squadron left to her outside the North Sea, and it removed a formidable menace to our trade routes. After 8 December, the *Dresden* (the *Dresden* was caught off Juan Fernandez on 14 March 1915, by the *Kent* and the *Glasgow*, and sunk in five minutes; the *Karlsruhe* had mysteriously blown up in the West Indies on 4 November 1914) was the sole enemy cruiser left at large, and she and the armoured merchantmen, the *Kronprinz Wilhelm* and the *Prince Eitel Friedrich*, were the only privateers still at work on the high seas. The British losses were small considering the magnitude of the victory. The *Invincible* was hit by eighteen shells, but had no casualties. The *Inflexible* was hit thrice, and had one man killed. The cruisers suffered more heavily, the *Kent*, for example, having four men killed and twelve wounded, and the *Glasgow* nine killed and four wounded. Every effort was made by the British ships to save life, but in the circumstances most of the efforts were vain. The only sign of a lost vessel was at first the slightly discoloured water. Then the wreckage floated up with men clinging to it, and boats were lowered and sailors let down the sides on bow-lines in order to rescue the survivors who floated past. The water was icy cold – about 40° – and presently many of the swimmers grew numb and went under. Albatrosses, too, attacked some of those clinging to the wreckage, pecking at their eyes and forcing them to let go. Altogether less than two hundred were saved, including the captain of the *Gneisenau*. Admiral von Spee perished, with two of his sons.

The victory was of supreme importance in the naval campaign, for it gave to Britain the command of the outer seas, and enabled her to concentrate all her strength in the main European battle-ground. Failure would have altered the whole course of the war in Africa, and most gravely interfered with the passage of troops and supplies to the Western Front. It is worthy, too, to be held in memory, along with Coronel, as an episode which maintained the high chivalrous tradition of the sea. Let us do honour to a gallant foe. The German admiral did his duty as Cradock had done his, the German sailors died as Cradock's men had died, and there can be no higher praise. They went down with colours flying, and at the last the men lined up on the decks of the doomed ships. They continued to resist after their vessels had become shambles. One captured officer reported that before the end, his ship had no upper deck left, every man there having been killed, and one turret blown bodily overboard by a 12-inch shell. But in all that hell of slaughter, which lasted for half a day, there was never a thought of surrender. Von Spee and Cradock lie beneath the same waters, in the final concord of those who have looked unshaken upon death.

party succeeded in occupying a stretch of shore, the necessity of dislodging him might gravely handicap our major strategy. Accordingly Yeomanry and Territorials entrenched themselves in the eastern counties, and had the dullness of their days enlivened by many rumours. Civilians were perturbed by the thought of how they should conduct themselves if their homes were violated, and there was much activity in the formation of national guards, and a considerable increase in recruiting for the new service armies.

Late on the afternoon of 2 November, eight German warships sailed from the Elbe base. They were three battle-cruisers – the *Seydlitz*, the *Moltke*, and the *Von der Tann*; two armoured cruisers – the *Blücher* and the *Yorck*; and three light cruisers – the *Kolberg*, the *Graudenz*, and the *Strassburg*. Except the *Yorck*, they were fast vessels, making at least 25 knots, and the battle-cruisers carried 11-inch guns. Cleared for action, they started for the coast of England, and early in the winter dawn ran through the nets of a British fishing fleet 8 miles east of Lowestoft. An old mine-sweeping gunboat, the *Halcyon*, was next sighted, and received a few shots, but the Germans had no time to waste on her. About eight o'clock they were opposite Yarmouth, and proceeded to bombard the wireless station and the naval air station from a distance of about 10 miles. For some reason or other they were afraid to venture farther inshore – probably they took their range from a line of buoys marked on the chart, and did not know that after the declaration of war these buoys had been moved 500 yards farther out to sea – so their shells only ploughed the sands and plumped in the water. In a quarter of an hour they grew tired of it, and moved away, dropping many floating mines, which later in the day caused the loss of one of our submarines and two fishing-boats. The enterprise was unlucky, for on the road back the *Yorck* struck a mine and went to the bottom with most of her crew. The raid was a reconnaissance, and a blow aimed at the *sangfroid* of

Britain. The latter purpose miscarried, for nobody in Britain gave it a second thought. To bombard the beach front of a watering-place seemed a paltry achievement, when at the moment the opportunity was present to interfere with Admiral Hood on the Belgian coast. It would have been wiser had the authorities taken it more seriously, and issued instructions to civilians as to what to do in case of a repetition of such attempts. For, having found the way, the invaders were certain to return.

They came again on 16 December, when a thick, cold mist lay low on our eastern coasts. Von Spee and his squadron had gone to their death at the Falkland Islands, and it behoved the German navy to strike a blow in return. The raiding force, which was under Rear-Admiral Funke, the second in command of the battle-cruiser squadron, included the *Derfflinger*, the newest of the battle-cruisers, and the *Von der Tann*. The *Blücher* was there, and the *Seydlitz* and the *Graudenz*, and there were also at least two light cruisers present. Before daybreak on the 16th the squadron arrived off the mouth of the Tees, and there divided its forces. The *Derfflinger*, the *Von der Tann*, and the *Blücher* went north to raid the Hartlepools, and the other two went south against Scarborough.

A few minutes before eight o'clock those citizens of Scarborough who were out of bed saw approaching from the north four strange ships. It was a still morning, with what is called in Scotland a *haar* on the water, and something of a sea running, for the last days had been stormy. Scarborough was entirely without defences, except an old Russian 60-pounder, a Crimean relic, which was as useful as the flint arrowheads in the local museum. It had once been a garrison artillery depot, and had a battery below the Castle, but Lord Haldane had altered this and made it a cavalry station. Some troops of the new service battalions were quartered in the place, and there was a wireless station behind the town. Otherwise it was an open seaside resort, as defenceless against an attack from the sea as a seal against a killer-whale. The ships poured shells into the coastguard station and the Castle grounds, where they seemed to suspect the presence of hostile batteries. Then they steamed in front of the town, approaching to some 500 yards from the shore. Here they proceeded to a systematic bombardment, aiming at every large object within sight, including the Grand Hotel and the gasworks, while many shells were directed towards the waterworks and the wireless station in the western suburbs. Churches, public buildings, and hospitals were hit, and some private houses were wrecked. For forty minutes the bombardment continued, and it was calculated that 500 shells were fired. Midway in their course the ships swung round and began to move northwards again, while the light cruisers went out to sea and began the work of mine-dropping. The streets were crowded with puzzled and scared inhabitants, and, as in every watering-place, there was a large proportion of old people, women, and invalids. At a quarter to nine all was over, and the hulls of the invaders were disappearing round the Castle promontory. They left behind them eighteen dead, mostly women and children, and about seventy wounded.

About nine o'clock the coastguard at Whitby, the little town on the cliffs north of Scarborough, saw two great ships steaming up fast from the south. Ten minutes later the newcomers opened fire on the signal station on the cliff head. Several dozen shells were fired in a few minutes, many striking the cliff, and others going too high and falling behind the railway station. Some actually went 4 miles inland, and awakened a sleepy little village. The old abbey of Hilda and Caedmon was struck but not seriously damaged; and on the whole, considering the number of shells it received, Whitby suffered little. The casualties were only five, three killed and two wounded. The invaders turned north-eastward and disappeared into the haze, to join their other division.

That other division had visited the Hartlepools, the only town of the three which came near to fulfilling the definition of a 'defended' place. It had a fort, with a battery of antiquated guns. It had important docks and large shipbuilding works, which were busy at the time on Government orders, and some companies of the new service battalions were billeted in the town. Off the shore was lying a small British flotilla – a gunboat, the *Patrol*, carrying 4-inch guns, and two destroyers, the *Doon* and the *Hardy*. About the same time as the bombardment of Scarborough began, the *Derfflinger*, the *Von der Tann*, and the *Blücher* came out of the mist upon the British flotilla and opened fire. The action took place on the north side of the peninsula on which Old Hartlepool stands. With great gallantry the small British craft tried to close and torpedo the invaders, but they were driven back with half a dozen killed and twenty-five wounded, and their only course was flight. The German ships approached the shore and fired on the battery. Then began the first fight on English soil with a foreign foe since the French landed in Sussex in 1690 – the first on the soil of Great Britain since the affair at Fishguard in 1797. The achievement deserves to be remembered. The garrison of the battery consisted of some Territorials of the Durham Royal Garrison Artillery and some infantry of the Durhams. The 12-inch shells of the *Derfflinger* burst in and around the battery, but the men stood to their outclassed guns without wavering, and aimed with success at the upper decks of the invaders. For more than half an hour a furious cannonade continued, in which some 1,500 shells seem to have been fired. One ship kept close to the battery, and gave it broadside after broadside; the other two moved farther north, shelled Old Hartlepool, and fired over the peninsula at West Hartlepool and the docks. The streets of the old town suffered terribly, the gasworks were destroyed, and one of the big shipbuilding yards was damaged, but the docks and the other yards were not touched. Churches, hospitals, workhouses, and schools were all struck. Little children going to school and babes in their mothers' arms were killed. The total death-roll was 119, and the wounded over 300; 600 houses were damaged or destroyed, and three steamers that night struck the mines which the invaders had laid off the shore, and went down with much loss of life. The spirit in which the inhabitants of the raided towns met the crisis was worthy of the highest praise. There was dire confusion, for nobody had been told what to do; there was some panic – it would have been a miracle if there had not been; but on the whole the situation was faced with admirable coolness and courage. The authorities, as soon as the last shots were fired, turned to the work of relief; the Territorials in Hartlepool behaved like veterans both during and after the bombardment; the girls in the telephone exchange worked steadily through the cannonade. It should be remembered that we cannot compare this attack on the east coast towns with the assaults in a land war on some city in the battle front. In the latter case the mind of the inhabitants has been attuned for weeks to danger, and preparations have been made for defence. But here the bolt came from the blue – the narrow, crowded streets of Old Hartlepool were a death-trap, and the ordinary citizen was plunged in a second from profound peace into the midst of a nerve-racking and unexpected war.

Somewhere between nine and ten on that December morning the German vessels rendezvoused and started on their homeward course. They escaped only by the skin of their teeth. Before the first shell was fired word of the attempt had reached the British Grand Fleet. Somewhere out in the *haar* Beatty with his battle-cruisers was moving to intercept the raiders, and behind came half a dozen of the great battleships. But for an accident of weather the German battle-cruiser squadron would have gone to the bottom of the North Sea. But the morning *haar* thickened, till a series of blind fog-belts stretched for a hundred miles east from our shores. This lamentable miscarriage was due solely to the weather, and not to any lack of skill and enterprise on the part of our admirals. Our destroyers had been in action with the raiders before dawn; as late as 11.30 p.m. one of our cruisers was in contact with the German light force, and just after noon the enemy was sighted by our battleships. But as the trap seemed about to close the fog thickened, and Admiral Funke slipped through. The German battle-fleet, which had followed the battle-cruisers, had turned for home early in the morning. The raiders returned safely to the Heligoland base, to be welcomed with Iron Crosses and newspaper eulogies of this new proof of German valour.

On that same day the Admiralty issued a message pointing out that 'demonstrations of this character against unfortified towns or commercial ports, though not difficult to accomplish, provided that a certain amount of risk is accepted, are devoid of military significance'. 'They must not,' it was added, 'be allowed to modify the general naval policy which is being pursued.' The first was a pardonable over-statement, unless we interpret the word 'military' in a narrow sense. These raids had a very serious military and naval purpose, which it would have been well to recognise. The German aim was to create such a panic in civilian England as would prevent the dispatch of the new armies to the Continent, and to compel Jellicoe and the Grand Fleet to move their base nearer the east coast, and undertake the duties of coast protection. The first was defeated by the excellent spirit in which England accepted the disaster. No voice was raised to clamour for the use of the new armies as a garrison for our seaboard. The second, though at first there was some natural indignation on the threatened coast, and a few foolish speeches and newspaper articles, had no chance of succeeding. In vain is the net spread in sight of the bird. The only result was that more stringent measures were taken to prevent espionage, that civilians were at last given some simple emergency directions, and that recruiting received the best possible advertisement.

Germany made much of the exploit, till she discovered that neutral nations, especially America, were seriously scandalised, and then she had recourse to explanations. Scarborough had been bombarded because it had a wireless station, Whitby because it had a naval signal station, Hartlepool because it had a little fort. Technically she could make out a kind of argument, and Hartlepool might fairly be said to have come within the category of a defended place. It was true that the fortifications were lamentably inadequate, but she could retort that that was Britain's business, not hers. But the real answer is that she did not aim at the destruction of military and naval accessories, except as an afterthought. The sea-front of Scarborough and the streets of Old Hartlepool were bombarded not because they were in the line of fire against a fort or a wireless station, but for their own sakes – because they contained a multitude of people who could be killed or terrorised. If Germany had the exact plans of the coast ports and of their condition at the time, as she certainly had, she knew very well how far they were from being fortified towns or military and naval bases. She selected them just because they were open towns, for 'frightfulness' there would have far greater moral effects upon the nation than if it had been directed against Harwich or Dover, where it might be regarded as one of the natural risks of war. Her performance was not a breach of a technicality, for it was only a logical extension of an admitted principle; but such a barbarous extension was in itself a breach of the unwritten conventions of honourable campaigning. ('Military proceedings are not regulated solely by the stipulations of international law. There are other factors – conscience, good sense. A sense of the duties which the principles of humanity impose will be the surest guide for the conduct of seamen, and will constitute the most effectual safeguard against abuse. The officers of the German navy – I say it with emphasis – will always fulfil in the strictest manner duties which flow from the unwritten law of humanity and civilisation.' – Baron Marschall von Bieberstein at the Hague Conference, 1907.) The slaughter of civilians to produce an impression was one of those things repellent to any man trained in the etiquette of a great service. The German navy had been justly admired, but it was beginning to show its parvenu origin. Individual sailors might conduct themselves like gentlemen, but there was no binding tradition of gentility in the service, and, as in the army, those at the head disliked and repudiated any such weakness. The last word was with the Mayor of Scarborough. 'Some newcomers,' he wrote, 'into honourable professions learn the tricks before the traditions.'

The British casualties by sea, apart from the losses in battle, were not serious during the last months of the year, but on the first day of 1915 there was a grave misfortune. On 31 December eight vessels of the Channel Fleet left Sheerness, and about three o'clock on the morning of 1 January in bright moonlight, the eight were steering in single line at a moderate speed near the Start Lighthouse. There was no screen of destroyers, and the situation invited an attack from submarines, several of which had been reported in these waters. The last of the line was the *Formidable*, Captain Loxley, a pre-Dreadnought of 15,000 tons, and a sister ship to the *Bulwark*, which had been blown up at Sheerness on 26 November. Some time after three she was struck by two torpedoes, and went down. Four boats were launched, one of which capsized, and out of a crew of some 800 only 201 were saved. The rescue of part of the crew was due to the courage and good seamanship of Captain William Pillar, of the Brixham trawler *Provident*, who in heavy weather managed to take the inmates of the *Formidable*'s cutter aboard his vessel. The misfortune showed that the lesson of the loss of the *Cressy*, *Hogue*, and *Aboukir* had been imperfectly learned. For eight battleships to move slowly in line on a moonlit night in submarine-infested waters without destroyers was simply to court destruction.

9

The Naval Attack on the Dardanelles

*The First Hint of an Eastern Diversion – Discussions in the War
Council – Lord Kitchener, Lord Fisher, and Mr Churchill – The
Dardanelles – Justification for the Naval Attack – Fortifications of
the Straits – The Naval Attack and Its Results*

Towards the close of 1914 the mind of the British Cabinet was
much exercised by the deadlock in the West. To some of its
members it seemed, in spite of Sir John French's hopefulness, that
the German defence was impenetrable except by an attrition so
slow that success would entail the bankruptcy of the conqueror.
They believed victory to be certain, but wished it to come soon,
and would fain have ended the war before the great drafts on
Britain's man-power fell due. In this impatience there was a sound
strategical instinct. There were no flanks to be turned in France
and Flanders, but vulnerable flanks might be found elsewhere.
The main gate of the enemy's beleaguered fortress was strongly
held, but there were various back doors which might be found
unguarded. Above all, they desired to make use of all the assets of
Britain, and in the campaign in the West, since Sir John French's
scheme of an advance by the coast road had been discarded, there
was no direct part which the British Navy could play. But in other
regions a joint enterprise might be possible, where the sea-power
of Britain could be used to decisive purpose. Accordingly, we find

during the winter a great scheme-making among Ministers and their technical advisers. Lord Fisher favoured a combined military and naval attack on the Schleswig-Holstein coast, for which he produced a colossal programme of new construction. His aim was to get behind the German right wing on land, and with the assistance of Russia to clear the Baltic. The enterprise seems to have been blessed at various times by Mr Lloyd George and Mr Churchill, but it faded from the air as it became clear that an immediate attack by Sir John French on a large scale was out of the question. The entry of Turkey into the war convinced the Government that, if a blow was to be struck in a new area, that area must be the Near East. Mr Lloyd George's fancy dwelt on Salonika. He was anxious, with the co-operation of Greece and Russia, to strike at the flank of the Teutonic League, and for the purpose to transfer a large British army to Serbia. The scheme was strongly opposed by military opinion, which pointed to the poor communications in Serbia for an advance and the extreme danger of depleting the British front in the West; and, though Lord Kitchener was prepared at one time to agree to a modification of it, the project died when Greece refused her assistance. A third alternative remained, which, compared with the other two, was sane and reasonable – to clear the Dardanelles and strike at Constantinople.

The Dardanelles campaign is one of the most pitiful, tragic, and glorious episodes in British history. As early as 1 September, Mr Winston Churchill had suggested to Kitchener the plan of seizing the Dardanelles by means of a Greek army, and so admitting a British fleet to the Sea of Marmora. On 25 November he proposed to the War Council to strike at the Gallipoli peninsula as a feint, but Kitchener decided that the movement was premature. But the matter remained in the minds of the War Council, and during December we find Kitchener discussing with Sir John Maxwell, then commanding in Egypt, the possibility of landing forces at Alexandretta in the Gulf of Iskanderun, to strike at the communications of any Turkish invasion of Egypt. On 2 January 1915, a new complexion was given to things by an appeal for help from Russia, then struggling on the Bzura and in the Caucasus. Kitchener resolved that Russia's request must be met, and next day pledged himself to a demonstration against the Turks, telling Mr Churchill that he considered the Dardanelles the only likely plan. On the 2nd, too, Lord Fisher had also informed the First Lord that he thought that the attack on Turkey held the field, 'but only if it is immediate'. Mr Churchill telegraphed to Vice-Admiral Carden on the 3rd asking if he considered that it was possible to force the Dardanelles by the use of ships alone, and received the answer that they might be forced 'by extended operations with a large number of ships'. As far back as 1906 the General Staff had reported on this very point and had come to an adverse decision, and Admiral Sir Henry Jackson, whom Mr Churchill had asked for a memorandum, was no less discouraging. On the 11th, Vice-Admiral Carden telegraphed his plan in detail, and the Admiralty Staff which examined it were more than dubious about its merits. At a meeting of the War Council on the 13th Mr Churchill explained the Carden scheme, and Kitchener declared that it was worth trying. The Council accordingly instructed the Admiralty to prepare for a naval expedition in February 'to bombard and take the Gallipoli peninsula, with Constantinople as its objective'.

It is clear that the chief patron of the scheme was Mr Churchill. His principal naval advisers were either hostile or half-hearted, and assented only on the understanding that in case of failure the attack could instantly be broken off. In the Council itself Lord Fisher and Sir Arthur Wilson kept silence, conceiving it to be their duty to answer questions when asked, but not to volunteer advice. But the former, though wavering sometimes between two opinions, was on the whole against the enterprise. He knew a good deal about the subject, having served under Hornby during the Russo-Turkish War when that admiral lay off Constantinople, and having, as First Sea Lord in 1904, fully investigated the whole problem of forcing the Dardanelles. The more he looked at Mr Churchill's policy the less he liked it, and on the 25th he wrote to the Prime Minister stating his objections. After a private meeting between Mr Asquith, Mr Churchill, and Lord Fisher on the 28th, a War Council was held, in which the First Lord carried his colleagues with him. For a moment it seemed as if Lord Fisher would resign, but he was persuaded to remain, apparently because he thought that the naval attack, even if it failed, need not involve serious losses. But on the feasibility of the operation he was still unconvinced, and he had with him the best naval opinion. Unfortunately, the naval authorities, out of a scrupulous regard for etiquette, left on the minds of the War Council the impression that they were not hostile to the scheme so much upon its technical merits as because they would have preferred a different objective in a totally different region. That appears to have been the view of Mr Asquith and Lord Kitchener; it cannot have been Mr Churchill's, who had precise knowledge of the technical naval objections but believed that new developments in gunnery had nullified them, and was prepared to force his opinion against the experts. That day, 28 January 1915, the decision to attack the Dardanelles by the fleet alone was finally ratified.

At this point it will be well to pause and consider two points which are vital if we are to form a judgement on the enterprise – the relation of such a plan to the general strategy of the war, and the kind of problem which an unsupported naval attack involved.

In the first place, it is necessary to be clear on the meaning of the terms 'subsidiary' and 'divergent' operations. The first is properly a term of praise; the second of blame. Every great campaign must produce one or more subsidiary operations. A blow may be necessary at the enemy's line of supply, or a halting neutral may require to have his mind made up for him, or some piece of enemy property, strategically valuable, deserves to be gathered in. Such operations are, strictly speaking, part of the main campaign, and success in them directly subserves the main object of the war. A 'divergent' operation, on the contrary, has no relation to the main effort, except that it is directed against the same enemy. Success in it is compatible with utter failure in the chief campaign, and does not necessarily bring the issue one step nearer. It usually involves some wasting of the force available for the main theatre, and it means a certain dissipation of the energy and brain-power of the high commands.

Our history is strewn with the wrecks of divergent operations, and a few instances may make their meaning clear. In the years 1793–94, when it was our business to scotch the Revolutionary Government of France by striking at its head, we set out on adventures in every quarter of the globe. We took six West Indian islands – strategically as important as the North Pole; we landed in Haiti; we sent a force under the Duke of York to the Netherlands; we held Toulon as long as we could; we seized Corsica; we sent an expedition to La Vendée. The consequence was that we succeeded nowhere, and the Revolutionary Government at the end of that time was stronger than ever. Next year, 1795, while things were going badly for us on other battle-grounds, we chose to send an expedition to Cape Town, to attack Demerara, and to make a disastrous landing on an island in Quiberon Bay. And so we continued to indulge our passion for outlandish geography, while France grew in strength and the star of Napoleon rose above the horizon. Take the year 1807. We sent a force under Sir Hume Popham to the Cape, which proceeded to South America, took Buenos Aires, and presently lost it. We projected an expedition to Valparaiso, and another against Mexico. These ventures, as a matter of fact, were utter failures; but had they been successful they would have in no way helped the main purpose of the war. For in Europe Napoleon was moving from strength to strength. 1807 was the year of Friedland and of the Treaty of Tilsit.

Let us attempt to set down the principles which govern legitimate subsidiary operations, and separate them from the illegitimate divergent type. There is first the question of locality. Obviously it is not necessary that the minor campaign should be fought in the same area as the major. Wellington wore down the strength of the French in the Peninsula, though the main theatre of war, the place where the big stake lay, was central Europe. In the American Civil War the eyes of the world were fixed on the lines of the Potomac, but the real centre of gravity was Vicksburg and the operations on the Mississippi. Nor, again, is it necessary that even the major campaign should be fought in or adjoining the enemy's home country. In the Seven Years' War France was conquered at Plassey and at Quebec, because it was for an overseas empire, for the domination of India and America, that the combatants fought. The locality of a subsidiary operation matters nothing, provided – and this is the first principle – the operation directly subserves the main object of the war. In other words, the operation, if successful, must be profitable. In the second place, there must be a reasonable chance of success. A subsidiary operation, thoroughly justified by general strategy, may be a blunder if it is undertaken with forces too weak to surmount the difficulties. If the force is not strong enough to effect the object, then, however desirable the object, the force would have been better left at home. Thirdly, any force used for the subsidiary operation must not seriously weaken the operations in the main theatre, unless the former operation is so vital that in itself it becomes the centre of gravity of the campaign.

Waterloo is rightly regarded as one of the decisive battles of the world, but the Allies at Waterloo won by a very narrow margin. At the time Wellington's seasoned veterans of the Peninsula were for the most part involved in the woods and swamps of the Canadian frontier. That was inevitable; but had they been sent there as part of a strategic purpose with the European situation what it was on Napoleon's return from Elba it would have exactly illustrated the danger we are discussing. In the present war it was clear from the start that Germany must be conquered in Europe, and that the main campaign must be that on the lines from the North Sea to the Alps, and from the Baltic to the Bukovina. Germany had set the battle plan, and her antagonists could not choose but accept the challenge. Any weakening of these lines so as to compromise their strength for the sake of a subsidiary operation was clearly inadvisable by all the principles of war.

Whether the Dardanelles expedition violated the second and the third of these canons will be discussed in due course. But the application of the first – the value of the objective sought, and its relation to the central purpose of the Allies – can be made clear by a few general considerations. What were the ends to be attained by the forcing of the Dardanelles? The Sea of Marmora and the winding straits that link it with the Ægean and the Euxine form a water frontier of some 200 miles between Asia and Europe. These straits are of the utmost importance to Turkey. Against a naval Power like Britain or France they were the last defence of the capital, and that capital, more than any other great city of the world, was the palladium of the Power which had its seat there. It was almost all that was left to the race of Osman of their once splendid European possessions. It had been the base for those proud expeditions against Vienna and the Hungarian plains when Turkey was still a conquering Power. It had been the prize for which her neighbours had lusted, and which she had still retained against all rivals. It was, in a real sense, the sign visible of Turkey's existence as a sovereign state. If Constantinople fell

Turkey would fall, and the doom of the capital was sealed so soon as the Allied battleships, with their communications secure behind them, entered the Sea of Marmora.

The strategic importance of the forcing of the Dardanelles in a war with Turkey was therefore clear beyond all doubt. But in how far would the fall of Constantinople influence the decision of the main European conflict? In the first place, it would to some extent simplify Russia's problem, and release troops for Poland and Galicia. There was the possibility that a mere threat to the capital might lead to a revolution which would overthrow the shaky edifice of Enver's rule. The bulk of the Turkish people did not share the passion for Germany felt by the Committee of Union and Progress, and advices from Constantinople during those days seemed to point to the imminence of a rising which would make a clean sweep of the Young Turk party and restore the Sultan to his old place at the side of France and Britain. Again, the opening of the passage between the Black Sea and the Ægean would give Russia the means for exporting her accumulated wheat supplies. The lack of these was increasing the cost of bread in western Europe, and the restriction of Russian exports had made the rate of exchange set violently against her, so that she was paying in some cases thirty times the normal price for her foreign purchases. She also stood in sore need of a channel for the entrance of war munitions. Archangel had been closed since January, the trans-Siberian line was a costly and circuitous route for all but her imports from Japan, while entries by Norway and Sweden were at the best precarious. But the main strategic value of the Dardanelles plan lay in its effect upon hesitating neutrals. Italy at the moment was still in the valley of indecision, and the downfall of Turkey and its influence upon the Balkan States would impel her to action. Turkey's defeat would have an effect upon the Balkan position like the addition of a new chemical to a compound – it would leave none of the constituents unaltered.

Greece, Rumania, and Bulgaria all had national interests and purposes which compelled them to keep a watchful eye on each other, and which made it difficult for any one of them to move without its neighbour. Bulgaria, who had borne the heavy end of the Turkish campaign, had lost the prize of victory. Three compacts had been violated to her hurt, and she was deeply distrustful of all the Great Powers, and especially of Russia. German financiers had befriended her in 1913, when France and Britain had stood aside, and her Stambolobists had always looked to Austria as their ally. A secret treaty with Austria had indeed been concluded a month after the outbreak of the war. With Greece and Serbia – especially with the latter – she had a bitter quarrel over the delimitation of territory after the Balkan wars, and she had little cause to forget Rumania's intervention. At the same time her geographical position made it highly perilous for her to join the Teutonic League, unless its victory were assured. Her attitude was therefore a circumspect neutrality; but the first Allied guns that spoke in the Sea of Marmora would compel her to a decision.

With Bulgaria decided, Greece and Rumania would soon follow suit. Rumania was faced with a complex situation from which she was slowly disentangling herself under the pressure of events. If her southern frontiers were safe it seemed likely that she would make her choice, and her geographical situation and her well-equipped army of nearly half a million would make her an invaluable ally. Greece in such circumstances could not stand apart. With Turkey out of action and the Balkans united on the Allies' side, the most critical part of the main campaign – the long front of Russia – would be greatly eased. When the Italian guns sounded on the Isonzo and the Rumanian force took the Austrian right wing in flank, the balance against Russian arms might be redressed.

In a speech made later in the year Mr Churchill defined the prize at which he aimed:

Beyond those 4 miles of ridge and scrub on which our soldiers, our French comrades, our gallant Australian and New Zealand fellow-subjects are now battling, lie the downfall of a hostile empire, the destruction of an enemy's fleet and army, the fall of a world-famous capital, and probably the accession of powerful allies. The struggle will be heavy, the risks numerous, the losses cruel; but victory when it comes will make amends for all. There never was a great subsidiary operation of war in which a more complete harmony of strategic, political, and economic advantages has combined, or which stood in truer relation to the main decision which is in the central theatre. Through the Narrows of the Dardanelles and across the ridges of the Gallipoli peninsula lie some of the shortest paths to a triumphant peace.

The language may have been over-coloured, but substantially the claim was just. A Dardanelles expedition directly subserved the main object of the war. An attack by ships alone, an attack that in case of failure could be promptly suspended, would not, it may fairly be argued, have weakened the Allies' strength in the main theatre, though Kitchener may well have reflected that in the East it was not wise for Britain to put her hand to the plough and then turn back. It remains to consider whether the enterprise fulfilled the third of the conditions of a wise subsidiary operation: whether the plan gave a reasonable chance of success.

A naval attack on the Dardanelles without the co-operation of a military force would be a battle of ships against forts, and it had long been widely held by experts that in such a contest the advantage would lie with the forts. This conclusion was so generally accepted that during the Spanish-American War the United States Navy Department repeatedly warned the admirals that battleships and heavy cruisers must not be risked in close-range action with forts. All that the navy ventured upon was a long-range bombardment of the Spanish coast fortifications, attacks that were little more than demonstrations, for no serious attempt was made to silence the land batteries. A few guns mounted on Socapa Point at Santiago, and very badly served, were sufficient to prevent Admiral Sampson from risking a close attack. It was the same in the Russo-Japanese War. Admiral Togo never risked his battleships and cruisers in a close attack on the sea batteries of Port Arthur. There were occasional long-range bombardments with no result, and the reduction of the fortress was due to the attack by land. Similarly Tsing-tau in the present war fell not to Admiral Kato's squadron, but to General Kamio's army.

It might be said, however, that though ships were not likely to silence forts, forts could not prevent ships running past them. The argument was not relevant to the case of the Dardanelles, where in the long run not only a passage, but the occupation of the passage, was necessary, as Hornby found in 1878. But in any case it was unsound, for the development of submarine mines and torpedo warfare had made it all but impossible to evade the fort. A minefield in a channel, protected by a few well-mounted guns, with searchlights and quick-firers to prevent mine-sweeping by night, was for a fleet a practically impassable barrier. The mine-field could not be disposed of until the fort had been destroyed.

Such being the accepted doctrine among naval and military students of the question, it may well be asked why the scheme of forcing the Dardanelles by a naval attack alone was ever accepted by the British Government. It was known that very high naval authority was opposed to it; it was equally true that certain naval authorities approved of it, and that Mr Churchill was its impassioned advocate. On what grounds? There was an idea abroad that new conditions had been introduced into the problem, and there was the usual tendency to exaggerate the effect of a new weapon. The Dreadnought, the long-range gun, the submarine had each been hailed as about to revolutionise warfare. It was presumed that the huge high-explosive shells of the modern warship would make land batteries untenable, not by silencing their guns one by one, but by acting like flying mines, the explosion of which would shatter the defences and produce a panic among the gunners. Once the forts were thus temporarily overcome, landing parties would complete the task, the mine-fields would be cleared, and the passage be won. It was also anticipated that with the long range of the newest naval guns the forts could be bombarded from a distance at which their own armament would be ineffective. The notion was that the outer forts at the entrance to the Straits could be silenced by the converging fire of a number of ships from the open sea, while the attack on the inner forts would be carried on by individual fire from ships in the Gulf of Saros, which, with airplanes to direct them, would send their shells over the hills of the Gallipoli peninsula. These two factors – aerial reconnaissance and the increased range of naval guns – were believed to have changed the whole conditions of the enterprise.

It would be unfair to say that there was no colour for this forecast. But it erred in strangely neglecting and underestimating other factors in the situation, and in unduly simplifying the problem. It was not a mere question of a duel between the guns of the fleet and those of the permanent fortifications. Had it been, there would have been much to be said for the optimistic view. But the defences of the Dardanelles had been organised on a system which took the fullest advantage of natural features, and was based on past experience and a scientific knowledge of modern warfare. It was no improvised Turkish expedient, but the work of the German General Staff. It contemplated an attack, not only by a fleet, but by a large military force acting in conjunction. When, therefore, the Allies, to the surprise of their enemies, decided upon a mere naval attack, the problem of the defence was immensely simplified.

To appreciate the difficulties of the attack we must consider briefly the topography of the Straits. Their northern shore is formed by the peninsula of Gallipoli, a tongue of land some 50 miles long, which varies in width from 12 to 2 or 3 miles. The country is a mass of rocky ridges rising to a height of over 700 feet from the sea. The hills are so steep and sharply cut that to reach their tops is in many places a matter of sheer climbing. There was little cultivation; there were few villages, and no properly engineered roads. Most of the land was covered with a dense scrub from 3 to 6 feet high, with stunted forests in the hollows. Communications were so bad that the usual way from village to village was not by land, but by boat along the inner or outer coast. At the head of the Dardanelles, on the European side, lay the town and harbour of Gallipoli, the headquarters of the naval defence of the Straits. The southern shore is also hilly. Near the entrance on the Asiatic side there is the flat and marshy plain of Troy, which is bounded on the east by hills running to 3,000 feet. On both sides the high ground overhangs the sea passage, and on the north side for about 12 miles the hills form a line of cliffs, with narrow half-moons of beach at the base, and here and there a stream making a gully in the rampart. As everywhere in the Mediterranean, there is practically no tide, but a strong current, rising to 4 knots, sets continuously down the Straits from the Sea of Marmora. North-easterly winds are prevalent, and before the days of steam these often closed the passage for weeks at a time to ingoing traffic.

There were two groups of forts. The first was at the entrance – on the north side, Cape Helles and Sedd-el-Bahr, with one or two adjacent batteries; on the opposite shore, Kum Kale and Orkanieh. None of these forts were heavily armed, for it was recognised that in any case they would be at a disadvantage against a long-range attack from a fleet in the open sea. The entrance forts were merely the outposts of the real defence. The second group was at the

Narrows. 14 miles from the mouth the Straits close in to a width of about ¾ mile. Up to this point their general course has been from south-west to north-east, but now the channel makes a short turn directly northward before resuming its original direction. There is thus within a distance of a few miles a sharp double bend, and guns placed in position at the water's edge could cross their fire against ships ascending the Straits, which would also be brought under end-on fire from guns at the top of the Narrows. At the entrance to the Narrows were the forts of Chanak, or Sultanieh Kalessi, on the Asiatic side, and Kilid Bahr, on the European. The slopes above the latter were studded with batteries, some commanding the approach to the Narrows, others commanding the seaway towards Gallipoli. Along both sides, but especially between Chanak and Nagara, the low ground was lined with batteries. It was possible to attack the forts at the entrance to the Narrows at fairly long range from the wider channel below the bend, but there was no room to bring any large number of ships into action at the same time. Once the entrance was passed all fighting must be at close range.

But the strength of the defence did not depend only on the batteries. An attacking fleet had other weapons to face besides the guns. There was first the obstruction of the channel by submarine mines. To get rid of these by sweeping was nearly impossible, for the light vessels, which alone could be employed, had to face not only the fire of the forts but that of mobile guns on the higher ground. Again, the descending current could be used to send down drift-mines upon the attacking ships. The artillery defence was further supplemented by howitzer batteries on the heights, difficult to locate, easy to move if located, and therefore almost impossible to silence. It was clear that a fleet endeavouring to force a channel thus defended was at the gravest disadvantage. There was only one way to complete success – the co-operation of a land army. By

On 3 November 1914, an Anglo-French squadron had appeared at the Dardanelles and for ten minutes bombarded the forts at the entrance. The order had been given by the British Admiralty, and the purpose seems to have been to draw the fire of the forts and ascertain if they possessed long-range guns. Such premature action was a blunder, for it put the enemy on the alert, and during the three months that followed no further step was taken, though by the end of January 1915 the island of Tenedos had been seized, while Greece tolerated the use of Lemnos, where the great inlet of Mudros supplied a valuable base for naval operations. By the middle of February a considerable naval force, French and British, had been concentrated at the entrance to the Straits. With two exceptions, the larger British ships were of the pre-Dreadnought class; but there were also present the *Inflexible*, which had been in the Battle of the Falkland Islands, and the new super-Dreadnought, the *Queen Elizabeth*. The latter belonged to the most recent and most powerful class of battleship in the world. She was one of a group of five which, when war began, were still in the builders' hands, and in the ordinary course she would not have been commissioned till the late summer of 1915. Her main armament was made up of eight 15-inch guns, so mounted as to give a fire of four guns ahead or astern, and of the whole, eight on either side.

The operations against the outer forts began on Friday 19 February. The ships engaged were the *Inflexible*, *Agamemnon*, *Cornwallis*, *Vengeance*, and *Triumph* – British; and the *Bouvet*, *Suffren*, and *Gaulois* – French; covered by a flotilla of destroyers. (*Inflexible* – 17,250 tons, eight 12-inch guns, sixteen 4-inch guns; *Agamemnon* – 16,750 tons, four 12-inch guns, ten 9.2-inch guns; *Cornwallis* – 14,000 tons, four 12-inch guns, twelve 6-inch guns; *Vengeance* – 12,950 tons, four 12-inch guns, twelve 6-inch guns; *Triumph* – 11,980 tons, four 10-inch guns, fourteen 7.5-inch guns; *Bouvet* – 12,200 tons, two 12-inch guns, two 10.8-inch guns, eight

5.5-inch guns, eight 4-inch guns; *Suffren* – 12,730 tons, four 12-inch guns, ten 6.4-inch guns; *Gaulois* – 11,260 tons, four 12-inch guns, ten 5.5-inch guns.) The naval force was under the command of Vice-Admiral Sackville Carden, and the French squadron was under Rear-Admiral Guépratte. Behind the battle-line lay the new mother-ship for seaplanes, the *Ark Royal*, named after Howard's flagship in the war with the Spanish Armada. From her, aircraft were sent up to watch the fire of the battleships and signal the result. The action began at 8 a.m. It was clear that the forts at Cape Helles, on the point of the peninsula, and at Kum Kale, on the opposite shore, were frequently hit, and at times seemed to be smothered in bursting shells. It was harder to make out what was happening to the low earthworks of the batteries about Sedd-el-Bahr. All morning the bombardment continued; it was like target practice, for not a single shot was fired in reply. Admiral Carden came to the conclusion that the forts had been seriously damaged, and at a quarter to three in the afternoon gave the order to close in. What followed showed that aerial observation of long-range fire was no easy matter. As the ships steamed nearer, the hitherto silent and apparently destroyed forts began to shoot. They made bad practice, for no one of the six ships that had shortened range was hit. By sundown the European batteries were quiet again, but Kum Kale was still firing, when, on account of the failing light, Admiral Carden withdrew the fleet.

For some days there was bad weather, but by the morning of Thursday 25 February, it had sufficiently improved for operations to be resumed. At 10 a.m. on that day the *Queen Elizabeth*, *Agamemnon*, and *Irresistible* (15,000 tons, four 12-inch and twelve 6-inch guns), and the French battleship *Gaulois*, renewed the long-range bombardment of the outer forts. It was clear that these had not been seriously damaged by the action of the 19th, and what injury had been done had been repaired in the interval. Once again the four forts, Sedd-el-Bahr, Cape Helles, Kum Kale, and Orkanieh, were attacked. Of these the first mounted six 10.2-inch guns, the second two 9.2-inch, the third four 10.2-inch and two 5.9-inch, and the fourth two 9.2-inch. Against the sixteen heavy guns of the forts the four ships brought into action twenty pieces heavier than anything mounted on the land, including the 15-inch guns of the *Queen Elizabeth*, the most powerful weapon ever used in naval war. The forts were thus greatly outmatched, and the long range of the *Queen Elizabeth*'s guns enabled her to come into the fight at a distance where nothing from the land could possibly touch her. In an hour and a half the *Queen Elizabeth* and the *Agamemnon* had silenced the Cape Helles guns, but not before these had hit the latter ship, a shell fired at a range of 6 miles bursting on board her, with a loss of three men killed and five wounded. This was the only casualty suffered during the first stage of the bombardment. At 11.30 a.m. the *Vengeance* and *Cornwallis* came into action, and, running into close range, silenced the lighter armament of the Cape Helles battery. The attack on the Asiatic forts was at the same time reinforced by two of the French ships, the *Suffren* and the *Charlemagne*, which poured in a heavy fire at a range of only 2,000 yards. Early in the afternoon the *Triumph* and the *Albion* (12,950 tons, four 12-inch guns, twelve 6-inch) attacked Sedd-el-Bahr at close range. It said much for the courage and discipline of the Turkish artillerymen that, though they faced overwhelming odds, their last gun was not silenced till after 5 p.m.

Little daylight remained, but, covered by the battleships and destroyers, a number of North Sea trawlers at once set to work to sweep for mines in the entrance. The work was resumed next morning at sunrise, and the mine-field was cleared for a distance of 4 miles up the Straits. Then the *Albion*, *Vengeance*, and *Majestic* (the oldest battleship type in the Navy; 14,000 tons, four 12-inch guns, twelve 6-inch) steamed in between the headlands, and opened a long-range fire on Fort Dardanos, a work on the Asiatic side some distance below the Narrows. It was not heavily armed, its best guns being four 5.9 Krupps. As the battleships opened fire, a reply came not only from Dardanos but from several un-located batteries at various points along the shore. The Turkish fire, however, did little harm, and we were able to attack the rear of the entrance forts and drive off several bodies of Turkish troops. One party near Kum Kale was driven across the bridge near the mouth of the River Mendere (the ancient Simois), and the bridge itself destroyed by shell fire. We believed that by this time the Turks had everywhere been forced to abandon the defences at the entrance, and landing parties of Royal Marines were sent ashore with explosives to complete the destruction of the guns in the forts. This they successfully accomplished, but near Kum Kale they encountered a detachment of the enemy, and, after a hot skirmish, had to fall back to their boats with a few casualties. On such slender basis the Turkish bulletins built up a report of landing parties everywhere repulsed with heavy loss. At this date it is clear that the Turks had nothing in the way of defences on the Gallipoli peninsula, apart from the shore forts.

The result of the day's operations was that we had cleared the entrance to the Straits. This was the easiest part of the problem, and only the beginning of the formidable task assigned to the Allied fleets. The real defence of the Dardanelles – the forts at the Narrows – had not been touched. Nevertheless, with that misleading optimism which has done so much to paralyse national effort, the press of France and Britain wrote as if the fall of the outer forts had decided the fate of Constantinople. In that city at the moment there was undoubtedly something of a panic among civilians, but the German and Turkish Staffs were in the best of spirits. They were greatly comforted by the time it had taken the powerful Allied fleet to destroy the outer forts, and they believed that the inner forts were impregnable. There long-range attacks would be impossible; no large number of ships could be brought simultaneously into action, and drifting mines and torpedoes could be used to supplement the artillery defence. Enver, not usually partial to the truth, was for once in a way correct when he told a correspondent: 'The real defence of the Straits is yet to come. That lies where the difficult waterway deprives ships of their power to manoeuvre freely, and obliges them to move in a narrow defile commanded by artillery and mines.'

For a few days there were strong northerly winds, but in spite of the rough weather the mine-sweepers continued their work below the Narrows. On Thursday 4 March, the battleships were again in action. Some attacked the forts inside the Straits, Dardanos and Soghandere, and a French cruiser in the Gulf of Saros demolished a look-out station at Cape Gaba Tepe. Among the ships engaged were the *Ocean* and the *Lord Nelson* (a sister ship of the *Agamemnon* – 16,500 tons, four 12-inch guns, ten 9.2-inch). A landing party of Royal Marines near Kum Kale were driven back to their boats by a superior Turkish force with the relatively large loss of twenty-two killed, twenty-two wounded, and three missing. On 5 March there was a demonstration against Smyrna, a British and French detachment, under Vice-Admiral Peirse, bombarding the outer forts. The attack was not pushed, and was only intended to induce Enver to keep a considerable force in that neighbourhood.

On 6 March the weather was again fine, with a smooth sea, and a preliminary attempt was made on the Narrows forts. On the preceding day some of the ships had entered the Straits and drawn the fire of the forts at Kilid Bahr. There was an explosion in one of them, and after that it ceased firing. On the morning of the 6th the *Vengeance*, *Albion*, *Majestic*, *Prince George* (a sister ship of the *Majestic*), and *Suffren* steamed into the Straits and attacked the forts on both sides just below the Narrows. The fire was chiefly directed against Dardanos on the Asiatic, and Soghandere on the European shore – works which may be regarded as the outposts of the main Narrows defence. The attacking ships were struck repeatedly by shells, but no serious damage was done, and there was no loss of life. This attack from inside the Straits was, however, a secondary operation. The main attack, from which great results were expected, was made by the *Queen Elizabeth*, *Agamemnon*, and *Ocean* from the Gulf of Saros, on the outer side of the Gallipoli peninsula. Lying off the point of Gaba Tepe, they sent their shells over the intervening hills, with airplanes directing their fire. Their target was two of the forts at Chanak, on the Asiatic side of the Narrows, about 12 miles off. These forts had a very heavy armament, including 14-inch guns, and it was hoped to destroy them by indirect fire, to which they had no means of replying. The Turks replied from various points on the heights of the peninsula with well-concealed howitzers and field guns, and three shells struck the *Queen Elizabeth*.

Next day, 7 March, the attack was renewed. The *Agamemnon* and *Lord Nelson*, firing at a range of from 12,000 to 14,000 yards, supported by four French battleships, the *Bouvet*, *Charlemagne*, *Gaulois*, and *Suffren*, attacked from inside the Straits and engaged the forts on both sides of the Narrows. Chanak, which the *Queen Elizabeth* had been trying to demolish the day before, brought its heavy guns into action. The *Gaulois*, *Agamemnon*, and *Lord Nelson* were hit several times, but we believed that we had put the forts below Chanak and Kilid Bahr out of action. Subsequent experience showed that it was a difficult matter permanently to silence forts. Under the heavy fire of the ships it was hard to keep the guns constantly in action, not so much on account of any serious damage, but because the batteries were flooded with stifling vapours from the shells, and it was necessary to withdraw the men until the air cleared. Further, the defenders had been ordered to economise ammunition, and to reserve their fire for the closer attack which they believed would follow. The fact, therefore, that a fort ceased firing was no proof that it had been really silenced. Again and again during these operations we heard of forts being silenced which next day or a few days after could bring most of their guns into action.

The following week saw nothing but minor operations. On the 10th an attempt was made to shell the Bulair defences at long range, and the British warships shelled some new batteries of light guns which the Turks had established near Morto Bay, on the European side of the entrance to the Straits. The Turkish Government sent out a report that the Allied fleets had been unsuccessfully bombarding the defences at Sedd-el-Bahr and Kum Kale. The Allied press treated this as an impudent fiction, and pointed out that the forts there had been destroyed many days before. But the Turkish communiqué told the truth. We had destroyed the forts, but we had not occupied the ground on both sides of the entrance. The Turks had accordingly entrenched themselves strongly near the ruins and mounted guns, and these we attacked on 10 and 11 March.

At that time, misled by the optimism of the newspapers, the ordinary man in France and Britain counted with certainty on the speedy news that our fleet was steaming through the Sea of Marmora on the way to Constantinople. When tidings came that the light cruiser *Amethyst* had on 15 March made a dash into the Narrows, he believed that the Turkish defence had collapsed. The *Amethyst*'s enterprise was part of a mine-sweeping expedition, and also a daring reconnaissance in which the little ship drew the fire of the upper forts. She got but a short way, and lost heavily in the attempt. But her exploit, magnified through Greek channels, made the world believe that the Narrows defences had been seriously damaged, and that the time was ripe for a determined effort to force a passage. The combined fleet had now grown to a formidable strength, and included a Russian cruiser, the *Askold*, which appeared on 3 March. Vice-Admiral Carden had been compelled by ill-health to relinquish the command, and Vice-Admiral John Michael de Robeck succeeded him.

The great effort was made on Thursday 18 March. It was a bright, clear day, with a light wind and a calm sea. At a quarter to eleven in the forenoon the *Agamemnon*, *Lord Nelson*, *Queen Elizabeth*, *Inflexible*, *Triumph*, and *Prince George* steamed up the Straits towards the Narrows. The first four ships engaged the forts of Chanak and the battery on the point opposite, while the *Triumph* and *Prince George* kept the batteries lower down occupied by firing at Soghandere, Dardanos, and Kephez Point. After the bombardment had lasted for an hour and a half, during which the ships were fired upon not only by the forts but by howitzers and field guns on the heights, the French squadron, *Bouvet*, *Charlemagne*, *Gaulois*, and *Suffren*, came into action, steaming in to attack the forts at short range. Under the combined fire of the ten ships the forts once more ceased firing. A third squadron then entered the Straits to push the attack further. This was made up of six British battleships, the *Albion*, *Irresistible*, *Majestic*, *Ocean*, *Swiftsure* (a sister ship of the *Triumph* – 11,980 tons, four 10-inch, fourteen 7.5-inch guns), and *Vengeance*. As they steered towards Chanak the four French ships were withdrawn in order to make room for them in the narrow waters. But in the process of this change all the forts suddenly began to fire again, which showed that none of them had been seriously damaged. According to Turkish accounts, only one big gun had been dismounted.

Then came the first disaster of the day. The French squadron was moving down to the open water inside the Straits, being still under fire from the inner forts. Three large shells struck the *Bouvet* almost simultaneously, and immediately after there was a loud explosion, and she was hidden in a cloud of smoke. The first impression was that she had been seriously damaged by shell fire, but her real wound was got from one of the mines which the Turks were now sending down with the current. They had waited to begin this new attack till the narrow waterway was full of ships. As the smoke cleared, the *Bouvet* was seen to be heeling over. She sank in three minutes in 36 fathoms of water, carrying with her most of her crew.

The attack on the forts continued as long as the light lasted. The mine-sweepers had been brought up the Straits in order to clear the passage in front, and to look out for drift-mines. An hour and a half after the *Bouvet* sank, the *Irresistible* turned out of the fighting line with a heavy list. She also had been struck by a mine, but she floated for more than an hour, and the destroyers took off nearly all her crew – a dangerous task, for they were the target all the time of Turkish fire. She sank at ten minutes to six, and a quarter of an hour later another drift-mine struck the *Ocean*. The latter sank almost as quickly as the *Bouvet*, but the destroyers were on the alert, and saved most of her crew. Several of the other ships had suffered damage and loss of life from the Turkish guns. The *Gaulois* had been repeatedly hit; her upper works were seriously injured, and a huge rent had been torn in her bows. The *Inflexible* had been struck by a heavy shell, which killed and wounded the majority of the men and officers in her fire-control station, and set her on fire forward.

As the sun set most of the forts were still in action, and during the short twilight the Allied fleet slipped out of the Dardanelles. The great attack on the Narrows had failed – failed, with the loss of three battleships and the better part of a thousand men.

At first it was the intention of Admiral de Robeck to continue the attack, and the British Admiralty assented. But on 19 March Sir Ian Hamilton, who had seen part of the action, telegraphed to Kitchener that he had been reluctantly forced to the conclusion that the Dardanelles could not be forced by battleships alone, and by the 22nd de Robeck had come round to the same opinion. Lord Fisher felt himself bound to accept the view of the admiral on the spot, and though Mr Churchill, supported by some of the younger naval officers, pressed for a renewal of the attack, he was compelled to bow to the opinion of his professional advisers. On the information at the disposal of the British Government it is hard to see what other course was open to them except to withdraw the fleet. Even if the enemy was running short of ammunition, the forts were sufficiently intact to protect the mine-field, and the mine-field barred the road for the great ships. Of the Allied fleet of sixteen battleships three had been sunk and four disabled long before they had come to the hardest part of their task. It is idle to discuss whether, had the action been persisted in even at the cost of more ships, the Turkish defence would have crumbled. Such discussions belong to the realm of pure hypothesis, and statesmen without a gift of prophecy must be content to decide on the gross and patent facts before them. Undoubtedly the Turks were gravely alarmed, and certain sections of the defence were ready to despair. But it is not less indubitable that, had the fleets attacked again, there would have been a stubborn resistance and such losses as would have left too weak a naval force for the joint operation now under contemplation. It was a gamble which no responsible Government could have justified to its people. (For Enver's reported view see Dardanelles Commission (Cd. 8490), p. 40. *Cf.* also Morgenthau's *Secrets of the Bosphorus*, chaps xvii–xviii.)

A month later the attempt on the Dardanelles was renewed, but the part played by the Navy was henceforth subsidiary to that of the Army, and the rest of this story – unsurpassed, for its heroism and tragedy, in the history of Britain – cannot be recorded here.

10

The Battle of Loos

The Russian Retreat from the Donajetz – Spring Offensives in the West – The French at Artois – Festubert – The Summer Stagnation – Loos – Sir John French Surrenders his Command

By the end of March the German Command had reached two important conclusions: that their forces in the West, though considerably outnumbered by the enemy, were competent to hold that front against any Allied attack; and that an effort must be made at once to bring about a decision against Russia. The desperate position of Austria, and the likelihood that in the near future Italy and Rumania might be added to the roll of their antagonists, forced the necessity of an immediate concentration of effort in the East upon their minds.

The issue proved that Germany had judged more shrewdly than the Allied Staffs. She alone was fully awake to the precise nature of the war in its present phase. All through the winter, when Britain was speculating how long German stores of food and explosives would last, she had been busy preparing her armoury. She found substitutes for materials which she had formerly imported, and the whole talent of her chemists was drawn upon for the purpose. All the human strength of the nation, which was not in the field, was employed directly or indirectly to make munitions. When we remember that she supplied 900 miles of front (with some assistance from Austria) in the East, more than 500 miles in the West, and equipped Turkey for the Dardanelles campaign, and that her use of shells was five or six times more lavish than that of her opponents, we may get some notion of the magnitude of the national effort. It was more impressive in its way than the muster of her great armies in August.

The decision to concentrate against Russia entailed many risks, but the German generals in the East, and the Austrian Conrad, believed that by a great effort Russia could be finally put out of action. Falkenhayn differed; she would be crippled, he thought, but no more; and he would consent only to a limited operation, which if necessary could be broken off to permit of a transfer of troops to the West. Yet the attack which opened on 2 May on the line of the Donajetz was so brilliantly directed and so overwhelmingly successful that at first it seemed as if Hindenburg's dream had come true. It was led by Mackensen, a master of speed and surprise, and his Chief of Staff was Seeckt, who after the war was to rebuild the German army. Tactically it was the forerunner of the method of infiltration. Although outnumbered by nearly half a million, Mackensen in three days was in open country, and in a fortnight had advanced 95 miles. By the end of May the Russians were behind the San and the Dniester. In June, Lemberg was retaken, and there was no enemy left in Galicia. The task was now to cut off the Warsaw salient, and on 4 August Warsaw fell.

The Russians were desperately short of equipment. Her total of heavy guns was far lower than the enemy's. Her field artillery was poorly supplied with shells; and at various times in the course of retreat its munitions gave out altogether, and it made no attempt to cope with the fire of the enemy. The Russians were terribly short also in machine guns, having at the most one to the enemy's four. As the retreat continued, even their musketry fire was in danger of starvation. Many of the new recruits took their places in the firing line without rifles; and captured rifles, preserved as souvenirs, were collected from the Red Cross detachments and wherever they could be found. Men had to wait in the trenches under heavy fire till they could get arms from wounded comrades. In one army a whole division had to face an attack without a single rifle, and the field artillery of that army was limited to two shells a day. In the words of a Russian private: 'We had only one weapon, the living breast of the soldier.' The fibre of the Russian soldier seemed a thing beyond the power of mortal calamity to weaken. He might perish in millions, but the survivors took up the weapons of the dead and cheerfully continued. But the effect on the Russian people – the relatives of the dead and missing in a thousand cities and a myriad villages – was tremendous, the more tremendous in that it wrought as slowly as the thawing of the ice in spring. There was as yet no weakening, but everywhere there was perplexity and confusion. In the circles of government the honest men laboured to purge the administration of its infinite corruption; many reputations were dimmed, suspicion fell upon the highest quarters, gossip was busy with all its tongues. The determination of the great people behind the bureaucrats was strong; and when in July, before the fall of Warsaw, Germany made overtures for peace, she was haughtily repulsed.

As the summer wore on Russia was retreating on better communications, and though Kovno, Brest-Litovsk, and Vilna were lost, the autumn saw a definite check in the German advance. For Germany the campaign had been a notable triumph, and Poland was now in her hands. But she had not attained her chief object. Russia had suffered bitterly between May and September, but the decisive victory for which Germany hoped had not been achieved.

* * *

In the West an Allied offensive in the spring and summer had been decided upon as early as November 1914. It was more than ever essential now that an attempt should be made to relieve the pressure on Russia, and to assure Italy, when she entered the alliance, of the vigour and resolution of her colleagues. It was true that the new armies of Britain were not ready, and that the munitionment everywhere fell short of what was required. But both Joffre and Sir John French believed that, even so, they had the power to break the enemy front and force a retirement. They conceived that what had been done on a small scale at Neuve Chapelle could be repeated at more vital points with deadly consequences. The result was a series of costly and futile attacks which continued through the summer, attacks based on a mistaken principle, delivered on various sections of a long front, but radically unco-ordinated. They did nothing to relieve the distress of Russia, and Germany was able to repel them without departing by a hairbreadth from the plan of campaign she had devised in March – a remarkable achievement for which she deserved the utmost credit, and a conspicuous example of the value of a unified over a disjointed command.

It was incumbent upon Joffre to develop a strategy which would distract the enemy from the Eastern Front by putting some more vital interest in jeopardy. One section was marked out above all others for such a venture. If the Tenth Army in Artois could advance over the plain of the Scheldt towards Douai and Valenciennes, the communications of the whole of the German front from Lille to Soissons would be in instant peril, and a wholesale retreat would be imperative. Elsewhere a blow might he struck at the local communications of one army, but here a blow was possible against the lines of supply of three armies. The history of the Allied summer offensive is, therefore, the history of the thrust of the French towards Lens and of the British towards Lille.

During the first week of May a huge weight of artillery was concentrated, not less than 1,100 guns of different types, and Foch, the commander of the army group, took personal charge of the operations. The German force opposed was certainly outnumbered by the French, and probably outgunned; but it had the advantage of holding one of the strongest positions on either the Western or Eastern front. We may describe its line as consisting of a number of almost impregnable fortresses, armed with machine guns, and linked together by an intricate system of trenches. By the end of May the French Battle of Artois had virtually closed. It had been a triumph for the fighting quality of the French infantry, and not less of the French gunners. But as a strategic movement it had failed. Much ground had been won at a terrible cost, but the enemy still held the ridges that commanded Lens. The marvellous artillery preparation had flattened and sterilised the landscape, but it had not overcome the enemy defence in depth. Strangely enough, even so good a soldier as Foch did not make the true deduction, and the underestimate of the German defence system was to continue for the better part of three years.

The British advance in May in the Festubert region was intended mainly as an auxiliary to the French effort in Artois. It was designed in the first place to detain the German forces opposite in position, and to prevent reinforcements in men and guns being sent south to Lens. But it had also a positive if subsidiary purpose. If successful, it would win the Aubers Ridge, for the sake of which we had fought Neuve Chapelle, and so threaten Lille and La Bassée, and if the French got to Lens we should be in a position to conform effectively to their advance. The Battle of Festubert, as it may well be called, would in other wars, looking at the casualties and the numbers engaged, have been a major action, but in this campaign it ranked only as an episode – one link in the long-drawn chain of the Allied attack. Ground was won, but we were far short of any real strategic point, and the losses had been out of all proportion to the gains. The British Commander-in-Chief thus summed up the results: 'Since 16 May the First Army has pierced the enemy's line on a total front of 4 miles. The entire first-line system of trenches has been captured on a front of 3,200 yards, and on the remaining portion the first and second lines of trenches are in our possession.' This epitome is the best comment on the Allies' failure.

Meanwhile, as May passed into June, there came news from the East of unvarying calamity. The first counter-movement in the West on Russia's behalf had done little to aid her; was it not the duty of France and Britain to attempt another? Their civilian peoples looked for it; the soldiers on the Western Front expected it daily. The Russian press asked what the Allies were doing, and we may believe that the heroic armies of Russia turned their eyes wearily westward in the hope that France and Britain would soon reap the fruit of their sacrifice. And yet nothing of value could be done. The Allies were not able to make a really effective diversion. Although their numbers were greater than the Germans', they were still behind them in machine guns, heavy pieces, and stores of shell. Against an enemy so firmly entrenched and so amply equipped mere numbers availed little. Could they have torn a wide rent in the Western Front, pushed their cavalry through, and harried vital communications, then indeed they might have brought great armies hurrying back from the Vistula. But to drive in tiny wedges could have no effect on the death-grapple in the East, any more than to beat a bull-dog with a light cane will make him slacken his grip.

The story of this summer in the West is, therefore, a chronicle of small things – small attacks followed by small counter-attacks, or local struggles for strong points where a week's advance was measured in yards. It was the winter's stalemate repeated, but the balance of the war of attrition was not now in the Allies' favour.

Trench fighting had now reached the rank of a special science. The armies had evolved in nine months a code of defensive warfare which implied a multitude of strange apparatus. The intricacy of the science meant a very hive of activity behind the lines. Any one journeying from the base to the first line might well be amazed at the immense and complex mechanism of modern armies. At first it seemed like a gigantic business concern, a sort of magnified American 'combine'. 50 miles off we were manufacturing on a colossal scale, and men were suffering from industrial ailments as they suffered in dangerous trades at home. There were more mechanics than in Sheffield, more dock labourers than in Newcastle. But all the mechanism resembled a series of pyramids which tapered to a point as they neared the front. Behind were the great general hospitals and convalescent homes; then came the clearing hospitals; then the main dressing stations; and last of all, the advanced and regimental dressing stations, where mechanism failed. Behind were the huge transport depots and repairing shops, the daily trains to railhead, the supply columns; and last, the hand-carts to carry ammunition to the firing line. Behind were the railways and the mechanical transport, but at the end a man had only his two legs. Behind were the workshops of the Flying Corps and the squadron and flight stations; but at the end of the chain was the solitary aeroplane coasting over the German lines, and depending upon the skill and nerve of one man. Though all modern science had gone to the making of the war, at the end, in spite of every artificial aid, it became elementary, akin in many respects to the days of bows and arrows.

Spring and summer brought easier conditions for the air services of the belligerent Powers; but the comparative stagnation in the Western theatre, where the service had been most highly developed, prevented any conspicuous action by this arm. The work of the winter in reconnaissance and destruction went on, and the story was rather of individual feats than of any great concerted activity. The importance of the air had revealed itself, and all the combatants were busied with new construction. In Britain we turned out a great number of new machines. We experimented with larger types, and we perfected the different varieties of aerial bomb. The enemy airplanes began to improve in speed and handiness, but where Germany advanced an inch we advanced an ell. Admirable as was the air work of all the Allies, the British service, under its Director-General, Sir David Henderson, had reached by midsummer a height of efficiency which was not exceeded by any other branch of the Army or Navy.

To a student of military affairs it seemed amazing that a department only a few years old, and with less than one year's experience of actual war, should have attained so soon to so complete an efficiency and so splendid a tradition. Young men gathered from all quarters and all professions became in a little while of one type. They had the same quiet voices, the same gravity, the same dulled eyes, with that strange look in them that a man gets from peering into infinite space. The air, like the deep sea, seemed to create its own gentility, and no service had ever a more perfect breeding.

* * *

In September a man with ample leisure and a passion for discomfort might have walked in a continuous ditch from the North Sea to the Alps. Two trenches, from 30 to 200 yards apart, represented the first lines of the opposing armies. Behind the British front there were second and third lines, and further positions at intervals in the rear. But the Germans had these, and something more. From the day when their High Command resolved to stand on the defensive in the West, they had expended immense ingenuity and labour in strengthening their position. The ramifications of their trenches were endless, and great redoubts, almost flush with the ground, consisting of a labyrinth of trenches and machine-gun stations, studded their front. The German lines in the West were, in the fullest sense of the word, a fortress. The day of manoeuvre battles had for the moment gone. There was no question of envelopment or outflanking, for there were no flanks to turn. The slow methods of fortress warfare – sap and mine, battery and assault – were all that remained to the offensive.

The past nine months had taught the Allies many lessons. They perceived the formidable nature of the enemy's defence. Though much inferior in numbers, his position and his weight of artillery made him impregnable to any ordinary attack. Guns must be met by guns of equal calibre and equal munitionment. Before infantry could advance, a section of the stronghold must be destroyed by bombardment. Further, it was clear that this destruction must be on a broad front. That was a moral which had been drawn in bitterness after the summer's campaign in Artois.

The plan which matured in September was for the Allies a change of policy. Foch and Sir John French had, indeed, early in the summer contemplated a great autumn offensive, but the battles in Artois had not augured well for its success. In July, Joffre had decided to postpone any forward movement till the following spring. But the situation in Russia suggested that the decision might well be revised, and the unexpected improvement in the supply of munitions strengthened the argument. In September there was for Britain a welcome change from the lean days of the early summer. In one branch of explosives alone the production was thirty times as great as it had been in the end of May. There was also a very clear superiority in numbers. By September Sir John French had nine divisions of the New Army in France, and some had been in training in the trenches since May. But in spite of this apparent

Archduke Franz Ferdinand, the heir to the Austro-Hungarian throne. (*All images in this section courtesy of the Library of Congress*)

Kaiser Wilhelm II of Germany.

Field Marshal Hindenburg
(left) and General
Ludendorff (right).

Sir Douglas Haig,
commander of the British
forces on the Western
Front.

General Joffre of the French army.

Marshal Foch, appointed as Allied Commander in Chief in 1918.

Winston Churchill, First Lord of the Admiralty at the start of the First World War.

Admiral Sir John 'Jacky' Fisher, First Sea Lord.

Admiral Beatty, commander of the Grand Fleet's battle-cruiser force.

Admiral Jellicoe, Commander-in-Chief of the Grand Fleet.

Admiral Scheer, commander of Germany's High Seas Fleet and Beatty and Jellicoe's opponent at the Battle of Jutland.

General Pershing, commander of the American Expeditionary Force in France.

strength it is certain that the Allied Staffs, under the influence of the false deduction from Neuve Chapelle, misread the problem before them. They realised in theory that a break-through would be a protracted operation, but they did not guess how protracted it would be. The conception of a breach in a sea-wall still dominated their minds, and they underestimated the strength of the enemy system of defence in depth. Their preparation was in reality only for the first assault; beyond that it faded into vagueness and improvisation.

Champagne and the *secteur* of Castelnau was chosen as the scene of the main attack. But to support the grand attack there must be others. The salient must be assaulted on its northern side, and the place chosen was the sector between La Bassée and Arras. Other subsidiary attacks were necessary for the same purpose, and these were entrusted to the British forces. They were strictly holding battles, and it was enough if they distracted and occupied the attention of the enemy.

Early in the month a general bombardment began along the whole Allied front. Its purpose was to serve as a screen behind which the preparations for attack could be made, and to puzzle the enemy as to which section of his line was chiefly threatened. The Allied aircraft were busy, for it was important that no German machines should reconnoitre over our lines. As the 25th of the month approached our airmen went farther afield, and bombed vital parts of the German railways. On Thursday 23 September, the main bombardment began. From La Bassée to Arras, and along the Champagne front, hell was loosed from thousands of pieces. At a quarter-past five on the 25th, on a fifteen-mile front, the blue-grey waves surged from the trenches. At the same moment, at lengthened ranges, the guns flung their curtain of fire between the enemy and his supports. Machine guns took heavy toll of the attack and the German artillery from far in the rear were 'watering' the path of the advance. The road was marked by piles of blue-grey dead, but the impetus did not slacken. By the end of the day, on a fifteen-mile front, the advance had been carried forward for an average of two and a half miles. Practically the whole German first line had gone, and the French held parts of the second line. But the enemy battle position was not pierced except in patches too small to be exploited.

The second great French effort was made on the 29th, and the place chosen was to the west of Navarin Farm, where the second position had already been pierced. Such an attack, so soon after the first, could not be delivered with the same vigour. Reconnaissances could not be so complete or the artillery concentration so strong. A gap was made in the last German position, but it was too narrow to use. The French were compelled to dig themselves shelter trenches and cling to their position. With this action the main operation closed.

The attack in the north which was launched on the 25th of September was a movement subsidiary to the great effort in Champagne. While it was under the general direction of Foch, the details were left to two different commands – the French Tenth Army and the British First and Second Armies. These were secondary attacks, designed to distract the attention of certain parts of the German front; and the fact that the Artois attack was not the main movement of the Allies was partly responsible for certain misfortunes in the handling of the troops. For what happened was that by accident the British force did find a real weakness in one section of the German front, and, had it been a major operation and the plans laid accordingly, a comprehensive disaster might have overtaken the enemy in the north. But for this success they were not prepared. Reserves were not ready in time, or in sufficient strength. It was the kind of misfortune which is frequent in an assault upon a long front, and it was made almost inevitable by the fact that the British army formed a quasi-independent command.

Attacks were delivered upon the 25th by the French Tenth Army and by the British at Ypres, Armentières, Neuve Chapelle, and Givenchy. Apart from local failures these may be considered to have won reasonable success. But the main British attack was directed against the German line from the La Bassée canal to the slopes in front of Grenay.

The landscape, as seen from some one of the slag-heaps behind the British front, was curiously open. The opposing trench lines showed up clearly in the coarse chalk, and the country seemed a dead-flat plain, scarred with roads and studded with the headgear of collieries and mean little red houses. But this openness was deceptive. Every acre was a possible fortress, and the Germans had strongly fortified posts such as Fosse 8 and the formidable Hohenzollern Redoubt, as well as a number of minor positions among the slag-heaps, pits, and other natural features. At 6.30 on 25 September, when the great bombardment slackened, the left of the 1st Corps found itself checked in this desperate country, but by midday it had driven forward in a broad salient and captured the chief works of the enemy. Upon the remainder of its front the 1st Corps had taken the whole German first line, and at three points had broken into the second. But it had used up all its reserves, and for the moment could do no more.

It was farther south, in the sector of the 4th Corps, that the advance reached its height. Here a brilliant advance resulted in the capture of Loos and – for a moment – the shaking of the whole German northern front. The Londoners, on the right, carried all before them. They had prepared assiduously for the day, working out the operations on a big model of the countryside, so that every battalion knew the lie of the land before it. Consequently, when one battalion lost all its officers, the men still carried out the plan with complete precision. As the French gunners watched the start, they were amazed to see one of the London Irish kick off a football from the parapet and dribble it across the thousand yards to the first German line. They learned that day that the stolid British had their own *panache*. Presently they had seized Loos Cemetery, and their left had swung into the outskirts of the village. Before eight o'clock they had joined hands with the Highlanders in the shattered streets beneath the twin Towers of Loos. The clearing of Loos did not take long. Before nine o'clock all resistance was at an end, the battalion headquarters had advanced, and Loos was in our hands.

But the Highlanders were not content. Their orders had been not only to take Loos, but to occupy the rising ground to the east – the broad down marked in the map as Hill 70. But the original plan had allowed for the attack to proceed beyond Hill 70, should circumstances be favourable, and though this had been modified on the eve of battle, the change had not been explained to all the troops, and the leading battalions were in doubt about their final objective. The rise begins just outside the village, and the crest of the flat top is about a mile from the church. The fire from the defence for a moment gave them pause, and the German infantry came out of their trenches as if to counter-attack. The sight spurred the Highlanders to a great effort. They streamed up the hill like hounds, with all battalion formation gone, the green tartans of the Gordons and the red of the Camerons mingled in one resistless wave. All the time they were under enfilading fire from south and north, but with the bayonet they went through the defence, and at nine o'clock were on the summit of the hill.

On the top, just below the northern crest, was a strong redoubt, destined to become famous in the succeeding days. The garrison surrendered – they seem scarcely to have resisted – but the Highlanders did not wait to secure the place. They streamed onward down the eastern side – now only a few hundreds strong – losing direction as they went. The attack had now passed outside the legitimate operations of war, and had reached a district which was a nest of fortifications. The Germans had a great array of machine guns on a small slope outside the village, and they were busy installing others on the railway embankment north-east of Lens. The Highlanders formed a mad salient, with no supports on south or north. The captured garrison had manned the crest of Hill 70, and assailed them with reverse fire; and from the unbroken positions south-east of Loos came a converging bombardment. The last stage of the Highland onslaught had been magnificent, but it had not been war, for there were no reserves to follow them. Had the supports been there, had their flanks been more secure, the enemy's northern front must have been pierced. In less than three hours the heroic brigade had advanced nearly 4 miles, and had passed beyond all but the last German trench line. Lens seemed already fallen, the enemy was feverishly getting away his heavy guns, and for one moment the fate of Lille and the plain of Douai trembled in the balance.

Between nine and ten a senior officer of the division took command on the hill and endeavoured to recall the van of the advance, which was lost in the fog and smoke of the eastern slopes, and to entrench himself on the summit. To retire the van was no light task. In the midst of encircling fire it was a forlorn hope, and few returned to the British lines on the hill. All down the slopes towards Lens lay the tartans, Gordon and Black Watch, Seaforth and Cameron, like the drift left on the shore when the tide has ebbed. The day has gone when a handful of men, like Cortés' adventurers, may conquer a kingdom. A modern battle is won by the superiority of numbers at the proper place and moment.

That night German counter-attacks were frequent against the whole of our new line, and upon the 26th we lost the Chalk Pit north-east of Loos and advanced ground towards Hulluch, which caused our line to bend sharply back from Hill 70 to the Loos–La Bassée road. On Hill 70 itself we lost some trenches, and our hold on the place was in jeopardy. It was a critical moment, for there were no reserves at hand. Had the Germans attacked in greater force we must have been driven out of Loos.

Monday the 27th was a day of cold rain and misty distances. German counter-attacks recaptured ground from which they were able to enfilade our line by machine-gun fire. But the great event of the day was the advance in the afternoon of the Guards Division in the area of the 4th Corps. The line on the Monday morning ran from a point between Hulluch and the Loos–La Bassée road, dipping back to that highway and continuing round the north-east end of Loos, to the western slopes of Hill 70. Nearly ¾ mile of ground had been lost on the left and centre during the Sunday, and it was the business of the Guards to win it back. It was the first time in the war that they had taken the field as a division, and great things were expected of them. These hopes were not disappointed. The ground had been well reconnoitred, and it was obvious that so soon as they crossed the ridge west of Loos they would come under a heavy bombardment. Accordingly the men were deployed in artillery formation. Once on the ridge the shrapnel tornado burst on them, but the Guards advanced with all the steadiness of parade. It was Fontenoy over again, and the wearied infantry and cavalrymen who had been holding the front cheered wildly as the ordered line of the Guards swept inexorably into Loos. Once through the town they had to face a storm of gas shells. When they gained the crest of Hill 70, and were outlined against the sky, they were greeted by a fierce bombardment, and by machine-gun fire from the redoubt. Realising that the line on the crest was too good a target for the enemy, the brigade entrenched itself about 100 yards to the west of it. Here it had the 3rd Cavalry Brigade on its right; but its left was in the air, since there was a gap in the front between the Hill and the strong point known as Pit 14 *bis*. Next day, the 28th, the 2nd Brigade renewed the assault on Pit 14 *bis*. The place was important, for, being situated on the northern slopes of Hill 70, so long as it was in German hands it enfiladed our whole position east of Loos. At 3.45 in the afternoon it was attacked from the south end of the Chalk Pit, while our guns were turned on the Bois Hugo. Once again the enemy's machine-gun fire proved deadly, and, though a small party managed to reach Pit 14 *bis*, the place could not be held. We fell back in the evening to the Chalk Pit and the spinney, thus connecting with the 3rd Brigade east of Loos.

The main phase of the battle was now drawing to a close. On the last day of September, Sir John French issued an order to his troops setting forth the details of the action. On a front of 6,500 yards we had everywhere carried the enemy's first line, and we had broken into his second line in many places. We had captured over 3,000 enemy rank and file and over fifty officers. We had taken twenty-six field guns and forty machine guns, besides great quantities of other war material. A substantial success it was beyond doubt, the most substantial the British army had seen since trench warfare began. Yet the exhilaration of victory, the sense that at last we were advancing, was tempered by a profound disappointment. We had had a great chance of which we had failed to take full advantage. There had been somewhere a colossal blundering. It is now clear that the whole offensive was in itself premature and mistaken, but such mistakes are inevitable for mortals who lack the gift of prophecy.

It is hard to avoid the conclusion that the superb drive and devotion of the troops of attack were frittered away by a certain fumbling and confusion in the mind of Headquarters. They anticipated some sort of success – or otherwise why was the cavalry massed in reserve? – but they had not considered fully the ways and means of it. They took the Germans by surprise, but were themselves caught unawares. They succeeded better than they had hoped, and were not ready to use the gifts of fortune. Of all the British actions in the war Loos was the one which did least credit to the High Command.

***

As a result of the blunders at Loos Sir John French was relieved of his command. He was transferred to the command of the forces at home, and Sir Douglas Haig was appointed as his successor.

Haig stood in the very first rank of British soldiers. He had played a chief part in the most hotly contested battles of the campaign – at First Ypres, at Neuve Chapelle, at Festubert, at Loos. Chary of speech, bold in design, resolute in execution, he had raised the First Army under his command to a foremost place among the British forces. He had the confidence of his men, and had earned the admiration of all who worked with him, for he was at once a scientific soldier after the most modern plan, and a true leader. Like Foch, from whom in many respects he was profoundly different, he was destined to develop through disaster and anxiety into a great soldier.

Sir John French received a viscounty, and took his title from Ypres, before which he had fought his greatest battle – a fitting choice, for his name will always be linked with that most miraculous achievement in the history of British campaigning.

11

The Blockade and the Commerce Raiders

The British Blockade – German Commerce Raiders – The Work of the British Fleet

The blockade of Germany maintained by British warships was one of our chief weapons in the campaign. It raised difficulties with America on points of law; towards the end of 1915 it was no less criticised by the British people on the point of fact. Critics urged that it was ineffective. Figures were quoted showing the enormously increased imports of the neutral countries adjoining Germany, principally in the way of foodstuffs. Our ring-fence was condemned as a farce, and the Foreign Office – which was not unnaturally suspected, as the sole begetter of the unfortunate Declaration of London – was enjoined to hand over the blockade to the sailors, who meant business. When these recommendations were examined they were found to fall under two heads. The first was the proposal to regularise our proceedings according to international law, and thereby placate the legally minded America. It was urged that there was nothing to prevent a large extension of our list of absolute and conditional contraband, since we had thrown over the Declaration of London. Further we might now declare a legal blockade. Even if it had been impossible before – which was not admitted by those who saw in the Baltic a 'closed sea' on a parallel with the American Great Lakes – the success of our submarines in these waters had enabled us now to make it effective. Ever since the summer there had been a real blockade of the German Baltic ports. We had wrecked there both the commerce and the troop transport of the enemy – it was difficult to find German or Swedish underwriters to undertake the risk. German ships had for the most part to keep within territorial waters, and this greatly increased the slowness and the risks of their voyages. The Danish press – which might be taken as an independent witness – had no doubt about the effectiveness in point of fact of the British Baltic blockade.

But a formal blockade would have given us no powers which we had not already arrogated, and the proclamation, while it might have satisfied a few American jurists, would have made the situation still more delicate with regard to European neutrals. More important was the second ground of criticism – that by way of adjacent neutrals a large amount of vital imports was still filtering through to Germany. It was possible for the Government to show that the figures of the critics were exaggerated; but the fact remained that Germany was making desperate attempts to get sea-borne food and raw materials for the purposes of war, and that our activities, while they had diminished this influx, had by no means put an end to it. It was easier to prove the unpleasant fact than to suggest a policy to prevent it. Talk about handing over the whole business to the Navy had little meaning, for before the Navy could act it must be given directions, and these directions were exactly what it was so hard to arrive at. What seemed to be in the minds of the critics was the action of Britain in the Napoleonic wars, when she stopped all commerce to the continent of Europe. But at that time the whole of Europe was openly or implicitly hostile, and unless we now wished to bring in all neutrals against us, this heroic remedy could scarcely be adopted. With Sweden, in particular, our relations were highly delicate; and Russia had no had many grave drawbacks. If the imports prior to the war were taken as the basis, then this involved not only imports required for home consumption, but those re-exported to Germany to meet the balance of trade. It permitted, for example, the German acquisition of foodstuffs, and so was in defiance of the preamble of the Order in Council of 11 March 1915, which announced that 'His Majesty had decided to adopt further measures to prevent commodities of any kind from reaching or leaving Germany'. If the basis were the home consumption of a particular article, then the following situation might occur. The limit from the point of view of our blockade might be reached early in any year, through a number of ships arriving in neutral ports carrying that article, part of which was secretly destined for Germany. Cargoes arriving later, honestly destined for neutral consumption, we should be compelled to turn back or confiscate. To meet these difficulties, central distributing agencies were arranged in the neutral states which had the control of all consignments. They were responsible to us for the behaviour of their own merchants, and they formed authoritative bodies with which we could negotiate, and arrange from week to week the details of lawful commerce. It was by no means a perfect scheme; but in the circumstances, when we could only seek a balance of difficulties, it was probably the best possible. In the words of Lord Robert Cecil, who in February 1916 entered the Cabinet as Minister of Blockade, we could stop up the holes in the dam as they appeared; but it was inevitable that a good deal of water should run through while the repairs were being made.

The criticism of our blockade policy was soon extended to other naval matters. On one point it was amply justified. The merchant shipping question had been allowed to drift, so that freights had risen to a crazy height, and shipowners made altogether excessive profits. It was urged that shipping companies should be made 'controlled establishments', so that the whole of their surplus earnings might be taken for the nation; but this plan, while it might have augmented our revenue, would not have met the real difficulty. It would have been well if the shipping trade had been taken over by the Government, who would have paid it a fixed rate of interest on its capital and drawn up a reasonable schedule of freights. Neutral freights had naturally followed the British lead, and risen to the same extravagant height, and it was idle to hope to lower them by any of the devices proposed – such as, for example, making their coaling facilities in the ports of the Empire depend upon their adherence to a tariff – unless our British scale was lowered and systematised. The reason why some such step was not taken seems to have been the departmentalism which is rampant in any time of stress. Every great question is inter-departmental, and no one can be settled speedily or wisely unless there is a strong central authority to colligate and harmonise the claims of the departments. Finally, in the early days of March, the critics fastened upon naval policy itself – not, indeed, the work of the fleets and the fighting admirals, but the alleged supineness of the Board of Admiralty in new construction. Mr Churchill returned from his battalion in the trenches to make a speech full of dark innuendoes, concluding with a demand for the reinstatement of Lord Fisher at Whitehall. He had a slender parliamentary and journalistic following, but those who most admired his courage and mental alertness could not but regard the performance as ill advised.

In the first months of 1916 speculation was rife, both among sailors and civilians, as to German naval plans. It was known that Germany had been busy at new construction, but it was not clear what form it would take. There were rumours of capital ships armed with 17-inch guns, of new mammoth submarines capable of voyaging a thousand miles from their bases without seeking supplies, and so beaked and armoured that they could sheer through any nets. It was believed that Germany contemplated in the near future an attack by sea and air as a complement to some great offensive by land. The most reasonable forecast seemed to be that she would lay a mine-field from some point on the British coast eastwards, and under its cover attempt a raid or a bombardment of our south-eastern shores. If our battleships and battle-cruisers hastened to cut off the raiders, they would be entangled in the mine-field and lose heavily. In this way she might hope to reduce our capital ships and prepare for future operations by her High Seas Fleet on more equal terms.

Colour was given to some such forecast by the very remarkable German mine-laying activity at the end of 1915 and during the first months of 1916. A new type of U-boat had been specially devised for the laying of mines under water. It carried the mines in a special air-tight chamber which could be shut off from the hull of the submarine, and opened from above the sea. As the mines descended they were automatically released from their sinker, which went to the bottom and acted as anchor. The mines, being lighter than water, floated at the end of the connecting chain, which kept them at the requisite distance below the surface. A mine-field laid in this way was impossible to trace, except by its consequences, and it necessitated sweeping operations on a far greater scale than hitherto. Hence there tended to be a shortage of smaller auxiliaries, mine-sweepers and the like, attached to the Grand Fleet. The campaign in the eastern Mediterranean, where our lines of communication lay on the sea, required a very large number of small vessels, and the dearth of skilled labour at home made it difficult to construct new ones in the time. Germany had correctly appreciated the situation, and laid her plans accordingly.

A second evidence of German naval activity was the dispatch of commerce raiders from her North Sea ports. In December 1915 a vessel of some 4,500 tons, which had been launched as a fruit-ship and christened the *Ponga*, but had been transformed into an auxiliary cruiser carrying 6-inch guns, slipped out of Kiel harbour. She was re-baptised the *Moewe*, after a gunboat sunk at Dar-es-Salaam. Her commander was Count von und zu Dohna-Schlodien, who had been the navigating officer on the battleship *Posen*. Disguised with false sides to look like a tramp, and flying the Swedish flag, she slipped through our watching cruisers in the fog, and, fetching a wide circuit round the north of Scotland, arrived in the Atlantic. There she began a remarkable predatory career. She took the *Corbridge* off Cape Finisterre on 11 January 1916, and presently added the *Author*, *Trader*, *Ariadne*, *Dromonby*, *Farringford*, and *Clan Mactavish*. The last vessel, which carried a 3-inch gun, put up a gallant fight, and lost eleven men killed. On 15 January the *Appam*, a vessel of nearly 8,000 tons, with the Governor of Sierra Leone on board, was taken in the seas off Madeira. Count Dohna, who behaved with humanity, put the crews and passengers of his different captures into the *Appam*, and sent her off under Lieutenant Berg to Norfolk, Virginia, where she duly arrived on 1 February, and raised a new legal conundrum for the American Government. Meantime the *Moewe* proceeded on her course, hunting the junction of the South American and West Indian trade routes, and added to her bag the *Westburn*, *Horace*, *Flamenco*, *Edinburgh*, and *Saxon Prince*, as well as the French *Maroni* and the Belgian *Luxembourg*. She sent the crews of these vessels in the *Westburn* to Santa Cruz, in Teneriffe, and after landing them blew the ship up. The *Moewe*, having done enough *pour chauffer la gloire*, turned towards home by the same route as she had come, and safely arrived at Kiel on 4 March. Her commander deserved all credit for a bold and skilful performance. He had captured fifteen vessels, and cost Britain at least £2 million. He brought home with him four British officers, twenty-nine marines and sailors, 166 men from the different crews, and some £50,000 in gold bars. He had proved that the right kind of disguise might give a ship the invisibility of the submarine, and his countrymen were entitled to acclaim his achievement.

Encouraged by his success, and before he had returned, Germany sent out another raider. This was the *Greif*, a big armed merchantman, carrying 7-inch and 4-inch guns, and fitted with torpedo tubes. Disguised as a tramp, and with the Norwegian colours painted on her sides, she made her way through the North Sea, and was steering a course for the Atlantic between the Shetlands and the Faroes, when, on the forenoon of 29 February, she was sighted by the *Alcantara*, a Royal Mail ship of over 15,000 tons, now used as an auxiliary cruiser. The *Alcantara* overhauled her, inquired her name and destination, and lowered a boat. Suddenly the false bulwarks were dropped, and the stranger opened fire at a range of about 1,000 yards. She discharged a torpedo, but without success; and then one of her shells wrecked the *Alcantara*'s steering gear, and a second torpedo found its mark. Meanwhile another British auxiliary, the *Andes*, appeared, and by her gun-fire put the *Greif* out of action. The destroyer *Comus* also joined in from long range, and made accurate shooting. The enemy, now blazing from stern to stern, presently blew up, probably when the fire reached her cargo of mines. From the sinking *Alcantara* the two cruisers rescued all but five officers and twenty-nine men, and picked up five of the Greif's officers and 115 of her crew.

The work of our fleet was so quiet and so little advertised that the ordinary Briton dwelling in the southern towns felt more remote from it than from the Flanders trenches. Only on the seaboard, especially in the north and east, was there evidence for the eye of an intricate and ceaseless activity. As our Army had grown so had our Navy. Men of every class and occupation – yacht owners, fishermen, leisured people with a turn for the sea – had been drawn into the net, and the Royal Navy now included as motley a collection of volunteers in its auxiliary branches as could be found in the ranks of the new battalions. How arduous and anxious was the work only those employed in it could tell. That it was carried on in all weathers and under all discouragements with no surcease of keenness, was a tribute not only to our national character, but to the masterful traditions of the great Service. Any army, compelled to twenty months of comparative inaction and an unsleeping defensive, would have gone to pieces. But any army was a ragged and amateur business as compared with the British fleet. The ordeal was sustained partly because a ship's life in war is not so different from a ship's life in peace, partly because of the tradition of discipline and wise ceremonial, and partly because of the expertness of the profession. A modern sailor has duties so intricate and technical that they provide his mind with constant occupation. Even in peace neither body nor brain can afford to rust.

The sea has formed the English character, and the essential England is to be found in those who follow it. They have not altered since the days of the Channel skippers who taught Drake his trade, and the adventurers who first drank bilge and ate penguins in far-away oceans. Our seamen have been unmoved by the political storms which raged on land. They have seen neither Puritans nor Cavaliers, Whigs nor Tories, but plain Englishmen who were concerned with greater things. From blue water they have learned mercifulness and a certain spacious tolerance for what does not affect their craft, but they have also learned in the grimmest of schools precision and resolution. The sea endures no makeshifts. If a thing is not exactly right it will be vastly wrong. Discipline, courage to the point of madness, contempt for all that is pretentious and insincere, are the teaching of the ocean and the elements, and they have been the qualities in all ages of the

British sailor. On the Navy, 'under the good Providence of God', it is written in the Articles of War, hang the peace and prosperity of our islands and our Empire. But in this struggle there were still greater issues, for on the British Navy especially depended whether law or rapine was henceforth to rule the world. To one who visited the Grand Fleet there came a sense of pride which was more than the traditional devotion of Englishmen to the senior service and the remembrance of a famous past. The great battleships far up in the northern waters, wreathed in mists and beaten upon by snowstorms, the men who for twenty months of nerve-racking strain had kept unimpaired their edge and ardour of mind, were indeed a shining proof of the might and spirit of their land. But in the task before them there was a high duty, which their forefathers, indeed, had shared, but which lay upon them with a more solemn urgency. They were the modern crusaders, the true defenders of the faith, doing battle not only for home and race and fatherland, but for the citadel and sanctities of Christendom.

12

Verdun and the Somme

Reasons for German Attack – French Defence – The Somme Region – Strategy of the Projective Battle – The First Day – The Attack of July the Fourteenth – Croat of the Uplands Won – The Autumn Attacks – The Weather Breaks – Summary of the Action

In January 1916 the Allies seemed in a favourable position for the campaign of the new year. They had considerably increased their strength in men and material. Great offensives had accordingly been planned for 1916 both in East and West: by Russia in the Dvinsk salient, and by France and Britain on both sides of the River Somme.

Faced with such a prospect it was impossible for the Teutonic League to sit still. Germany, in the weeks before Christmas 1915, had to face a problem scarcely less difficult than that which had confronted her after her initial failure at the Marne. She had the prestige of her dynasty to think of, and the whole military and bureaucratic system built round it. She had in her mind two wavering neutrals, who must be constantly presented with new proofs of her might. Above all, she was faced with her dwindling man power, and an economic stress which could not be indefinitely endured. It was becoming clear that the first great movement of 1916 must be undertaken on her initiative. At Christmas, Falkenhayn had presented to the Emperor a memorandum in which he enumerated cogently and lucidly the factors in the case. A breakthrough in the ordinary sense was not contemplated. He sought to inflict on France the utmost injury with the least expense to Germany, and for this a section at once acutely sensitive and highly embarrassing for the defence was required. Germany must be free to accelerate or draw out her offensive, to intensify it or break it off from time to time as suited her purpose. Two such areas suggested themselves – Belfort and Verdun, and the argument leaned towards the latter.

On 20 February the guns opened. History had never seen so furious a fire. It blotted out the French first lines, it shattered the communication trenches, it tore the woods into splinters, and altered the very shape of the hills. At a quarter to five in the evening the German infantry moved forward to what they had been told would be an easy and uncostly triumph.

France performed no greater feat in the war than the defence of Verdun. Pétain, and subsequently Nivelle, refused to give way, and for months miraculously held their ground. What shall be said of the soldiers themselves who for these long months rolled back the invader? Not the Ypres salient or the nightmare Labyrinth was more dreadful than those shattered Meuse uplands, churned into grey mud by the punctual shells till they seemed like some lunar desert where life was forbidden. It was a struggle on the defensive, a contest of stark endurance waged with the knowledge that ground must some time be ceded, but with the resolve that the cession should be dearly bought. Such a task puts the sternest strain on human nature. It requires not the exhilaration of hot blood and high spirits, but cold patience and disciplined sacrifice. The glib commentators who before the war praised French *élan* and denied French fortitude were utterly put to shame. It was the fortitude and the stoicism of the French that were their most shining endowments. They showed it under Castelnau at Nancy of the landscape – may carry the eye for 30 miles. There were few detached farms, for it was a country of peasant cultivators who clustered in villages. Not a hedge broke the long roll of cornlands, and till the higher ground was reached the lines of tall poplars flanking the great Roman highroads were the chief landmarks. At the lift of country between Somme and Ancre copses patched the slopes, and sometimes a church spire was seen above the trees from some woodland hamlet. The Somme winds in a broad valley between chalk bluffs, faithfully dogged by a canal – a curious river which strains, like the Oxus, 'through matted rushy isles', and is sometimes a lake and sometimes an expanse of swamp. The Ancre is such a stream as may be found in Wiltshire, with good trout in its pools. On a hot midsummer day the slopes are ablaze with yellow mustard, red poppies, and blue cornflowers; and to one coming from the lush flats of Flanders, or the 'black country' of the Pas-de-Calais, or the dreary levels of Champagne, or the strange, melancholy Verdun hills, this land wore a habitable and cheerful air, as if remote from the oppression of war.

Till midsummer in 1916 the Picardy front had shown little activity. There had been local raids and local bombardments, but the trenches on both sides were good, and a partial advance offered few attractions to either. This long stagnation led to one result: it enabled the industrious Germans to excavate the chalk hills on which they lay into a fortress which they believed to be impregnable. Their position was naturally strong, and they strengthened it by every device which science could provide. Their High Command might look uneasily at the Aubers ridge and Lens and Vimy, but it had no doubts about the Albert heights. From Arras southward they held in the main the higher ground. The front consisted of a strong first position, with firing, support, and reserve trenches, and a labyrinth of deep dug-outs; a less strong intermediate line covering the field batteries; and a second position some distance behind, which was of much the same strength as the first. Behind lay fortified woods and villages which could be readily linked up with trench lines to form third and fourth positions. They were well served by the great network of railways. It was a fortress to which no front except the West could show a parallel. The Russian soldiers who in the early summer were brought to France stared with amazement at a ramification of trenches compared with which the lines in Poland and Galicia were like hurried improvisations.

The aim of the Allied Command must be clearly understood. It was not to recover so many square miles of France; it was not to take Bapaume or Péronne or Saint-Quentin; it was not even in the strict sense to carry this or that position. All these things were subsidiary and would follow in due course, provided the main purpose succeeded. That purpose was simply to exercise a steady and continued pressure on a certain section of the enemy's front. For nearly two years the world had been full of theories as to the possibility of breaking the German line. Gradually it had been accepted that an attack should proceed by stages, with, as a prelude to each, a complete artillery preparation, and that, since the struggle must be long drawn out, fresh troops should be used at each stage. The policy was that of 'limited objectives', but it did not preclude an unlimited objective in the event of some local enemy weakness suddenly declaring itself. A strategical problem is not, as a rule, capable of being presented in a simple metaphor, but it may be said that, to the view of the Allied strategy, the huge German salient in the West was like an elastic band drawn very tight. Each part of such a band has lost elasticity, and may be severed by friction which would do little harm to the band if less tautly stretched.

The coming attack was allotted to the Fourth Army, under General Sir Henry Rawlinson. Behind in the back areas lay the nucleus of another army, called first the Reserve, and afterwards the Fifth, under General Sir Hubert Gough, which at this time was mainly composed of cavalry divisions. It was a cadre which would receive its complement of infantry when the occasion arose. The French striking force lay from Maricourt astride the Somme to opposite the village of Fay.

About the middle of June on the whole front held by the British, and on the French front north and south of the Somme, there began an intermittent bombardment of the German lines. There were raids at different places, partly to mislead the enemy as to the real point of assault, and partly to identify the German units opposed to us. During these days, too, there were many fights in the air. It was essential to prevent German airplanes from crossing our front and observing our preparations. Our own machines scouted far into the enemy hinterland, reconnoitring and destroying. On Saturday 24 June, the bombardment became intenser. It fell everywhere on the front; German trenches were obliterated at Ypres and Arras as well as at Beaumont Hamel and Fricourt.

All the last week of June the weather was grey and cloudy, with a thick fog on the uplands, which made air work unsatisfactory. There were flying showers of rain and the roads were deep in mire. As the hours passed in mist and wet, it seemed as if the fates were unpropitious. Then, on the last afternoon of June, there came a sudden change. The pall of cloud cleared away and all Picardy swam in the translucent blue of a summer evening. That night the orders went out. The attack was to be delivered next morning three hours after dawn.

The first day of July dawned hot and cloudless, though a thin fog, the relic of the damp of the past week, clung to the hollows. The British aim, in the opening stage of the battle, was the German first position. The main assault was to be delivered between Maricourt and the Ancre; the attack from that river to Gommecourt was meant to be subsidiary. It is clear that the Germans expected the movement of the Allies, and had made a fairly accurate guess as to its terrain. They assumed that the area would be from Arras to Albert. In all that stretch they were ready with a full concentration of men and guns. South of Albert they were less prepared, and south of the Somme they were caught napping. The history of the first day was therefore the story of two separate actions in the north and south, in the first of which the Allies failed and in the second of which they brilliantly succeeded. By the evening the first action had definitely closed, and the weight of the Allies was flung wholly into the second.

Let us first tell the tale of the desperate struggle between Gommecourt and Thiepval. The divisions in action there had to face a chain of fortified villages – Gommecourt, Serre, Beaumont Hamel, and Thiepval – and enemy positions which were generally on higher and better ground. The Ancre cut the line in two, with steep slopes rising from the valley bottom. Each village had been so fortified as to be almost impregnable, with a maze of catacombs, often two stories deep, where whole battalions could take refuge, underground passages from the firing line to sheltered places in the rear, and pits into which machine guns could be lowered during a bombardment. On the plateau behind, with excellent direct observation, the Germans had their guns massed. As our men began to cross no-man's-land, the Germans seemed to man their ruined parapets, and fired rapidly with automatic rifles and machine guns. Moreover, they had machine-gun pits far in front of their parapets, connected with their trenches by deep tunnels secure from shell fire. The British moved forward in line after line, dressed as if on parade; not a man wavered or broke rank; but minute by minute the ordered lines melted away under the deluge of high-explosive, shrapnel, rifle, and machine-gun fire. By the evening, from Gommecourt to Thiepval, the attack had been everywhere checked, and our troops – what was left of them – were back again in their old line. They had struck the core of the main German defence.

Farther south an attempt was made to cut off the salient of Fricourt by an advance on the fortified villages of Ovillers and La Boiselle, and up the long shallow depression which our men called Sausage Valley towards Contalmaison. This, if Mametz were carried, would pinch it so tightly that it must fall. Mametz was carried that day, but Ovillers and La Boiselle held out. Fricourt fell on the 2nd, but the struggle for Ovillers and La Boiselle continued. On the morning of the 3rd the situation was that between Thiepval and Fricourt we had not pierced many parts of the German front line, while south of Fricourt we were advancing against the enemy's second position. Farther to the south below the junction points of Montauban, where on 1 July was seen for the first time in the campaign the advance in line of British and French troops, the French had advanced with lightning speed and complete success.

In the northern sector La Boiselle was finally taken on the 5th, and Contalmaison taken by storm on the 7th, though Ovillers did not finally fall until the 16th, when the gallant remnant of its garrison – two officers and 124 guardsmen – surrendered. In the southern sector the problem was to clear out the fortified woods with which this part of the country was patched, curiously clean-cut woods like the copses in the park of a country house. By the 12th we had taken virtually the whole of Mametz Wood and the wood of Bernafay. They were not acquired without a grim struggle. The woods were thick with undergrowth which had not been cut for two seasons, and though our artillery played havoc with the trees it could not clear away the tangled shrubbery beneath them. The Germans had filled the place with machine-gun redoubts, connected by concealed trenches, and in some cases they had machine guns in positions in the trees. Each step in our advance had to be fought for, and in that briery labyrinth the battle tended always to become a series of individual combats. Every position we won was subjected at once to a heavy counter-bombardment. Meantime the wood of Trônes had become a Tom Tiddler's Ground, which neither antagonist could fully claim or use as a base. It was at the mercy of the artillery fire of both sides, and it was impossible in the time to construct shell-proof defences.

Meanwhile in the French sector the advance had been swift and continuous. Their artillery, even the heavies, was now far forward in the open, and old peasants beyond the Somme, waiting patiently in their captivity, heard the guns of their countrymen sounding daily nearer.

The next step was for the British to attack the enemy second position before them. At dawn on Friday the 14th began the second stage of the battle. The day of the attack was of fortunate omen, for 14 July was the anniversary of the fall of the Bastille, the fête-day of France. The front chosen for attack was from a point south-east of Pozières to Longueval and Delville Wood, a space of some 4 miles. Incidentally, it was necessary for our right flank to clear the wood of Trônes. Each village in the second line had its adjacent or enfolding wood – Bazentin-le-Petit, Bazentin-le-Grand, and at Longueval the big wood of Delville. In the centre, a mile and more beyond the German position, the wood of Foureaux, which we called High Wood, hung like a dark cloud on the sky line. At 3.25 a.m., when the cloudy dawn had fully come, the infantry attacked. So complete was the surprise that in the dark the battalions which had the farthest road to go came within 200 yards of the enemy's wire with scarcely a casualty. When the German barrage came it fell behind them. The attack failed nowhere.

The great event of the day fell in the late afternoon, when the cavalry came into action against High Wood, the first time our mounted men had been used in eighteen months. The final advance, about 8 p.m., was made partly on foot and partly on horseback, and the enemy in the corn were ridden down, captured, or slain with lance and sabre. The cavalry then set to work to entrench themselves, to protect the flank of the advancing infantry in High Wood. It was a clean and workmanlike job, and the news of it exhilarated the whole line. That cavalry should be used at all seemed to forecast the end of the long trench fighting and the beginning of a campaign in the open.

On Saturday 15 July, we were busy consolidating the ground won, and at some points pushing farther. High Wood was last under pressure of counter-attacks, but we had by that time consolidated our line behind it. This position was held with extraordinary resolution by the enemy, and it was two months before the whole wood was in our possession. On the right, around Longueval and Delville Wood, was waged the fiercest contest of all. The struggle which began on that Saturday before dawn was to last for thirteen days, and to prove one of the costliest episodes of the whole battle. The situation was an ideal one for the defence. Longueval lay to the south-west of the wood, a straggling village with orchards at its northern end where the road climbed towards Flers. Delville itself was a mass of broken tree trunks, matted undergrowth, and shell holes. It had rides cut in it, running from north to south and from east to west, which were called by such names as 'The Strand' and 'Princes Street', and along these were the enemy trenches. The place was terribly at the mercy of the enemy guns, and on the north and south-east sides the Germans had a strong trench line, some 70 yards from the trees, bristling with machine guns. The South Africans, after desperate attacks, clung to the south-east corner, from where they refused to be dislodged. Their assault had been splendid, but their defence was a greater exploit. They hung on without food or water, while their ranks were terribly thinned, and at the end, when one battalion had lost all its officers, they repulsed an attack by the German 5th Division, the *corps d'élite*

We were now fighting on the watershed. At Thiepval we held the ridge that overlooked the village from the south-east. We held all the high ground north of Pozières, which gave us a clear view of the country towards Bapaume, and our lines lay 300 yards beyond the Windmill. We had all the west side of High Wood and the ground between it and the Albert–Bapaume road. We were half-way between Longueval and Ginchy, and our pincers were encircling Guillemont. At last we were in position over against, and in direct view of, the German third line. On Sunday 3 September, at twelve noon, the whole Allied front pressed forward. Guillemont was at last taken. South of the Somme a new French army came into action and carried the German front line on a new front of nearly 3 miles. Our advance was continued during the next few days, and though in High Wood and round Delville and Ginchy we made no progress our main object had been achieved.

By 10 September the British had made good the old German second position, and had won the crest of the uplands, while the French in their section had advanced almost to the gates of Péronne, and their new army on the right had begun to widen the breach. That moment was in a very real sense the end of a phase, the first and perhaps the most critical phase of the Somme battle. The immense fortifications of her main position represented for Germany the accumulated capital of two years. She had raised these defences when she was stronger than her adversaries in guns and in men. Now she was weaker, and her capital was gone. Thenceforth the campaign entered upon a new stage, new alike in strategical and tactical problems. From Thiepval to Chaulnes the enemy was in improvised positions. The day of manoeuvre battles had not come, but in that section the rigidity of the old trench warfare had vanished. Haig's aim was to push eastward till he secured a good defensive position, and then turn north against the flank and rear of the German positions beyond the Ancre. It looked as if he were soon to attain the first half of his purpose.

been parked in secluded spots at the back of the front. The world is now familiar with those strange machines, which, shaped like monstrous toads, crawled imperturbably over wire and parapets, butted down houses, shouldered trees aside, and humped themselves over the stoutest walls. They were an experiment which could only be proved in practice, and the design in using them at this stage was principally to find out their weak points, so as to perfect their mechanism for the future. Their main tactical purpose was to clear out redoubts and nests of machine guns which, as we had found to our sorrow at Loos, might hang up the most resolute troops. The things had been kept a profound secret, and until the very eve of the advance few in the British army had even heard of them. The Germans manning their parapets saw through the thin mist inhuman shapes crawling towards them, things like gigantic slugs, spitting fire from their mottled sides. And ere they could collect their dazed wits the British bayonets were upon them.

On the left and centre the attack was instantly successful. The Canadians, after beating off the German counter-attack, carried Courcelette in the afternoon. Farther south there was fierce fighting in the old cockpit of High Wood, but at last the place was swept clear. Flers was taken with little trouble by the New Zealanders. They were preceded by a tank which waddled complacently up the main street of the village, with the enemy's bullets rattling harmlessly off its sides, followed by cheering and laughing British troops. Farther south we advanced our front for nearly a mile and a half. Only on the right wing in the area of Ginchy was our success incomplete. There, and in High Wood, we incurred most of the casualties of the day. The check was the more regrettable since complete success in this area was tactically more important than elsewhere. But after all deductions were made the day's results were in a high degree satisfactory. We had broken in one day through three of the enemy's main defensive systems, and on a front of over 6 miles had advanced to an average depth of a mile. It was the most effective blow yet dealt at the enemy by British troops.

For the next week there was a lull in the main operations while the hammer was swung back for another blow. On Sunday the 24th our batteries opened again, this time against the uncaptured points in the German third line like Morval and Lesboeufs, against intermediate positions like Gueudecourt, and especially against Thiepval, which we now commanded from the east. By the evening of the 25th the British had stormed an enemy front of 6 miles between Combles and Martinpuich to a depth of more than a mile. The fall of Morval gave them the last piece of uncaptured high ground on that backbone of ridge which runs from Thiepval through High Wood and Ginchy. The next day Combles fell, while on the British left Thiepval itself was carried, as well as the north-west corner of Mouquet Farm and the Zollern Redoubt on the eastern crest. The German pivot had gone, the pivot which they had believed impregnable.

On the evening of 26 September the Allied fortunes in the West had never looked brighter. The enemy was now in his fourth line, without the benefit of the high ground, and there was no chance of retrieving his disadvantages by observation from the air. A hundred captured documents showed that the German *moral* had been shaken, and that the German machine was falling badly out of gear. In normal seasons at least another month of fine weather might be reasonably counted on, and in that month further blows might be struck with cumulative force. In France they spoke of a 'Picardy summer' – of fair bright days at the end of autumn when the ground was dry and the air of a crystal clearness. A fortnight of such days would suffice for a crowning achievement. The hope was destined to fail. The guns were scarcely silent after the great attack of the 26th when the weather broke, and October was one long succession of tempestuous gales and drenching rains.

To understand the difficulties which untoward weather imposed on the Allied advance, it is necessary to grasp the nature of the 50 square miles of ground which three months' fighting had given them, and over which lay the communications between their firing line and the rear. From a position like the north end of High Wood almost the whole British battle-ground on a clear day was visible to the eye. To reach the place from the old Allied front line, some 4 miles of bad roads had to be traversed. They would have been bad roads in a moorland parish, where they suffered only the transit of the infrequent carrier's cart; for at the best they were mere country tracks, casually engineered, and with no solid foundation. But here they had to support such a traffic as the world had scarcely seen before. Not the biggest mining camp or the vastest engineering undertaking had ever produced one tithe of the activity which existed behind each section of the battle line. It was not the German guns which made the trouble on the ground between the Albert–Péronne road and the British firing fine. Casual bombardments vexed us little. It was the hostile elements and the unkindly nature of Mother Earth.

The country roads had been rutted out of recognition by endless transport, and, since they never had much of a bottom, the toil of the road-menders had nothing to build upon. New roads were hard to make, for the chalky soil was poor, and had been so churned up by shelling and the movement of guns and troops that it had lost all cohesion. There was no stone in the countryside and little wood, so repairing materials had to be brought from a distance, which still further complicated the problem. The problem was hard enough in fine weather; but let the rain come and soak the churned-up soil, and the whole land became a morass. There was no *pavé*, as in Flanders, to make a firm causeway. Every road became a watercourse, and in the hollows the mud was as deep as a man's thighs. An army must be fed, troops must be relieved, guns must be supplied, and so there could be no slackening of the traffic. Off the roads the ground was a squelching bog, dug-outs crumbled in, and communication trenches ceased to be.

Weather is a vital condition of success in operations where great armies are concerned, for men and guns cannot fight on air. In modern war it is more urgent than ever, since aerial reconnaissance plays so great a part, and Napoleon's 'fifth element', mud, grows in importance with the complexity of the fighting machine. Again, in semi-static trench warfare, where the same area remains for long the battlefield, the condition of the ground is the first fact to be reckoned with. Once we grasp this, the difficulty of the October campaign, waged in almost continuous rain, will be apparent. But no words can convey an adequate impression of the Somme area after a week's downpour. Its discomforts had to be endured to be understood.

The next advance of the British army had two distinct objectives. The first – the task of the Fourth Army – was to carry the two spurs which ascended from the main Thiepval–Morval ridge behind which the German fourth position lay. The month of October provided a record in wetness, spells of drenching rain being varied by dull, misty days, so that the sodden land had no chance of drying. The carrying of the spurs – meant as a preliminary step to a general attack – proved an operation so full of difficulties that it occupied all our efforts during the month, and with it all was not completed. The story of these weeks is one of minor operations, local actions with strictly limited objectives undertaken by only a few battalions. In the face of every conceivable difficulty we moved slowly up the intervening slopes.

The struggle of those days deserves to rank high in the records of British hardihood. The fighting had not the swift pace and the brilliant successes of the September battles. Our men had to strive for minor objectives, and such a task lacks the impetus and exhilaration of a great combined assault. On many occasions the battle resolved itself into isolated struggles, a handful of men in a mud hole holding out and consolidating their ground till their post was linked up with our main front. Rain, cold, slow reliefs, the absence of hot food, and sometimes of any food at all, made those episodes a severe test of endurance and devotion.

Our second task, in which we brilliantly succeeded, was to master completely the Thiepval ridge.

On 9 November the weather improved. The wind swung round to the north and the rain ceased, but owing to the season of the year the ground was slow to dry, and in the area of the Fourth Army the roads were still past praying for. Presently frost came and a powder of snow, and then once more the rain. But in the few days of comparatively good conditions the British Commander-in-Chief brought the battle to a further stage, and won a conspicuous victory. The fortress village of Beaumont-Hamel was taken and the naval division carried Beaucourt. It was the last attack, with which concluded the Battle of the Somme. The weather had now fallen like a curtain upon the drama.

***

Before 1 July, Verdun had been the greatest continuous battle fought in the world's history; but the Somme surpassed it both in numbers of men engaged, in the tactical difficulty of the objectives, and in its importance in the strategical scheme of the campaign. By what test are we to judge the result of a battle in modern war? In the old days of open fighting there was little room for doubt, since the retreat or rout or envelopment of the beaten army was too clear for argument. Now, when the total battle-front was 3,000 miles, such easy proofs were lacking; but the principle remained the same. A battle is final when it ends in the destruction of the enemy's fighting strength. A battle is won – and it may be decisively won – when it results in achieving the strategic purpose of one of the combatants, provided that purpose is, on military grounds, a wise one. Hence the amount of territory occupied and the number of important points captured are not necessarily sound criteria at all. The success or defeat of a strategic purpose, that is the sole test. Judging by this, Tannenberg was a victory for Germany, the Marne for France, and the First Battle of Ypres for Britain. The Battle of the Somme was no less a victory, since it achieved the purpose of the Allies.

In the first place, it relieved Verdun, and enabled Nivelle to advance presently to a conspicuous success. In the second place, it detained the main German forces on the Western Front. In the third place, it drew into the battle, and gravely depleted, the surplus man-power of the enemy, and struck a shattering blow at his *moral*. For two years the German behind the shelter of his trench-works and the great engine of his artillery had fought with comparatively little cost against opponents far less well equipped. The Somme put the shoe on the other foot, and he came to know what the British learned at Ypres and the French in Artois – what is meant to be bombarded out of existence, and to cling to shell-holes and the ruins of trenches under a pitiless fire. It was a new thing in his experience, and took the heart out of men who, under other conditions, had fought with skill and courage. Further, the Allies had dislocated his whole military machine. Their ceaseless pressure had crippled his Staff work, and confused the organisation of which he had justly boasted.

The Battle of the Somme had, therefore, fulfilled the Allied purpose in taxing to the uttermost the German war machine. The place became a name of terror. Though belittled in communiqués, and rarely mentioned in the press, it was a word of ill-omen to the whole German people, that 'bloodbath' to which many journeyed and from which few returned. Of what avail their easy conquests on the Danube when this deadly cancer in the West was eating into the vitals of the nation? Winter might give a short respite – though the Battle of the Ancre had been fought in winter weather – but spring would come, and the evil would grow malignant again. Germany gathered herself for a great effort, marshalling for compulsory war work the whole male population between seventeen and sixty, sending every man to the trenches who could walk on sound feet, doling out food supplies on the minimum scale for the support of life, and making desperate efforts by submarine warfare to cripple her enemies' strength. She was driven to stake her last resources on the game.

In every great action there is a major purpose, a reasoned and calculated purpose which takes no account of the accidents of fortune. But in most actions there come sudden strokes of luck which turn the scale. But in the elaborate and mechanical warfare of to-day they come rarely, and at the Battle of the Somme they did not fall to the lot of Foch or Haig. They did what they set out to do; step by step they drove their way through the German defences; but it was all done by hard and stubborn fighting, without any bounty from capricious fortune. Germany had claimed that her line was impregnable; they broke it again and again. She had counted on her artillery machine; they crippled and outmatched it. She had decried the fighting stuff of the new British armies; we showed that it was a match for her Guards and Brandenburgers. The major purpose was attained. Like some harsh and remorseless chemical, the waxing Allied energy was eating into the German waning mass. Its sure and methodical pressure had the inevitability of a natural law. It was attrition, but attrition in the acute form – not like the slow erosion of cliffs by the sea, but like the steady crumbling of a mountain to which hydraulic engineers have applied a mighty head of water. And it was a law of life and of war that the weakness of the less strong would grow *pari passu* with the power of the stronger.

to make periodical sweeps through the North Sea, and to be first upon the scene should the enemy appear. They were the advance guard, the *corps de choc* of the Grand Fleet; they were the hounds which must close with the quarry and hold it till the hunters of the Battle Fleet arrived. Hence the task of their commander was one of peculiar anxiety and strain. At any moment the chance might come, so he must be sleeplessly watchful. He would have to make sudden and grave decisions, for it was certain that the longed-for opportunity would have to be forced before it matured. The German hope was by attrition or some happy accident to wear down the superior British strength to an equality with their own. A rash act on the part of a British admiral might fulfil that hope; but, on the other hand, without boldness, even rashness, Britain could not get to grips with her evasive foe. So far Sir David Beatty and the battle-cruisers had not been fortunate. From the shelter of the mine-strewn waters around Heligoland Germany's warships made occasional excursions, for they could not rot for ever in harbour; her battle-cruisers had more than once raided the English coasts; her battleships had made stately progresses in short circles in the vicinity of the Jutland and Schleswig shores. But so far Sir David Beatty had been unlucky. At the Battle of the Bight of Heligoland on 28 August 1914, his great ships had encountered nothing more serious than enemy light cruisers. At the time of the raid on Hartlepool in December of the same year he had just failed, owing to fog, to intercept the raiders. In the Battle of the Dogger Bank on 24 January 1915, the damage done to his flagship had prevented him destroying the whole German fleet of battle-cruisers. It was clear that the enemy, if caught in one of his hurried sorties, would not fight unless he had a clear advantage. Hence, if the battle was to be joined at all, it looked as if the first stage, at all events, must be fought by Britain against odds.

On Tuesday afternoon, 30 May, the bulk of the British Grand Fleet left its bases on one of its customary sweeps. On this occasion it put to sea with hope, for the Admiralty had informed it that a large German movement was contemplated. It sailed in two sections. To the north were twenty-four Dreadnoughts of the Battle Fleet under Sir John Jellicoe – the 1st, 2nd, and 4th Battle Squadrons; one Battle-Cruiser Squadron, the 3rd, under Rear-Admiral the Honourable Horace Hood; the 1st Cruiser Squadron, under Rear-Admiral Sir Robert Arbuthnot; the 2nd Cruiser Squadron, under Rear-Admiral Heath; the 4th Light Cruiser Squadron, under Commodore Le Mesurier; and the 4th, 11th, and 12th Destroyer Flotillas. Farther south moved the Battle-Cruiser Fleet, under Sir David Beatty – the six vessels of the 1st and 2nd Battle-Cruiser Squadrons, under Rear-Admiral Brock and Rear-Admiral Pakenham; the 5th Battle Squadron, four vessels of the Queen Elizabeth class, under Rear-Admiral Evan-Thomas; the 1st, 2nd, and 3rd Light Cruiser Squadrons; and the 1st, 9th, 10th, and 13th Destroyer Flotillas. It will be noticed that the two sections of the Grand Fleet were not sharply defined by battleships and battle-cruisers, for Sir John Jellicoe had with him one squadron of battlecruisers, and Sir David Beatty had one squadron of the largest battleships. On the morning of the last day of May the German High Seas Fleet also put to sea, and sailed north a hundred miles or so from the Jutland coast. First went Admiral von Hipper's battle-cruisers, five in number, with the usual complement of cruisers and destroyers. Following them came the Battle Fleet, under Admiral von Scheer – fifteen Dreadnoughts and six other vessels, accompanied by three cruiser divisions and seven torpedo flotillas. With a few exceptions, all the capital ships of the German navy were present in this expedition. We know the purpose of Scheer from his own narrative. He hoped to engage and destroy a portion of the British fleet which might be isolated from the rest, for German public opinion demanded some proof of naval activity now that the submarine campaign had languished.

Sir John Jellicoe, as early as October 1914, had taken into review the new conditions of naval warfare, and had worked out a plan to be adopted when he met the enemy's fleet – a plan approved not only by his flag officers but by successive Admiralty Boards. The German aim, as he forecast it, would be to fight a retreating action, and lead him into an area where they could make the fullest use of mines, torpedoes, and submarines. He was aware of the weakness of his own fleet in destroyers and cruisers, and was resolved not to play the enemy's game. Hence he might be forced to give the appearance of refusing battle and not closing with a retreating foe.

> I intend to pursue what is, in my considered opinion, the proper course to defeat and annihilate the enemy's battle fleet without regard to uninstructed opinion or criticism. The situation is a difficult one. It is quite within the bounds of possibility that half of our battle fleet might be disabled by under-water attack before the guns opened fire at all if a false move is made, and I feel that I must constantly bear in mind the great probability of such attack and be prepared tactically to prevent its success.

The German methods had, therefore, from the start a profound moral effect in determining the bias of the Commander-in-Chief's mind. A second principle was always in his thoughts, a principle derived from his view of the general strategy of the whole campaign, for Jellicoe had a wider survey than that of the professional sailor. It was no question of a partiality for the defensive rather than the offensive. The British Grand Fleet, in his view, was the pivot of the Allied strength. So long as it existed and kept the sea, it fulfilled its purpose, it had already achieved its main task; if it were seriously crippled, the result would be the loss not of one weapon among many, but of the main Allied armoury. It was, therefore, the duty of a wise commander to bring the enemy to battle – but on his own terms; no consideration of purely naval results, no desire for personal glory, must be allowed to obscure the essential duty of his solemn trusteeship. The psychology of the Commander-in-Chief must be understood, for it played a vital part in the coming action.

The fourth week of May had been hot and bright on shore, with low winds and clear heavens; but on the North Sea there lay a light summer haze, and on the last day of the month loose grey clouds were beginning to overspread the sky. Sir David Beatty, having completed his sweep to the south, had turned north about 2 p.m., according to instructions to rejoin Jellicoe. The sea was dead calm, like a sheet of glass. His light cruiser squadrons formed a screen in front of him from east to west. But at 2.20 p.m. the *Galatea* (Commodore Alexander-Sinclair), the flagship of the 1st Light Cruiser Squadron, signalled enemy vessels to the east. Beatty at once altered course to south-south-east, the direction of the Horn Reef, in order to get between the enemy and his base.

Five minutes later the *Galatea* signalled again that the enemy was in force, and no mere handful of light cruisers. At 2.35 the watchers in the *Lion* saw a heavy pall of smoke to the eastward, and the course was accordingly altered to that direction, and presently to the north-east. The 1st and 3rd Light Cruiser Squadrons spread in a screen before the battle-cruisers. A seaplane was sent up from the *Engadine* at 3.8, and at 3.30 its first report was received. Flying at a height of 900 feet, within 2 miles of hostile light cruisers, it was able to identify the enemy. Sir David Beatty promptly formed line of battle, and a minute later came in sight of Hipper's five battle-cruisers. Evan-Thomas and the 5th Battle Squadron were at the time more than 5 miles away, and, since their speed was less than that of the battle-cruisers, would obviously be late for the fight; but Beatty did not wait, considering, not unnaturally, that his six battle-cruisers were more than a match for Hipper.

***

Of all human contests, a naval battle makes the greatest demands upon the resolution and gallantry of the men and the skill and coolness of the commanders. In a land fight the general may be 30 miles behind the line of battle, but the admiral is in the thick of it. He takes the same risks as the ordinary sailor, and, as often as not, his flagship leads the fleet. For 300 years it had been the special pride of Britain that her ships were ready to meet any enemy at any time on any sea. If this proud boast were no longer hers, then her glory would indeed have departed.

At 3.30 that afternoon Sir David Beatty had to make a momentous decision. The enemy was in all likelihood falling back upon his main Battle Fleet, and every mile the British admiral moved forward brought him nearer to an unequal combat. For the moment the odds were in his favour, since he had six battle-cruisers against Hipper's five, as well as the 5th Battle Squadron, but presently the odds might be heavily against him. He was faced with the alternative of conducting a half-hearted running fight with Hipper, to be broken off before the German Battle Fleet was reached, or of engaging closely and hanging on even after the junction with Scheer had been made. In such a fight the atmospheric conditions would compel him to close the range and so lose the advantage of his heavier guns, and his own battle-cruisers as regarded turret armour and deck-plating were far less stoutly protected than those of the enemy, which had the armour of a first-class battleship. Sir David Beatty was never for a moment in doubt. He chose the course which was not only heroic, but right on every ground of strategy. Twice already by a narrow margin he had missed bringing the German capital ships to action. He was resolved that now he would forgo no chance which the fates might send.

Hipper was steering east-south-east in the direction of his base. Beatty changed his course to conform, and the fleets were now some 23,000 yards apart. The 2nd Light Cruiser Squadron took station ahead with the destroyers of the 9th and 13th Flotillas; then came the 1st Battle-Cruiser Squadron, led by the *Lion*; then the 2nd; and then Evan-Thomas, with the 5th Battle Squadron. Beatty formed his ships on a line of bearing to clear the smoke – that is, each ship took station on a compass bearing from the flagship, of which they were diagonally astern. At 3.48 the action began, both sides opening fire at the same moment. The range was 18,500 yards, the direction was generally south-south-east, and both fleets were moving at full speed, an average perhaps of 25 knots. The wind was from the south-east, the visibility for the British was good, and the sun was behind them. They had ten capital ships to the German five. The omens seemed propitious for victory.

In all battles there is a large element of sheer luck and naked caprice. In the first stage, when Beatty had the odds in his favour, he was destined to suffer his chief losses. A shot struck the *Indefatigable* (Captain Sowerby) in a vital place, the magazine exploded, and in two minutes she turned over and sank. The German gunnery at the start was uncommonly good; it was only later, when things went ill with them, that their shooting fell off. Meantime the 5th Battle Squadron had come into action at a range of 20,000 yards, and engaged the rear enemy ships. From 4.15 onward for half an hour the duel between the battle-cruisers was intense, and the enemy fire gradually grew less rapid as ours increased. At 4.18 the German battle-cruiser third in the line was seen to be on fire. Presently the *Queen Mary* (Captain Prowse) was hit, and blew up. She had been at the Battle of the Bight of Heligoland; she was perhaps the best gunnery ship in the fleet; and her loss left Beatty with only four battlecruisers. Happily she did not go down before her superb marksmanship had taken toll of the enemy. The haze was now settling on the waters, and all that could be seen of the foe was a blurred outline.

Meantime, as the great vessels raced southwards, the lighter craft were fighting a battle of their own. Eight destroyers of the 13th Flotilla – the *Nestor, Nomad, Nicator, Narborough, Pelican, Petard, Obdurate,* and *Nerissa* – together with the *Moorsom* and *Morris* of the 10th, and the *Turbulent* and *Termagant* of the 9th, moved out at 4.15 for a torpedo attack, at the same time as the enemy destroyers advanced for the same purpose. The British flotilla at once came into action at close quarters with fifteen destroyers and a light cruiser of the enemy, and beat them back with the loss of two destroyers. This combat had made some of them drop astern, so a full torpedo attack was impossible. The *Nestor, Nomad,* and *Nicator,* under Commander the Honourable E. B. S. Bingham, fired two torpedoes at the German battle-cruisers, and were sorely battered themselves by the German secondary armament. They clung to their task till the turning movement came which we shall presently record, and the result of it was to bring them within close range of many enemy battleships. Both the *Nestor* and the *Nomad* were sunk, and only the *Nicator* regained the flotilla. Some of the others fired their torpedoes, and apparently the rear German ship was struck. The gallantry of these smaller craft cannot be overpraised. That subsidiary battle, fought under the canopy of the duel of the greater ships, was one of the most heroic episodes of the action.

We have seen that the 2nd Light Cruiser Squadron was scouting ahead of the battle-cruisers. At 4.38 the *Southampton* (Commodore Goodenough) reported the German Battle Fleet ahead. Instantly Beatty recalled the destroyers, and at 4.42 Scheer was sighted to the south-east. Beatty put his helm to port and swung round to a northerly course. From the pursuer he had now become the pursued, and his aim was to lead the combined enemy fleets towards Sir

John Jellicoe. The 5th Battle Squadron, led by Evan-Thomas in the *Barham*, now hard at it with Hipper, was ordered to follow suit. Meanwhile the *Southampton* and the 2nd Light Cruiser Squadron continued forward to observe, and did not turn till within 13,000 yards of Scheer's battleships, and under their fire. At five o'clock Beatty's battle-cruisers were steering north, the *Fearless* and the 1st Destroyer Flotilla leading, the 1st and 3rd Light Cruiser Squadrons on his starboard bow, and the 2nd Light Cruiser Squadron on his port quarter. Behind him came Evan-Thomas, attended by the *Champion* and the destroyers of the 13th Flotilla.

It is not difficult to guess at the thoughts of Scheer and Hipper. They had had the good fortune to destroy two of Beatty's battle-cruisers, and now that their whole fleet was together they hoped to destroy more. The weather conditions that afternoon made Zeppelins useless, and accordingly they knew nothing of Jellicoe's presence in the north, though they must have surmised that he would appear sooner or later. They believed they had caught Beatty cruising on his own account, and that the gods had delivered him into their hands. From 4.45 till 6 o'clock to the mind of the German admirals the battle resolved itself into a British flight and a German pursuit.

The case presented itself otherwise to Sir David Beatty, who knew that the British Battle Fleet was some 50 miles off, and that it was his business to coax the Germans towards it. He was now facing heavy odds, eight capital ships as against at least nineteen, but he had certain real advantages. He had the pace of the enemy, and this enabled him to overlap their line and to get his battle-cruisers on their bow. In the race southwards he had driven his ships at full speed, and consequently his squadron had been in two divisions, for Evan-Thomas's battleships had not the pace of the battle-cruisers. But when he headed north he reduced his pace, and there was no longer a tactical division of forces. The eight British ships were now one fighting unit. It was Beatty's intention to nurse his pursuers into the arms of Jellicoe, and for this his superior speed gave him a vital weapon. Once the northerly course had been entered upon the enemy could not change direction, except in a very gradual curve, without exposing himself to enfilading fire from the British battle-cruisers at the head of the line. Though in a sense he was the pursuer, and so had the initiative, yet as a matter of fact his movements were mainly controlled by Sir David Beatty's will. That the British admiral should have seen and reckoned with this fact in the confusion of a battle against odds is not the least of the proofs of his sagacity and fortitude.

Unfortunately the weather changed for the worse. The British ships were silhouetted against a clear western sky, but the enemy was shrouded in mist, and only at rare intervals showed dim shapes through the gloom. The range was about 14,000 yards. The two leading ships of Evan-Thomas's squadron were assisting the battle-cruisers, while his two rear ships were engaged with the first vessels of the German 3rd Battle Squadron, which developed an unexpected speed. As before, the lesser craft played a gallant part. At 5.5 the *Onslow* and the *Moresby*, which had been helping the *Engadine* with the seaplane, took station on the engaged bow of the *Lion*, and the latter struck with a torpedo the sixth ship in the German line and set it on fire. She then passed south to clear the range of smoke, and took station on the 5th Battle Squadron. At 5.33 Sir David Beatty's course was north-north-east, and he was gradually hauling round to the north-eastward. He knew that the Battle Fleet could not be far off, and he was heading the Germans on an easterly course, so that Jellicoe should be able to strike to the best advantage.

At 5.50 on his port bow he sighted British cruisers, and six minutes later had a glimpse of the leading ships of the Battle Fleet 5 miles to the north. He at once changed course to east and increased speed, bringing the range down to 12,000 yards. He was forcing the enemy to a course on which Jellicoe might overwhelm him.

* * *

The first stage was now over, the isolated fight of the battle-cruisers, and we must turn to the doings of the Battle Fleet itself. When Sir John Jellicoe at the same time as Beatty took in the *Galatea*'s signals, he was distant from the battle-cruisers between 50 and 60 miles. He at once proceeded at full speed on a course south-east by south to join his colleague. The engine rooms made heroic efforts, and the whole fleet maintained a speed in excess of the trial speeds of some of the older vessels. It was no easy task to effect a junction at the proper moment, since there was an inevitable difference in estimating the rendezvous by 'reckoning', and some of Beatty's messages, dispatched in the stress of action, were obscure. Moreover, the thick weather made it hard to recognise which ships were enemy and which were British when the moment of meeting came. What a spectacle must that strange rendezvous have presented had there been any eye to see it as a whole! Two great navies on opposite courses at high speeds driving toward each other: the German unaware of what was approaching; the British Battle Fleet, mile upon mile of steel giants whose van was far out of sight of its rear, 12 miles wrong in its reckoning, and so making contact almost by accident in a drift of smoke and sea-haze!

The 3rd Battle-Cruiser Squadron, under Rear-Admiral Hood, led the Battle Fleet. At 5.30 Hood observed flashes of gun-fire and heard the sound of guns to the south-westward. He sent the *Chester* (Captain Lawson) to investigate, and at 5.45 this ship engaged three or four enemy light cruisers, rejoining the 3rd Battle-Cruiser Squadron at 6.5. Hood was too far to the south and east, so he turned north-west, and five minutes later sighted Beatty. At 6.11 he received orders to take station ahead, and at 6.22 he led the line, 'bringing his squadron into action ahead in a most inspiring manner, worthy of his great naval ancestors'. He was now only

8,000 yards from the enemy, and under a desperate fire. At 6.34 his flagship, the *Invincible*, was sunk, and with her perished an admiral who in faithfulness and courage must rank with the nobler figures of British naval history. This was at the head of the British line. Meantime the 1st and 2nd Cruiser Squadrons accompanying the Battle Fleet had also come into action. The *Defence* and the *Warrior* had crippled an enemy light cruiser, the *Wiesbaden*, about six o'clock. The *Canterbury*, which was in company with the 3rd Battle-Cruiser Squadron, had engaged enemy light cruisers and destroyers which were attacking the destroyers *Shark*, *Acasta*, and *Christopher* – an engagement in which the *Shark* was sunk. At 6.16 the 1st Cruiser Squadron, driving in the enemy light cruisers, had got into a position between the German and British Battle Fleets, since Sir Robert Arbuthnot was not aware of the enemy's approach, owing to the mist, until he was in close proximity to them. The *Defence* perished, and with it Arbuthnot. The *Warrior* passed to the rear disabled, and the *Black Prince* received damage which led later to her destruction.

Meantime Beatty's lighter craft had also been hotly engaged. At 6.5 the *Onslow* sighted an enemy light cruiser 6,000 yards off, which was trying to attack the *Lion* with torpedoes, and at once closed and engaged at a range from 4,000 to 2,000 yards. She then closed the German battle-cruisers, but after firing one torpedo she was struck amidships by a heavy shell. Undefeated, she fired her remaining three torpedoes at the enemy Battle Fleet. She was taken in tow by the *Defender*, who was herself damaged, and in spite of constant shelling the two gallant destroyers managed to retire in safety. Again, the 3rd Light Cruiser Squadron, under Rear-Admiral Napier, which was well ahead of the enemy on Beatty's starboard bow, attacked with torpedoes at 6.25, the *Falmouth* and the *Yarmouth* especially distinguishing themselves. One German battlecruiser was observed to be hit and fall out of the line.

The period between 6 o'clock and 6.40 saw the first crisis of the battle. The six divisions of the Grand Fleet had approached in six parallel columns, and it was Jellicoe's business to deploy as soon as he could locate the enemy. A few minutes after six he realised that the Germans were on his starboard side, and in close proximity; he resolved to form line of battle on the port wing column on a course south-east by east, and the order went out at 6.16. His reasons were – to avoid danger in the mist from the German destroyers ahead of their Battle Fleet; to prevent the *Marlborough*'s division on the starboard wing from receiving the concentrated fire of the German Battle Fleet before the remaining divisions came into line; and to obviate the necessity of turning again to port to avoid the 'overlap' which formation on the starboard wing would give the enemy van. This decision has been vehemently criticised, but without justification. It may well be doubted whether to have formed line towards instead of away from the enemy would have substantially lessened the time of closing the enemy, and it would beyond doubt have exposed the British starboard division to a dangerous concentration of fire. As it was, the *Hercules* in the starboard division was in action within four minutes. The movement took twenty minutes to perform, and during that time the situation was highly delicate. But on the whole it was brilliantly carried out, and by 6.38 Scheer had given up his attempt to escape to the eastward, and was bending due south.

At 5.40 Hipper, under pressure from Evan-Thomas and the destroyers, had turned six points to starboard; at 5.55, being now overlapped by Beatty, who had closed the range, he turned sharp east; at six he bent south; at 6.12 he went about on a north-north-east course; and about 6.15 he came in contact with Hood's battle-cruisers, and realised that Jellicoe had arrived. For a quarter of an hour there was heavy fighting, during which his flagship, the *Lützow*, was badly damaged and the *Derfflinger* silenced. By 6.33

he was steering due south, followed by Scheer. The turn on interior lines gave him the lead of Beatty, who bent southward on a parallel course. The 1st and 2nd Battle-Cruiser Squadrons led; then the 3rd Battle-Cruiser Squadron; there followed the six divisions of the Battle Fleet – first the 2nd Battle Squadron, under Vice-Admiral Sir Thomas Jerram; then the 4th, under Vice-Admiral Sir Doveton Sturdee, containing Sir John Jellicoe's flagship, the *Iron Duke*; and finally the 1st, under Vice-Admiral Sir Cecil Burney. Evan-Thomas's 5th Battle Squadron, which had up to now been with Beatty, intended to form ahead of the Battle Fleet, but the nature of the deployment compelled it to form astern. The *Warspite* had her steering-gear damaged, and drifted towards the enemy's line under a furious cannonade. For a little she involuntarily interposed herself between the *Warrior* and the enemy's fire. She was presently extricated; but it is a curious proof of the caprices of fortune in battle that while a single shot at the beginning of the action sank the *Indefatigable*, this intense bombardment did the *Warspite* little harm. Only one gun turret was hit, and her engines were uninjured.

At 6.40 then, the two British fleets were united, the German line was headed off on the east, and Beatty and Jellicoe were working their way between the enemy and his home ports. Scheer and Hipper were now greatly outnumbered, and it seemed as if the British admirals had won a complete strategic success. But the fog was deepening, and the night was falling, and such conditions favoured the German tactics of retreat.

***

The third stage of the battle – roughly, two hours long – was an intermittent duel between the main fleets. Scheer had no wish to linger, and he moved southwards at his best speed, with the British line shepherding him on the east. He was definitely declining battle.

Beatty had succeeded in crumpling up the head of the German line, and its battleships were now targets for the majority of his battle cruisers. The visibility was becoming greatly reduced. The mist no longer merely veiled the targets, but often shut them out altogether. This not only made gunnery extraordinarily difficult, but prevented the British from keeping proper contact with the enemy. At the same time, such light as there was was more favourable to Beatty and Jellicoe than to Scheer. The German ships showed up at intervals against the sunset, as did Cradock's cruisers off Coronel, and gave the British gunners their chance.

Hipper and his battle-cruisers were in serious difficulties. At 6.15 he was compelled to leave the *Lützow*, and since by this time neither the *Derfflinger* nor the *Seydlitz* was fit for flag duties, he remained in a destroyer till a lull in the firing enabled him to board the *Moltke*. From seven o'clock onward Beatty was steering south, and gradually bearing round to south-west and west, in order to get into touch with the enemy. At 7.14 (Scheer having ordered Hipper to close the British again) he sighted them at a range of 15,000 yards – three battlecruisers and two battleships of the König class. The sun had now fallen behind the western clouds, and at 7.18 Beatty increased speed to 22 knots, and re-engaged. The enemy showed signs of great distress, one ship being on fire and one dropping astern. The destroyers at the head of the line emitted volumes of smoke, which covered the ships behind with a pall, and enabled them at 7.37 to turn away and pass out of Beatty's sight. At that moment he signalled Jellicoe, asking that the van of the battleships should follow the battle-cruisers. At 7.58 the 1st and 3rd Light Cruiser Squadrons were ordered to sweep westwards and locate the head of the enemy's line, and at 8.20 Beatty altered course to west to support. He located three battleships, and engaged them at 10,000 yards' range. The *Lion* repeatedly hit the leading ship, which turned away in flames with a heavy list to port, while the *Princess Royal* set fire to one battleship, and the third ship, under the attack of the *New Zealand* and the *Indomitable*, hauled out of the line heeling over and on fire. Once more the mist descended and enveloped the enemy, who passed out of sight to the west.

To turn to the Battle Fleet, which had become engaged during deployment with the leading German battleships. It first took course south-east by east; but as it endeavoured to close it bore round to starboard. The aim of Scheer now was escape and nothing but escape, and every device was used to screen his ships from British sight. Owing partly to the smoke palls and the clouds emitted by the destroyers, but mainly to the mist, it was never possible to see more than four or five enemy ships at a time. The ranges were, roughly, from 9,000 to 12,000 yards, and the action began with the British Battle Fleet in divisions on the enemy's bow. Under the British attack the enemy constantly turned away, and this had the effect of bringing Jellicoe to a position of less advantage on the enemy's quarter. At the same time it put the British fleet between Scheer and his base. In the short periods, however, during which the Germans were visible, they received a heavy fire and were constantly hit. Some were observed to haul out of line, and at least one was seen to sink. The German return fire at this stage was poor, and the damage caused to our battleships was trifling. Scheer relied for defence chiefly on torpedo attacks, which were favoured by the weather and the British position. A following fleet can make small use of torpedoes, as the enemy is moving away from it; while the enemy, on the other hand, has the advantage in this weapon, since his targets are moving towards him. Many German torpedoes were fired, but the only battleship hit was the *Marlborough*, which was, happily, able to remain in line and continue the action.

The 1st Battle Squadron, under Sir Cecil Burney, came into action at 6.17 with the 3rd German Battle Squadron at a range of 11,000 yards, but as the fight continued the range decreased to 9,000 yards. This squadron received most of the enemy's return fire, but it administered severe punishment. Take the case of the *Marlborough* (Captain George P. Ross). At 6.17 she began by firing seven salvos at a ship of the Kaiser class; she then engaged a cruiser and a battleship; at 6.54 she was hit by a torpedo; at 7.3 she reopened the action; and at 7.12 fired fourteen salvos at a ship of the König class, hitting her repeatedly till she turned out of line. The *Colossus*, of the same squadron, was hit, but only slightly damaged, and several other ships were frequently straddled by the enemy's fire. The 4th Battle Squadron, in the centre, was engaged with ships of the König and the Kaiser classes, as well as with battle-cruisers and light cruisers. Sir John Jellicoe's flagship, the *Iron Duke*, engaged one of the König class at 6.30 at a range of 12,000 yards, quickly straddled it, and hit it repeatedly from the second salvo onwards till it turned away. The 2nd Battle Squadron in the van, under Sir Thomas Jerram, was in action with German battleships from 6.30 to 7.20, and engaged also a damaged battle-cruiser.

At 7.15, when the range had been closed and line ahead finally formed, came the main torpedo attack by German destroyers. In order to frustrate what he regarded as the most serious danger, Jellicoe ordered a turn of two points to port, and presently a further two points, opening the range by about 1,750 yards. This caused a certain loss of time, and Scheer seized the occasion to turn well to starboard, with the result that contact between the battle fleets was presently lost. Jellicoe received Beatty's appeal at 7.54, and ordered the 2nd Battle Squadron to follow the battle-cruisers. But mist and smokescreens and failing light were fatal hindrances to the pursuit, and even Beatty had soon to give up hope of sinking Hipper's damaged remnant.

By nine o'clock the enemy had completely disappeared, and darkness was falling fast. He had been veering round to a westerly course, and the whole British fleet lay between him and his home ports. It was a strategic situation which, but for the fog and the coming of night, would have meant his complete destruction. Sir John Jellicoe had now to make a difficult decision. It was impossible for the British fleet to close in the darkness in a sea swarming with torpedo craft and possibly with submarines, and accordingly he was compelled to make dispositions for the night which would ensure the safety of his ships and provide for a renewal of the action at dawn. For a night action the Germans were the better equipped as to their fire system, their recognition signals, and their searchlights, and he did not feel justified in presenting the enemy with a needless advantage. On this point Beatty, to the south and westward, was in full agreement. In his own words: 'I manoeuvred to remain between the enemy and his base, placing our flotillas in a position in which they would afford protection to the fleet from destroyer attack, and at the same time be favourably situated for attacking the enemy's heavier ships.' He informed Jellicoe of his position and the bearing of the enemy, and turned to the course of the Battle Fleet.

* * *

Jellicoe moved the Battle Fleet on a southerly course, with its four squadrons in four parallel columns a mile apart, so as to keep in touch. The destroyer flotillas were disposed from west to east 5 miles astern. The battle-cruisers and the cruisers lay to the west of the Battle Fleet; the 2nd Light Cruiser Squadron north of it; and the 4th Light Cruiser Squadron to the south. The main action was over, and Jellicoe was now wholly out of touch with the enemy. His light craft were ordered to attend the Battle Fleet and not to attempt to find touch; hence he was in the position of a warder in the centre of a very broad gate, and an alert enemy had many opportunities of slipping past his flanks.

The night battle was waged on the British side entirely by the lighter craft. It began by an attack on our destroyers by German light cruisers; then at 10.20 an enemy cruiser and four light cruisers came into action with our 2nd Light Cruiser Squadron, losing the *Frauenlob* and severely handling the *Southampton* and the *Dublin*. The 4th Destroyer Flotilla about 11.30 lost the *Sparrowhawk*, and later the *Tipperary*, but at midnight sunk the old battleship *Pommern*. The 12th Flotilla was in action between one and two in the morning, and torpedoed two enemy battleships. The 9th Flotilla lost the *Turbulent*, and after 2 a.m. the 13th Flotilla engaged four Deutschlands. The German ships made good their escape, but they lost in the process out of all proportion to the British light craft. No ships in the whole battle won greater glory than these. 'They surpassed,' wrote Sir John Jellicoe, 'the very highest expectations that I had formed of them.' An officer on one of the flotillas has described that uneasy darkness:

We couldn't tell what was happening. Every now and then out of the silence would come *bang*, *bang*, *boom*, as hard as it could go for ten minutes on end. The flash of the guns lit up the whole sky for miles and miles, and the noise was far more penetrating than by day. Then you would see a great burst of flame from some poor devil, as the searchlight switched on and off, and then perfect silence once more.

'The searchlights at times made the sea as white as marble, on which the destroyers moved "black",' wrote an eye-witness, 'as cockroaches on a floor.'

At earliest dawn on 1 June the British fleet, which was lying south and west of the Horn Reef, turned northwards to collect its light craft, and to search for the enemy. It was ready and eager to renew the battle, for it had still twenty-two battleships untouched, and ample cruisers and light craft, while Scheer's command was scarcely any longer a fleet in being. But there was to be no second 'Glorious First of June', for the enemy was not to be found. He had slipped in single ships astern of our fleet during the night, and was then engaged in moving homewards like a flight of wild duck that had been scattered by shot. He was greatly helped by the weather, which at dawn on 1 June was thicker than the night before, the visibility being less than 4 miles. About 3.30 a.m. a Zeppelin passed over the British fleet, and reported to Scheer the position of the British squadrons. All morning till eleven o'clock Sir John Jellicoe waited on the battle-ground, watching the lines of approach to German ports, and attending the advent of the enemy. But no enemy came. 'I was reluctantly compelled to the conclusion,' wrote Sir John, 'that the High Seas Fleet had returned into port.' Till 1.15 p.m. the British fleet swept the seas, picking up survivors from some of our lost destroyers. After that hour waiting was useless, so the fleet sailed for its bases, which were reached next day, Friday 2 June. There it fuelled and replenished with ammunition, and at 9.30 that evening was ready for further action.

* * *

The German fleet, being close to its bases, was able to publish at once its own version of the battle. A resounding success was a political necessity for Germany, for she needed a fillip for her new loan, and it is likely that she would have claimed a victory if any remnant of her fleets had reached harbour. As it was, she was overjoyed at having escaped annihilation, and the magnitude of her jubilation may be taken as the measure of her fears. It is of the nature of a naval action that it gives ample scope for fiction. There are no spectators. Victory and defeat are not followed, as in a land battle, by a gain or loss of ground. A well-disciplined country with a strict censorship can frame any tale it pleases, and hold to it for months without fear of detection at home. Germany claimed at once a decisive success. According to her press the death-blow had been given to Britain's command of the sea. The Emperor soared into poetry.

> The gigantic fleet of Albion, ruler of the seas, which, since Trafalgar, for a hundred years has imposed on the whole world a bond of sea tyranny, and has surrounded itself with a nimbus of invincibleness, came into the field. That gigantic Armada approached, and our fleet engaged it. The British fleet was beaten. The first great hammer blow was struck, and the nimbus of British world supremacy disappeared.

Germany admitted certain losses – one old battleship, the *Pommern*; three small cruisers, the *Wiesbaden*, *Elbing*, and *Frauenlob*; and five destroyers. A little later she confessed to the loss of a battle-cruiser, *Lützow*, and the light cruiser *Rostock*, which at first she had kept secret 'for political reasons'.

It was a striking tribute to the prestige of the British Navy that the German claim was received with incredulity in all Allied and in most neutral countries. But false news, once it has started, may be dangerous; and in some quarters, even among friends of the Allies, there was at first a disposition to accept the German version. The ordinary man is apt to judge of a battle, whether on land or sea, by the crude test of losses. The British Admiralty announced its losses at once with a candour which may have been undiplomatic, but which revealed a proud confidence in the invulnerability of the Navy and the steadfastness of the British people. These losses were: one first-class battle-cruiser, the *Queen Mary*; two lesser battle-cruisers, the *Indefatigable* and *Invincible*; three armoured cruisers, the *Defence*, *Black Prince*, and *Warrior*; and eight destroyers, the *Tipperary, Ardent, Fortune, Shark, Sparrowhawk, Nestor, Nomad,* and *Turbulent*. The class and displacement of the lost ships were as follows:

	Tons	
Queen Mary	Battle-cruiser	27,000
Indefatigable	"	18,750
Invincible	"	17,250
Defence	Armoured cruiser	14,600
Black Prince	"	13,550
Warrior	"	13,550
Tipperary	Destroyer	1,430
Ardent	"	935
Fortune	"	935
Shark	"	935
Sparrowhawk	"	935
Nestor	"	1,000
Nomad	"	1,000
Turbulent	"	430
Total		113,300

More vital than the ships was the loss of thousands of gallant men, including some of the most distinguished of the younger admirals and captains.

Sir John Jellicoe at the time estimated the German losses as two battleships of the largest class, one of the Deutschland class, one battle-cruiser, five light cruisers, six destroyers, and one submarine. He overstated the immediate, and understated the ultimate damage. The German account was formally accurate, but her real loss was infinitely greater. The *Seydlitz* and the *Derfflinger* limped home almost total wrecks; the battleship *Ostfriesland* struck a mine; the *Moltke* and the *Von der Tann* took weeks to repair; almost every vessel had been hit, some of them grievously. Scheer has declared that, apart from the two battle-cruisers, the fleet was ready to take to sea by the middle of August; but the truth is that it was never again a fighting fleet. Jutland, which had at first the colour of victory, was an irremediable disaster. After the war was over, Captain Persius wrote in the *Berliner Tageblatt*: 'The losses sustained by us were immense, in spite of the fact that luck was on our side, and on June 1, 1916, it was clear to every one of intelligence that the fight would be, and must be, the only one to take place.' The fact was recognised by reasonable minds everywhere, and it was only the ignorant who imagined that the loss of a few ships could weaken British naval prestige. There was much to praise in the German conduct of the action. The German battle-cruiser gunnery was admirable; Scheer's retreat when heavily outnumbered was skilfully conducted, and his escape in the night, even when we admit his special advantages, was a brilliant performance. But the one test of success is the fulfilment of a strategic intention, and Germany's most signally failed. From the moment of Scheer's return to port the British fleet held the sea. The blockade which Germany thought to break was drawn tighter than ever. Her secondary aim had been so to weaken the British fleet that it should be more nearly on an equality with her own. Again she failed, and the margin of British superiority was in no way impaired. Lastly, she hoped to isolate and destroy a British division. That, too, failed. The British Battle-Cruiser Fleet remained a living and effective force, while the German Battle-Cruiser Fleet was only a shadow. The result of the battle of 31 May was that Britain was more than ever confirmed in her mastery of the waters.

Nevertheless the fact that the only occasion on which the main fleets met did not result in the annihilation of the enemy was a disappointment and a surprise to the British people, and criticism has been busy ever since with the British leadership. It has been asked why the Admiralty at 5.12 p.m. on 31 May ordered the Harwich force to sea, and then cancelled the order for ten hours

– and this when Jellicoe had long before asked that all available ships and torpedo craft should be ordered to the scene of the Fleet's action as soon as it was known to be imminent. Beatty's dash and resolution have been universally commended, but he has been criticised for allowing Evan-Thomas's squadron to lag so far behind that it scarcely joined in the first stages of the battle-cruiser action, and for the lack of precision in his messages to Jellicoe before their junction. But it is the conduct of the Commander-in-Chief which has principally been called in question. He has been accused of a lack of ardour in engaging the enemy, as shown in his deploying to port instead of to starboard; in his turning away between 7.15 and 7.30 p.m. on 31 May to avoid torpedo attacks; and in his refusal of a night battle. On the first and third of these points it would appear that the bulk of expert naval opinion is on his side; on the second the arguments are more evenly balanced, and the matter will long continue in dispute. Even had no turn away been ordered, it is doubtful whether the range could have been kept closed, owing to the bad light and Scheer's persistent turning to starboard. But from the controversy there emerges a larger issue, on which naval historians must eternally take sides. Was Jutland fought in the true Trafalgar tradition? Had the British Commander-in-Chief the single-hearted resolve to destroy the enemy at all costs, content to lose half or more than half his fleet provided no enemy ship survived? It is idle to deny that the destruction of the High Seas Fleet would have been of incalculable value to the Allies, for it would have taken the heart out of the German people; would have crippled, even if it did not prevent, the submarine campaign which in the next twelve months was to sink 25 out of every 100 merchantmen that left our shores; and would have opened up sea communication with Russia and thereby prevented the calamity of the following year. Was such a final victory possible at Jutland had Jellicoe handled the Battle Fleet as Beatty handled his battle-cruisers?

The answer must remain a speculation. It is probable, indeed, that no risks accepted by the Commander-in-Chief would have altered a result due primarily to weather conditions and the late hour when the battle was joined. But the fact remains that Jellicoe's policy was that of the limited offensive. He was convinced that his duty was not to press the enemy beyond a point which might involve the destruction of his own weapon. The situation, as he saw it, had changed since the days of Trafalgar. Then only a relatively small part of the British fleet was engaged; now the Grand Fleet included the great majority of the vessels upon which Britain and her Allies had to rely for safety. There was ever present to his mind, in his own words,

> the necessity for not leaving anything to chance in a Fleet action, because our Fleet was the one and only factor that was vital to the existence of the Empire, as indeed of the Allied cause. We had no reserve outside the Battle Fleet which could in any way take its place should disaster befall it, or even should its margin of superiority over the enemy be eliminated.

Moreover, the British Navy had already achieved its main purpose; was any further gain worth the risk of losing that victory? It was a war of peoples, and even the most decisive triumph at sea would not end the contest, while a defeat would strike from the Allied hands the weapon on which all others depended. Such considerations are of supreme importance; if it be argued that they belong to statesmanship rather than to naval tactics, it may be replied that the commander of the British Grand Fleet should be statesman as well as seaman. A good sailor, of proved courage and resolution, chose to decide in conformity with what he regarded as the essential interests of his land and against the tradition of the service and the natural bias of his spirit, and his countrymen may well accept and respect that decision.

* * *

Following close upon the greatest naval fight of all history came the news of a sea tragedy which cost Britain the life of her foremost soldier. It had been arranged that Lord Kitchener should undertake a mission to Russia to consult with the Russian commanders as to the coming Allied offensive, and to arrange certain details of policy concerning the supply of munitions. On the evening of Monday 5 June, he and his party embarked in the cruiser *Hampshire*, which had returned three days before from the Battle of Jutland. About 8 p.m. that evening the ship sank in wild weather off the western coast of the Orkneys, having struck a mine in an unswept channel. Four boats left the vessel, but all were overturned. One or two survivors were washed ashore on the inhospitable coast, but of Kitchener and his colleagues no word was ever heard again.

The news of his death filled the whole Empire with profound sorrow, and the shock was felt no less by our Allies, who saw in him one of the chief protagonists of their cause. The British army went into mourning, and all classes of the community were affected with a grief which had not been paralleled since the death of Queen Victoria. Labour leader, trade-union delegate, and the patron of the conscientious objector were as heartfelt in their regret as his professional colleagues or the army which he had created. He died on the eve of a great Allied offensive, and did not live to see the consummation of his labours. But in a sense his work was finished, for more than any other man he had the credit of building up that vast British force which was destined to be the determining factor in the war.

Germany and the United States

The Effect on America of Germany's New Submarine Policy – America Declares War

The ripening of American opinion against the aims and methods of the Teutonic League was a slow process, for the great republic had a long road to travel from her historic isolation to the point of junction with the Allies. But the wiser statesmen in Europe saw that, behind the academic decorum of America, the forces of enlightenment were at work, and they possessed their souls in patience. For with a strong people a slow change is a sure change.

The initial atrocities in Belgium and France had induced in the greater part of the educated class in America the conviction that Germany was a menace to civilisation. But such a conviction was still far removed from the feeling that America was called on to play an active part in the war. Her pride was first wounded by Germany's insistence that as a neutral the United States had no right to trade in munitions with the Allied Powers. The American view was well stated in the official presentation of America's case issued after she entered the struggle by the Committee of Public Information.

If, with all other neutrals, we refused to sell munitions to belligerents, we could never in time of a war of our own obtain munitions from neutrals, and the nation which had accumulated the largest reserves of war supplies in times of peace would be assured of victory. The militarist state that invested its money in arsenals would be at a fatal advantage over a free people that invested its money in schools. To write into international law that neutrals should not trade in munitions would be to hand over the world to the rule of the nation with the largest armament factories.

Then came the sinking of the *Lusitania*, and the preposterous demand that America should surrender her right of free travel by sea. Concurrent with the prevarications and belated apologies of Berlin ran a campaign of German machination and outrages in the New World. To quote again from the same document:

In this country official agents of the Central Powers – protected from a criminal prosecution by diplomatic immunity – conspired against our internal peace, placed spies and *agents provocateurs* throughout the length and breadth of our land, and even in high positions of trust in departments of our Government. While expressing a cordial friendship for the people of the United States, the Government of Germany had its agents at work both in Latin America and in Japan. They bought and subsidized papers and supported speakers there to arouse feelings of bitterness and distrust against us in those friendly nations, in order to embroil us in war. They were inciting to insurrection in Cuba, in Haiti, and in Santo Domingo; their hostile hand was stretched out to take the Danish Islands; and everywhere in South America they were abroad sowing the seeds of dissension, trying to stir up one nation against another, and all against the United States. In their sum these various operations amounted to direct assault of the Monroe doctrine.

When on 4 May 1916, Germany grudgingly promised that ships should not be sunk without warning, it seemed as if the controversy was settled. But meantime two currents of opinion in America had been growing in volume. One was the desire to make this war the last fought under the old bad conditions of national isolation, to devise a League to Enforce Peace, which would police the world on behalf of international justice. Of such ideals Mr Wilson was a declared champion. The second was the conviction that this war was in very truth America's war; that the Allies were fighting for America's interests, the greatest of which was the maintenance of public right. To this creed Mr Root and Mr Roosevelt had borne eloquent testimony. In the light of it the various diplomatic wrangles with Britain over her naval policy became things of small moment.

As long as militarism continues to be a serious danger, peaceful neutral nations, by insisting on the emancipation of commerce from interference by sea-power, would be adopting a suicidal policy ... The control of commerce in war is now exercised by Great Britain because she possesses a preponderant navy. Rather than that control should be emasculated, Great Britain must be allowed to continue its exercise ... We are more than ever sure that this nation does right in accepting the British blockade and defying the submarine. It does right, because the war against Britain, France, and Belgium is a war against the civilization of which we are a part. To be *fair* in such a war would be a betrayal. (These quotations are taken from the American weekly paper, the *New Republic*, of 7 August 1915, and 17 February 1917.)

The Presidential election in the autumn of 1916 caused public discussion on the question to languish, but it did not stop the steady growth of opinion. Then came the revival of German submarine activity in the early winter, and the hectoring German peace proposals, which boasted so loudly of German conquests, and asked the world to accept them as the basis of all negotiations. Mr Wilson, secure in power by his second election, and pledged to the ideal of a League of Nations, dispatched his own request to the belligerents to define their aims, for he saw very clearly that the hour of America's decision was drawing nigh. The interchange of notes which followed cleared the air, and established the fact that American and Allied opinion were moving in the same channels. On 22 January the President, in an eloquent address to the Senate, outlined the kind of peace which America could guarantee. The area of agreement had been defined, and the essential difference was soon to leap into blinding clarity. For on 31 January, as we have seen, Germany tore up all her former promises, and informed Washington that she was about to enter upon an unrestricted submarine campaign.

The Rubicon had been reached, and there could be no turning back. The German Ambassador was handed his passports on 3 February, and Mr Gerard summoned from Berlin. On the same day the President announced to both Houses of Congress the severance of diplomatic relations with Germany. He showed by his speeches that he took the step unwillingly. He drew a distinction between the German people and the German Government – the old distinction to which idealists in democratic countries were apt to cling till facts forced them to relinquish it. He declared that he could not believe that the German Government meant 'to do in fact, what they have warned us they feel at liberty to do', and that only 'actual overt acts' would convince him of their hostile purpose. But he ended with the solemn announcement that if American ships were sunk and American lives were lost he would come again to Congress and ask for power to take the necessary steps for the protection of his people.

The immediate result of the German decree was that American passenger ships were deterred from sailing for Europe. This brought the situation home very vividly to the dwellers on the eastern states, but had only a remote interest for the inhabitants of the west and the middle west. At first there was no very flagrant offence against American shipping, though the *Housatonic* was sunk on 3 February and the *Lyman M. Law* on 13 February. But the situation was none the less intolerable, and on the 26th Mr Wilson again addressed Congress, pointing out that Germany had placed a practical embargo on America's shipping, and asking for authority to arm her vessels effectually for defence. What he contemplated was an armed neutrality which should stop short of war. On 1 March the House of Representatives gave this authority by 403 votes to 13, but in the Senate a similar vote was held up by a handful of pacificists, and could not be passed before the session came automatically to an end on 4 March. Nevertheless an overwhelming majority of the Senate signed a manifesto in favour of the Bill.

Meantime various events had roused the temper of the country. On 26 February the *Laconia* was sunk and eight Americans were drowned. On 1 March there was published an order which had been issued on 19 January by Herr Zimmermann, of the German Foreign Office, to the German Minister in Mexico. The latter was instructed to form an alliance with Mexico in the event of war breaking out between Germany and the United States, and to offer as a bribe the provinces of Texas, Arizona, and New Mexico. In the same document it was suggested that efforts might be made to seduce Japan from the Allies and bring her into partnership with Germany. Such proposals inspired the deepest resentment in the west and the middle west, where the submarine atrocities were least realised. There was another consideration which was beginning to impress thoughtful Americans. Even if she avoided war, America would be forced one day or another to negotiate a settlement with Germany. Peace would not come to her automatically on the conclusion of hostilities, and her position in peace negotiations would depend on how the war ended. Mr Wilson realised that his present policy could not endure. In his inaugural address of 5 March he said:

> We have been obliged to arm ourselves to make good our claim to a certain minimum of right and of freedom of action. We stand firm in armed neutrality, since it seems that in no other way we can demonstrate what it is we insist upon and cannot forgo. We may be drawn on by circumstances, not by our own purpose or desire, to a more active assertion of our rights as we see them, and a more immediate association with the great struggle itself.

The order for arming merchant ships was issued by the American Government on 12 March. A week later came the 'overt acts' of which the President had spoken. On the 16th the *Vigilancia* was sunk and five American lives lost. On the 17th the *City of Memphis* and the *Illinois* followed suit. On the 21st the *Healdton* was torpedoed off the Dutch coast and outside the prohibited zone, and seven Americans perished. On 1 April came the loss of the *Aztec*, when twenty-eight Americans were lost. The defiance was flagrant and unmistakable. The feeling against Germany rose to fever heat. At last the country was ripe for the final step. In the words of the official statement:

> Judging the German Government now in the light of our own experience through the long and patient years of our honest attempt to keep the peace, we could see the Great Autocracy and read her record through the war. And we found that record

damnable ... With a fanatical faith in the destiny of German *Kultur* as the system that must rule the world, the Imperial Government's actions have through years of boasting, double-dealing, and deceit, tended towards aggression upon the rights of others ... Its record ... has given not only to the Allies but to liberal peoples throughout the world the conviction that this menace to human liberties everywhere must be utterly shorn of its power for harm. For the evil it has effected has ranged far out of Europe – out upon the open seas, where its submarines, in defiance of law and the concepts of humanity, have blown up neutral vessels and covered the waves with the dead and dying, men and women and children alike. Its agents have conspired against the peace of neutral nations everywhere, sowing the seeds of dissension, ceaselessly endeavouring by tortuous methods of deceit, of bribery, false promises, and intimidation, to stir up brother nations one against the other, in order that the liberal world might not be able to unite, in order that the Autocracy might emerge triumphant from the war. All this we know from our own experience with the Imperial Government. As they have dealt with Europe, so they have dealt with us and with all mankind.

The case against Germany was plain, and an event had occurred which made an alliance easier with Germany's foes. On 9 March the Revolution broke out in Petrograd; by 16 March the autocracy had fallen and a popular Government ruled in Russia. The issue was now clear, not as a strife between dynasties, but as the eternal war of liberty and despotism, and no free people could be deaf to the call. The special session of Congress was advanced by a fortnight, and on 2 April Mr Wilson asked it for a declaration of war.

The President's message on that day will rank among the greatest of America's many famous state documents. Couched in terms of studious moderation and dignity, it stated not only the case of America against Germany, but of civilisation against barbarism and popular government against tyranny. He began with an indictment of the submarine campaign, recalling the promise given on 4 May 1916, and its complete reversal by the decree of 31 January 1917.

> Vessels of every kind, whatever their flag, their character, their cargo, their destination, their errand, have been ruthlessly sent to the bottom without warning and without thought of help or mercy for those on board, the vessels of friendly neutrals along with those of belligerents. Even hospital ships [notably the *Britannic*, the *Gloucester Castle*, and the *Asturias* (sunk 20 March). The Belgian relief ships were the *Camilla*, the *Trevier*, the *Feistein*, and the *Storstad*] and ships carrying relief to the sorely bereaved and stricken people of Belgium, though the latter were provided with safe-conduct through the proscribed areas by the German Government itself, and were distinguished by unmistakable marks of identity, have been sunk with the same reckless lack of compassion or of principle.

Germany had swept away the last fragments of international rights, and her new warfare was not against commerce only but against mankind.

On 6 April, by a majority of 373 votes to 50, the House of Representatives passed the resolution, which ran as follows:

> Whereas the Imperial German Government have committed repeated acts of war against the Government and the people of the United States of America: Therefore be it resolved by the Senate and the House of Representatives of the United States of America in Congress assembled: That a state of war between the

United States and the Imperial German Government which has been thrust upon the United States is hereby formally declared; and that the President be, and he is hereby authorized and directed to employ the entire naval and military forces of the United States and the resources of the Government to carry on war against the Imperial German Government; and to bring the conflict to a successful termination all the resources of the country are hereby pledged by the Congress of the United States.

The entrance of America into the war on the Allied side meant an immediate increase of strength in certain vital matters. She was the greatest workshop on earth, and the high mechanical talent of her people was invaluable in what was largely a war of engineers. She had immense wealth to put into the common stock. She had a powerful fleet, though one somewhat lacking in the lighter type of vessel which was the chief need of the moment, and she had a great capacity for shipbuilding. Her army was small, but its officers were among the most highly trained in the world, and her reserves of man-power gave her the chance of almost unlimited expansion. It would be some time before she could make her potential strength actual, but in the meantime she solved the worst financial difficulties of the Allies, and her accession made ultimate victory something more than probable. Like her cousins of Britain, she was a nation slow to move, but on the path she had chosen she would walk resolutely to the end of the journey.

Germany, however, intervened to dislocate Nivelle's plan. Ludendorff, aware of his diminishing manpower, set himself to reorganise his armies, and to prepare the way for that victory on land which he believed must follow the submarine triumph. Across the chord of his great salient in the West from Lens to Rheims he built a gigantic series of defences, which were named after the heroes of German mythology, and which Britain knew as the Hindenburg Line. Then he withdrew his front towards it, devastating all the area relinquished.

By the beginning of the second week of March the Allies were conscious of a general movement in the enemy lines everywhere between the Aisne and Arras. On the morning of 17 March the Allied commanders, French and British, ordered a general forward movement on a front of 45 miles. The movement was, indeed, greater, for it embraced virtually the whole line from Arras to north of Soissons – 70 miles as the crow flies, well over 100 if the sinuosities of the front trenches were followed. The next few days revealed to our soldiers some of the most surprising sights of the campaign. They were beyond the old tortured battlefield, with its infinite ramification of trenches. Henceforward, up to the new Siegfried Line, there was open country. The fields were not pitted with shell-holes; the trees were not splintered into matchwood; the villages had not been levelled by the Allied artillery. But the enemy himself in falling back had made a great destruction, destroying roads, mining certain areas, levelling buildings which might give billets to the Allies, cutting down woods which could afford cover. Every house in town and hamlet had been looted of all goods that could be removed, and what could not be taken away had been smashed up or defiled. During those days the Allies had literally to grope their way forward. They were advancing, over country in which all means of communication had been destroyed, against an enemy whose armies were still intact. Strong detachments of his infantry and cavalry occupied points of advantage along the line of advance; his guns, which had been withdrawn to prepared positions, were available at any moment to cover and support a sudden counter-stroke, while the broken country made the progress of the Allied artillery slow. He had a most formidable defensive system, upon which he could fall back should his counter-stroke miss its aim; while the Allies, as they moved forward, left prepared defences farther and farther behind them. The position craved wary walking, and those were anxious days for the Allied High Commands. Their cavalry felt their way gingerly through a country full of unknown perils. The infantry behind them prepared, as they advanced, successive lines of resistance in the event of a counter-attack. Behind them, again, the engineers and labour battalions did wonderful work in restoring roads and bridges and pushing on light railways, so that presently the difficulties of the old battlefield were conquered.

The retreat of the Germans was, all things considered, a brilliant performance; but scarcely less brilliant was the work of the Allies, which nipped in the bud the counter-stroke that had been one object of that retreat. By 5 April the Allies were almost everywhere in front of the Siegfried Line which the enemy believed to be impregnable. It was obvious that he would fight desperately for all parts of it, but especially for the pivots on which its security depended. These pivots were the positions about Arras in the north, and those in the south around Laon and the Chemin des Dames.

* * *

The eyes of the Allied generals were fixed on the pivots, and Britain's concern was that northern one where, at the hamlet of Tilloy-lez-Mofflaines, the Siegfried Line branched off from the old front. Between that point and Lens the original lines were very strong, consisting of three main systems, each constructed on the familiar pattern of four parallel lines of trenches, studded with redoubts, and linked up with numerous switches. A special and very powerful switch line ran for 5½ miles from the village of Feuchy northward across the Scarpe to beyond Thelus, and so constituted what was virtually a fourth line of defence. The whole defensive belt was from 2 to 5 miles deep; but the German Command were not content with it. They had designed an independent line running from Drocourt, south-east of Lens, to the Siegfried Line at Quéant, which should be an alternative in case of an assault on the Arras salient. But at the beginning of April this position, which was to become famous as the Drocourt–Quéant line, was not yet completed. It was intended as a protection for Douai and Cambrai, the loss of which would have made the whole Siegfried system untenable. But it was designed only *pro majore cautela*, for there was every confidence in the mighty ramified defences between Lens and Tilloy, and in the resisting power of the northern Siegfried sector.

The plan devised at Chantilly in November 1916 had, as we have seen, to be wholly recast, in view of the different policy and the enlarged powers of the new French Commander-in-Chief, and the German retreat to the Hindenburg Line. The position now was that the Arras attack, which Haig had regarded as only a preparation for the main campaign in Flanders, became the principal task of the British Army during the first half of 1917. This action, at the same time, was conceived as a movement subsidiary to the greater effort of the French in the south. It was admittedly an attack in a region where, except for an unexampled piece of fortune, good strategic results could scarcely be obtained. The success of the British depended on what the French could do on the Aisne. If the latter failed, then the former, too, must fail in the larger strategic sense, however valuable might be certain of their local gains. If, however, Nivelle succeeded, the pressure from Arras in the north would beyond doubt greatly contribute to the enemy's discomfiture. The danger of the whole plan was that the issue might be indeterminate, and the fighting at Arras so long protracted, without any decisive success, that the chances of the more vital Flanders offensive later in the summer might be imperilled. This, as we shall see, was precisely what happened.

Haig had a formidable problem before him. The immediate key of the area was Vimy ridge, the capture of which was necessary to protect the flank of any advance farther south. It was clear that no strategic result could be obtained unless the Drocourt–Quéant switch was breached, and that meant an advance of well over 6 miles. But this position was still in the making; and, if the fates were kind, and the first three German systems could be carried at a rush, there was good hope that the Drocourt–Quéant line would never be manned, and that the drive of the British, assisted by the great French attack on the Aisne, might bring them to Douai and Cambrai. It was a hope, but no more. A result so far-reaching demanded a combination of fortunate chances, which as yet had not been vouchsafed to us in any battle of the campaign.

The British front of attack was slightly over 12 miles long, from Givenchy-en-Gohelle in the north to a point just short of Croisilles in the south. In the third week of March a systematic cutting of the enemy's wire began, and our heavy artillery shelled his back areas and communications. About Wednesday 4 April, the British guns woke along the whole sector. There was a steady bombardment of all the enemy positions, more especially the great fortress of the Vimy ridge. Wonderful counter-battery work was done, and battery after battery of the enemy was put out of action, located partly by direct observation from the air, and partly by our new device for sound identification. These were days of clear, cold spring weather, with the wind in the north-east, and from dawn to dark our airplanes fought a mighty battle on their own account. In the history of air-fighting, that week must rank as an epoch, for it was a last desperate struggle on the enemy's part to defend his side of the line against our encroaching supremacy. It was a week of heavy losses, for at all costs the foe must be blinded, and the British airmen kept up one continuous offensive.

Zero hour was 5.30 on the morning of Easter Monday. At the appointed moment the British guns broke into such a fire as had been yet seen on no battle-ground on earth. It was the first hour of the Somme repeated, but a hundredfold more awful. As our men went over the parapets they felt as if they were under the protection of some supernatural power, for the heaven above them was one canopy of shrieking steel. There were now no enemy front trenches; soon there were no second-line trenches; only a hummocky waste of craters and broken wire. Within forty minutes all the German first position was captured, and our men were moving steadily against the second, while our barrage crept relentlessly before them. On the left wing the Canadians with a bound reached the crest of Vimy, and swarmed on to the tableland from which the ground fell away to the flat industrial area between Lens and Douai. Before nine o'clock all the Vimy ridge was ours, except its northern corner and the high point marked Hill 145. By 9.30 the whole of the German second position had fallen, except a short length west of Bailleul. By the evening the Feuchy switch line had now gone, and the enemy front had been utterly destroyed. He had no prepared position short of the Drocourt–Quéant line, and that was still in the making.

But the weather was on his side. The ground was sodden, and our guns took time to bring up. He was holding it with machine guns in pockets, which prevented the use of cavalry for what was the true duty of cavalry. Had we possessed a light type of tank in reasonable numbers the rout could have been made complete.

future operations. Likewise he had to prepare for that great assault upon the German right wing in Flanders which he had long ago determined should be the main British enterprise of the summer. The fighting of May was, therefore, in a different category from that of April. The initial impetus had gone, the main strategical end had not been attained, and, as during the last phase of the Somme, it was an affair of local offensives and limited objectives.

Nivelle's plan had been to force the Aisne heights in one bold assault from west, south, and south-east; at the same moment to carry the Rheims heights from the north; and simultaneously to launch his centre through the gap between the two into the plain of Laon. Next day a fresh army would attack the Moronvillers *massif* to distract the German counter-attack, and protect his own right flank. In the centre he would use the new French tanks – machines less stout and solid than the British, but believed to possess greater speed. The plan was doomed from the start. In the first place, it was not the culmination of an arpeggio of attack, as had been proposed; for Franchet d'Esperey, who attacked on 14 April near Saint-Quentin, failed utterly, being brought up sharp against the strongest part of the Siegfried defences. In the second place, the scheme was known in full detail to the enemy. Never was a defence more amply forewarned. In the third place, the aim which Nivelle set before himself demanded forces in the perfection of physical and moral well-being – an army of 'shock-troops'; and the French armies were weary, dispirited, out of temper, doubtful of their leader, and in the mood to listen to treasonable tales. Small blame to them, for they had been too highly tried. But, even had there been none of these attendant misfortunes, the plans of the French general would still have been open to censure. He proposed to break through a strong enemy defence, but his tactical methods were not different from those already used for less ambitious objectives. His main conception was right: trench warfare could be ended, an enemy front could be not only pierced but crumbled; but he had not discovered the means. The result of his offensive was that though there had been considerable gains of ground, the major strategy had failed. The road to Laon was as firmly barred as ever.

The result was to produce grave discouragement among the French people. Nivelle was invited to resign, declined, and on 15 May was replaced by Pétain, while Fayolle succeeded to Pétain's old group command in the central sector. Foch followed Pétain as Chief of the General Staff in Paris. Pétain on his succession to office found a grim problem before him. The battle had been like a chemical which when added to a compound produces an explosion, and the superb *moral* of the soldiers of France seemed to be in the gravest jeopardy. As early as February Nivelle had complained of pacificist and communist propaganda among his troops. There were evil elements in French life which seized the occasion of the fatigue and disillusionment of the soldier to instill the poison of cowardice and treason. The rank and file had many grievances. Leave was hard to get, and when it was granted the *permissionnaire* found such difficulties in reaching his family that most of his scanty time was taken up by the journey. Intense bitterness was roused by letters from home, which told the peasant of the struggle of his womenkind to keep his farm in cultivation; while the workmen of the towns were exempted by thousands for munition making. There was dire confusion in the medical services during the battle, and wounded were sent all over France to spread despondency by the tale of their needless sufferings.

The first signs of revolt appeared about 20 May, not in the troops fighting on the Aisne, but in corps which had been some months in reserve. The contagion spread to the men in the line, and in certain divisions nearest Paris the mutiny seemed to have something of the character of a first step in political revolution.

The crisis showed Pétain at his best. He insisted on reforming flagrant abuses. The penal measures used were few; less than a dozen suffered death as mutineers. But Pétain set himself to a great work of education and exhortation. In two months he visited and addressed the officers and men of over one hundred divisions, and created a profound impression. He had no tricks to win popularity, no easy geniality, none of the air of the *bon enfant*; he was always grave and dignified, always the general-in-chief. But such was the atmosphere of calm resolution which he bore with him, such the simplicity and sincerity of his voice and eyes, that he moved audiences which the most finished orations would have left untouched. Honestly and gravely he told them of the peril of their country and the cause for which they and their Allies fought. By the middle of June the danger was past. But one consequence remained, which was to affect the whole strategy of 1917. The armies of France were convalescent, but they had still to be nursed hack to perfect health. For the rest of the year it was plain that Britain must bear the chief burden.

16

The Third Battle of Ypres and Cambrai

Haig's Flanders Policy – Battle of Messines – 'The Pill-boxes' – British Attacks – The Weather – Capture of Passchendaele – Battle of Cambrai – Enemy Counter-Attack – Close of 1917 Campaign

The Battle of Arras had died down before the end of May, and Sir Douglas Haig, having protracted the fighting in that area so long as the French on the Aisne required his aid, was now free to turn his attention to the plan which he had elaborated seven months before. This was an offensive against the enemy forces in Flanders, with the aim of clearing the Belgian coast and turning the northern flank of the whole German defence system in the West. It was a scheme which, if successful, promised the most profound and far-reaching results. It would destroy the worst of the submarine bases; it would restore to Belgium her lost territory, and thereby deprive the enemy of one of his cherished bargaining assets; it would cripple his main communications with the depots of the lower Rhineland. It offered the chance of a blow at a vital spot within a reasonable time. It was true that conditions had changed since the plan was first matured. The two months' conflict at Arras had used up a certain part of the British reserves. More important, the disastrous turn of the Russian situation would enable the Germans to add greatly to their strength both in munitions and in men. Time, therefore, was the essence of the business. The blow must be struck at the earliest possible hour, for delay meant aggrandisement for the enemy.

For twelve months the front between the sea and the Lys had been all but stagnant. It had been for the first two years the chief cockpit of British arms, and the enemy had spent infinite ingenuity and labour on perfecting his defences. In the half-moon of hills round Ypres and the ridge of Wytschaete and Messines he had view-points which commanded the whole countryside, and especially the British line within the Salient. Any preparations for attack would be conducted under his watchful eye. Moreover, the heavy, waterlogged clay of the flats where our front lay was terribly at the mercy of weather, and in rain became a bottomless swamp, so that any attack must be in the position of a horseman taking a stiff fence from a bad jumping-off ground. Lastly, the Germans were acutely conscious of the importance of the terrain, and there was little chance of taking them by surprise.

The British front was held by the Second Army, which had not altered its position since the spring of 1915. The Second Army was fortunate in its leader. Sir Herbert Plumer, now sixty years of age, had in the highest degree the traditional virtues of the British soldier, and especially of those county line regiments which have always been the backbone of the British army. Moreover, for a year and more he had been making ready for the offensive in which he was to play the chief part. Methodical and patient preparation had been carried by him to the pitch of genius.

The Wytschaete–Messines ridge had seen no fighting since the close of 1914. But for nearly two years an offensive had been going on underground. As early as July 1915 it had been resolved to make use of the clay stratum below our position for extensive mining operations, and in January 1916 we had gone seriously to work. We used in our tunnelling companies some of the best expert talent in the world, men who in private life had received large salaries from mining corporations. It was work attended by endless difficulties and dangers. Water-bearing strata would suddenly be encountered, which necessitated damming and pumping work on a big scale. The enemy was busy counter-mining, and we had to be ever on the watch to detect his progress, and by *camouflets* to blow in his galleries.

From the last days of May a pitiless bombardment had assailed the enemy area, devastating his front line and searching out his rear positions. The last remnants of Wytschaete and Messines villages disappeared. The woods on the slopes ceased to be tattered, and became fields of stumps. Our raiding activity was unceasing, and from dazed prisoners and from many captured letters we learned of the miseries of the enemy. British aircraft spent their days over the German hinterland, and prevented any enemy planes from learning the extent of our preparation. On the evening of Wednesday 6 June, the weather broke in a violent thunderstorm. Torrents of rain fell, and from the baked earth rose a warm mist which enfolded the ground like a cloak. During the night the heavens were overcast, so that the full moon was not seen, and only a luminous glow told of its presence. But at 2.30 a.m. on the 7th the skies cleared, the moon rode out, and to a watcher on the hills to the west the whole landscape stood forth in a sheen made up of moonlight and the foreglow of dawn. As the dawn broadened our guns seemed to cease, though the enemy's were still active. The air was full of the hum of our bombing and reconnoitring 'planes flying eastward, and our balloons were going up – tawny patches against the June sky. Then came a burst of German high explosives, and then, at precisely ten minutes past three, a sound compared to which all other noises were silence.

From Hill 60 in the north to the edge of Messines, with a shock that made the solid earth quiver like a pole in the wind, nineteen volcanoes leaped to heaven. Nineteen sheets of flame seemed to fill the world. For a moment it looked as if the earth, under a magician's wand, had been contorted into gigantic toadstools. The black cloud-caps seemed as real as the soil beneath them. Then they shook and wavered and thinned, leaving a brume of dust, rosy and golden atop with the rising sun. And at the same moment, while the ears were still throbbing with the concussion of the mines, every British gun opened on the enemy. Flashes of many colours stabbed the wall of dust, the bursts of shrapnel stood out white against it, and smoke barrages from our trenches burrowed into its roots. The sun was now above the horizon, and turned the fringes of the cloud to a hot purple and crimson. No battle had ever a more beautiful and terrible staging. And while the débris of the explosion still hung in the air the British divisions of assault went over their parapets. They entered at once upon a world like the nether pit – poisonous with gas fumes, twisted and riven out of all character, a maze of quarried stone, moving earth, splintered concrete, broken wire, and horrible fragments of humanity. In most places the German front lines had been blown out of existence. A few nerve-shattered survivors were taken prisoner in the dug-outs that had escaped destruction, and here and there a gallant machine-gun officer, who had miraculously survived, obeyed his orders till death took him.

It was a day everywhere of complete success. Before darkness fell the whole of the line was in our hands, and Plumer had gained his final objective. During the night we secured our gains, and on the morning of the 8th cleared a few remaining lengths of German trench. Not till that evening was there any sign of a counter-stroke. At 7 p.m., after an intense bombardment, the Germans attacked along nearly the whole length of our new line, and at every point were repulsed. The surprise and shock of the action of the 7th had been too great to permit of a speedy recovery. That evening we attacked again on both our flanks, clearing out some of the strong points north of the Ypres–Comines canal, and forcing the enemy on the south back to the line of the River Warnave.

Sir Herbert Plumer's task had been brilliantly and fully accomplished. In a single day's fighting he had advanced 2½ miles on a front of nearly 10; he had wiped out the German salient, and carried also its chord; he had stormed positions on the heights which the enemy regarded as impregnable; his losses were extraordinarily small, and he had taken 7,200 prisoners, sixty-seven guns, ninety-four trench mortars, and 294 machine guns. The Battle of Messines will rank in history as a perfect instance of the success of the limited objective.

***

The preliminary work of Messines was over by 12 June, but it was not till late in July that the day for the major advance could be fixed. The plan, as it was finally put into action, bristled with difficulties which might have deterred a less stout-hearted commander than Sir Douglas Haig. It was in some degree a race against time. If a true strategic purpose was to be effected before winter, the first stages must be quickly passed. The high ground east of the Salient must be won in a fortnight, to enable the British to move against the German bases in West Flanders and clear the coast-line. Moreover, it was now evident that the Russian front was crumbling; already divisions and batteries had come westward, and those left behind had been skimmed for shock-troops. Soon the process would proceed more rapidly, and the British would be faced with an accumulation of reserves strong enough to bar their way. Again, the nature of the terrain made any offensive a gamble with the weather. A dry autumn like that of 1914 would be well enough, but a repetition of the Somme experience must spell disaster. The Salient was, after Verdun, the most tortured of the Western battlefields.

In Flanders the nature of the ground did not permit of a second Siegfried Line. Deep dug-outs and concrete-lined trenches were impossible because of the waterlogged soil, and he was compelled to find new tactics. The solution was the 'pill-box'. These were small concrete forts, sited among the ruins of a farm or in some derelict piece of woodland, often raised only a yard or two above the ground level, and bristling with machine guns. The low entrance was at the rear, and the ordinary pill-box held from twenty to forty men. It was easy to make, for the wooden or steel framework could be brought up on any dark night and filled with concrete. They were echeloned in depth with great skill; and, in the wiring, alleys were left so that an unwary advance would be trapped among them and exposed to enfilading fire. Their small size made them a difficult mark for heavy guns, and since they were protected by concrete at least 3 feet thick, they were impregnable to the ordinary barrage of field artillery. The enemy's plan was to hold his first line – which was often a mere string of shell-craters linked by a trench – with few men, who would fall back before an assault. He had his guns well behind, so that they should not be captured in the first rush, and would be available for a barrage when his opponents were entangled in the 'pill-box' zone. Finally, he had his reserves in the second line, ready for the counter-stroke before the attack could secure the ground won. It will be seen that these tactics were admirably suited for the exposed and contorted ground of the Salient. Any attack would be allowed to make some advance; but if the German plan worked well, this advance would be short-lived, and would be dearly paid for. Instead of the cast-iron front of the Siegfried area, the Flanders line would be highly elastic, but would spring back into position after pressure with a deadly rebound.

Throughout July the preparations for the great Salient battle were being assiduously pressed on. All the month our bombardment

continued, till every corner of the Salient was drenched with our fire. We made constant raids and gas attacks, the latter with deadly effect. The front of attack was 15 miles long, from the Lys river to a little north of Steenstraate, but the main effort was planned for the 7½ miles between Boesinghe and the Zillebeke–Zandvoorde road. The task of the British Fifth Army was, by a series of bounds, to capture the enemy's first defences situated on the forward slope of the rising ground, and his second position sited along the crest, and at the same time to secure the crossings of the Steenebeek, the muddy ditch which flows by Saint-Julien to join the Sint-Jansbeek, north-east of Bixschoote. If this could be done at once and the weather favoured, a strong defensive flank could be formed for a breakthrough in the direction of Thourout towards the north-east.

On the morning of Monday the 30th came a heavy thunderstorm, and rain fell in the afternoon. All day the Allied bombardment continued at its height, and during the drizzling night. The rain stopped towards dawn, but a thick mist remained, and the ground was plashy and the skies overcast as zero hour drew near. There was a short lull in the firing after three; but precisely at 3.50 a.m. on the 31st the whole Allied front broke into flame. Under cover of discharges of thermit and blazing oil, and a barrage of exceptional weight, the infantry crossed their parapets, and the battle began. The whole of the German front position fell at once. According to plan, the next day should have seen a second blow with cumulative force. But the weather had joined the enemy. From midday on 1 August for four days and four nights without intermission fell the rain. Even when it stopped on the 5th there followed days of sombre skies and wet mists and murky clouds. The misery of our troops, huddled in their impromptu lines or strung out in shell-holes, cannot be pictured in words. Nor can the supreme disappointment of the High Command. After months of thought and weeks of laborious preparation, just when a brilliant start had been made, they saw their hopes dashed to the ground. An offensive was still possible, but it could not be the offensive planned. The time-schedule was fatally dislocated.

For a fortnight we held our hand. To advance was a stark impossibility till the countryside was a little drier, for though we had won positions on the heights, our communications ran through the spongy Salient. In the middle of the month there was a short break in the storms, and Haig took advantage of it for a new attack. He began by a highly successful subsidiary action in the south, designed to threaten an important position of the enemy, and prevent him massing all his strength before the Salient. Next day, the 16th, saw the second stage of the Ypres struggle. The Fifth Army was directed against the German third position, the Gheluvelt–Langemarck line, which ran from the Menin road along the second of the tiers of ridges which rimmed the Salient on the east. The attack took place at dawn, 4.45 a.m., and on the Allies' left and left centre had an immediate success. But north and north-east of Saint-Julien, and between the Wieltje–Passchendaele and the Ypres–Zonnebeke roads, it came up against the full strength of the 'pill-boxes'. A number fell to us, and all day we struggled on in the mud, losing heavily from the concealed machine-gun fire. In some places our men reached their final objectives, but they could not abide in them. Enemy counter-attacks later in the morning forced us back, and at the close of the day we were little beyond our starting-point. On the British right the fighting was still more desperate. In the area about the woods, Inverness Copse, Glencorse Wood, and Polygon Wood, we made but little progress. This second stage of the battle was beyond doubt a serious British check. We had encountered a new tactical device of the enemy, and it had defeated us. The Fifth Army had fought with the most splendid gallantry, but its courage had been largely fruitless.

For almost the first time in the campaign there was a sense of discouragement abroad on our front. Men felt that they were being sacrificed blindly; that every fight was a soldiers' fight, and that such sledge-hammer tactics were too crude to meet the problem. For a moment there was a real ebb of confidence in British leadership. Haig accordingly brought upon the scene the man who was rapidly coming to recognition as the most accomplished of army commanders. The front of the Second Army was extended northward, and Sir Herbert Plumer took over the attack upon the southern portion of the enemy front on the Menin road. The better part of a month was spent in preparation, while Plumer patiently thought out the problem. Sorely tried – too sorely tried – divisions were taken out of the line to rest, and the dispositions on the whole front of assault were readjusted. Especially our artillery tactics were revised, in order to cope with the 'pill-boxes'. In the early days of September the weather improved, and the sodden Salient began slowly to dry. That is to say, the mud hardened into something like the *séracs* of a glacier, and the streams became streams again, and not lagoons. But the process was slow, and it was not till the third week of the month that the next stage in the battle could begin.

The new 8-mile front of attack ran from the Ypres–Staden railway north of Langemarck to the Ypres–Comines canal north of Hollebeke. On the left and centre our objectives were narrowly limited, averaging about ¾ mile; but Plumer on the right had the serious task of pushing for a mile along the Menin road. The 'pill-box' problem had been studied, and a solution, it was believed, had been found, not by miraculous ingenuity but by patience and care. The little fortalices had been methodically reconnoitred, and our heavy barrage so arranged as to cover each mark. Even when a direct hit was not attained, it was believed that the concussion of the great shells might loosen some of the lesser structures, while fumes, smoke, and gas would make the life of the inmates difficult. One famous division followed with complete success another plan. Having located the 'pill-box', the field-gun barrage lengthened on both sides of it; which enabled the advancing troops, hugging their barrage, to get round its unprotected rear.

At 5.40 a.m. on the 20th the attack was launched. The ground was knee-deep in mud, but the whole British line pressed forward. This day's battle cracked the kernel of the German defence in the Salient. It showed a limited advance, and the total of 3,000 prisoners had been often exceeded in a day's fighting; but every inch of the ground won was vital. We had carried the southern pillar on which the security of the Passchendaele ridge depended. Few struggles in the campaign were more desperate, or carried out on a more gruesome battlefield. The maze of quagmires, splintered woods, ruined husks of 'pill-boxes', water-filled shell-holes, and foul creeks which made up the land on both sides of the Menin road was a sight which to the recollection of most men must seem like a fevered nightmare. It was the classic soil on which during the First Battle of Ypres the 1st and 2nd Divisions had stayed the German rush for the Channel. Then it had been a broken but still recognisable and featured countryside; now the elements seemed to have blended with each other to make of it a limbo outside mortal experience and almost beyond human imagining. Only on some of the contorted hills of Verdun could a parallel be found. The battle of 20 September was a proof to what heights of endurance the British soldier may attain.

We struck again on 26 September. The weather was fine, and for a brief week it ceased to be an element in the German defensive. Our front of attack was the 6-mile stretch from north-east of Saint-Julien to south of the Tower Hamlets. The new advance was as precise and complete as its predecessor of the 20th. The last days of fine weather were employed by the Germans in some of the most resolute counter-attacks of the battle. The last took place on 3 October, close to the Menin road, but it was broken up by our guns before it reached our lines.

That night the weather broke, and a gale from the south-west brought heavy rains. It was the old ill-luck of our army, for on the 4th we had planned the next stage of the battle. But if the weather was ill-timed, not so was our attack. The enemy had brought up three fresh divisions, with a view to recovering his losses of the 26th. Ten minutes past six was his zero hour, and by good fortune and good guiding six o'clock was ours. Our barrage burst upon his infantry when it was forming up for the assault, and cut great swathes in its ranks. While the Germans were yet in the confusion of miscarried plans, our bayonets were upon them. Like Messines and the first day of Arras, that was a day of perfect success. By midday every objective had been gained. The enemy, caught on the brink of an attack of his own, was not merely repulsed: a considerable part of his forces was destroyed.

But October had set in, storm followed storm, and Haig had to reconsider his plan of campaign. Weather and a dozen other malignant accidents had wrecked the larger scheme of a Flanders offensive. Gone was the hope of clearing the coast or of driving the enemy out of his Flemish bases. What had been laboriously achieved at the end of ten weeks had been in the programme for the first fortnight. The weather had compelled us to make our advance by stages, widely separated in time, with the result that the enemy had been able to bring up his reserves and reorganise his defence. Our pressure could not be cumulative, and we had been unable to reap the full fruits of each success. There was, therefore, no chance of any decisive operation in the Flanders area, and it became a serious question for Haig whether the Ypres operations should be continued. If October should bring the kind of weather which it had shown the year before on the Somme, the Salient would be an ugly fighting ground. The extremity of Russia was permitting more and more German divisions to be transferred to the West, which would not make our task easier. On the other hand, we had not won the last even of the limited preliminary objectives; for we did not control the whole Passchendaele ridge, and it might well be urged that, till we did, we had not secured our own position or made difficult the enemy's against the coming winter. Also events of high importance were in train in Italy, and the attack towards Cambrai in November had been decided upon – which made it essential to fix the enemy's attention on the Flanders front. Balancing the pros and cons of the matter, Haig resolved to continue his offensive on a modified scale till the end of October, or such time as would give our men the chance of reaching Passchendaele.

The last stages of the Third Battle of Ypres were probably the muddiest combats ever known in the history of war. It rained incessantly – sometimes clearing to a drizzle or a Scots mist, but relapsing into a downpour on any day fixed for our attack. Such fighting was the last word in human misery, for the country was now one irreclaimable bog, and the occasional hours of watery sunshine had no power to dry it. On 30 October came the attack on Passchendaele itself. Rain again interfered with our operations but some days of dry weather followed, and on 6 November two Canadian Divisions swept forward again, carried the whole of Passchendaele, and pushed northward to the Goudberg spur. Four days later they increased their gains, so that all the vital part of the main ridge of West Flanders was in British hands. We dominated the enemy's hinterland in the flats towards Roulers and Thourout, and he had the prospect of a restless winter under our direct observation. The Third Battle of Ypres had wiped out the Salient where for three years we had been at the mercy of the German guns.

The great struggle which we have considered was strategically a British failure. We did not come within measurable distance of our major purpose, and that owing to no fault in generalship or fighting virtue, but through the maleficence of the weather in a land where weather was all in all. We gambled upon a normal August, and we did not get it. The sea of mud which lapped around the Salient was the true defence of the enemy. Consequently the battle, which might have had a profound strategic significance in the campaign, became merely an episode in the war of attrition, a repetition of the Somme tactics, though conspicuously less successful and considerably more costly than the fighting of 1916. Third Ypres was the costliest battle up to date fought by a British army, for the casualties from 31 July to 10 November were in killed, wounded, and missing 230,000 men. For the gain of a trivial ridge and a few miles of mud the price might well be deemed fantastic; but such a judgement would miss the true reason of the action. It was fought out of dire necessity, at the entreaty of France, lest a worse thing should befall. One outstanding fact in the struggle was the superb endurance and valour of the new British armies, fighting under conditions which for horror and misery had scarcely been paralleled in war. Ypres was indeed to Britain what Verdun was to France – the hallowed soil which called forth the highest virtue of her people, a battle-ground where there could be no failure without loss of honour.

The battlefield of the old Salient was now as featureless as the Sahara or the mid-Atlantic. All landmarks had been obliterated; the very ridges and streams had changed their character. The names which still crowded the map had no longer any geographical counterpart; they were no more than measurements on a plane, as abstract as the points of the mathematician. It was war bared to the buff, stripped of any of the tattered romance which has clung to older fields. And yet in its very grossness it was war sublimated, for the material appanages had vanished. The quaint Flemish names belonged not now to the solid homely earth; they seemed rather points on a spiritual map, marking advance and retreat in the gigantic striving of the souls of peoples.

* * *

But splendid as the record had been, the British High Command could not contemplate the situation with much comfort. Many German divisions had been broken at Ypres, but the stagnation of the winter war would give them time to rest and refit. Already large enemy forces had been brought from Russia, more were on their way, and there were many more to come. If the enemy were left in peace, he had it in his power to create a dangerous situation for the spring. Moreover, Italy, fighting desperately on the Piave, deserved by all the laws of war some relief in the shape of an Allied diversion. Weary as his troops might be, Sir Douglas Haig was not able to grant them the rest which they had earned and most urgently required.

If another blow was to be struck, it must not be delayed. If the British could strike at once in an unexpected quarter, they might have the benefit of a real surprise, and at the moment the thoughts of the Allied Command, like that of the German General Staff, were running on some means of breaking the rigidity of trench warfare and restoring the element of the unexpected. Should such a blow succeed, it would have a real effect upon the *moral* of the enemy, for after Third Ypres he would not anticipate a fresh Allied effort yet awhile. It would give him an uneasy winter, for it would not permit him to reduce the strength of any part of his front, as had been his former practice, and so would cripple that heavy local concentration which might be looked for in the spring. In deciding the question a final consideration affected Sir Douglas Haig. The

British tanks had greatly increased in number and efficiency. At Third Ypres ground and weather had prevented their effective use, and decreased their reputation in the enemy's eyes. But a terrain might be found where they could work freely, and, if so, they might form a further element of surprise.

A suitable area was found in that section of the Siegfried Line which lay in front of Havrincourt Wood, between the Bapaume–Cambrai road and the Scheldt canal. The merits of this area for a surprise attack were many. In the first place, it was dry, open country, where tanks could operate. In the second place, behind the British lines, notably in the big wood of Havrincourt, there were places where they might be concealed without the knowledge of the Germans. In the third place, the sector was very thinly held by the enemy. Finally, any considerable British advance would endanger a vital part of the enemy's front, and seriously hamper his communications. Cambrai, a main centre, would be brought under our guns, as would the great lateral railway which ran through it. The British tactical plan was conceived on novel lines. There was to be no preliminary bombardment. Tanks were relied upon to break through the enemy's wire, and the six infantry divisions allotted for the attack were to advance on a 6-mile front, supported as far as possible by our guns shooting at unregistered targets. The German defences were complicated and very strong. First came certain forward positions in the nature of outposts. Behind lay the Siegfried Line proper. Acres of dense wire lay before it, wire nowhere less than 50 yards wide; it was calculated that to cut it with artillery would take five weeks and cost 20 millions of money. A mile or so behind that lay the famous Siegfried Reserve Line, tunnelled to a great depth and heavily wired. Between 3 and 4 miles to the east ran the final German position, covering Cambrai.

Haig's object was not the capture of Cambrai; that might happen, but his advance in the direction of the town was rather to secure his right flank. His main objective was towards the north-east, Bourlon, and the Arras–Cambrai road. He hoped to break through all the enemy's lines of defence on the first day; and, since he believed that no serious German reinforcements could appear before forty-eight hours, he considered that he would have time to exploit and secure any success. The cavalry were to be kept ready to go through and disorganise the enemy communications, and he arranged with Pétain to have a French force of infantry and cavalry within call in the event of fortune providing one of those happy chances which he had hitherto been denied. It may fairly be said in criticism of the Cambrai plan that it contemplated a limited and local operation, which in the nature of things could not be limited and localised, much less easily broken off. It designed a raid with a few divisions; but such a raid must inevitably develop into a battle and demand supports, and these supports could only come from troops who *ex hypothese* were in no condition for a new and desperate conflict.

Secrecy was vital in the matter, and Byng directed the preparations with consummate skill. Till the very eve of the battle few even in the Tank Corps knew the plan. Tuesday 20 November dawned with heavy clouds that promised rain before evening. At twenty minutes past six a solitary gun broke the silence. It was the signal, and from just north of the Bapaume road to the hamlet of Gonnelieu in the south a long line of tanks crept forward into the fog, their commander, General Elles, leading them like an admiral in his 'flagship'. Gas and smoke were released everywhere from the Scarpe to Saint-Quentin, and in front of the tanks a dense smoke barrage blinded the enemy's guns. The British artillery broke loose and deluged the German rear with shells, while, behind the tanks, quietly and leisurely moved the six divisions of assault. The enemy was taken utterly unawares. The tanks cut great lanes in his wire, broke up his machine-gun nests, and enfiladed his trenches, while the British infantry followed to complete the work. At once the outposts went, the main Siegfried Line followed soon, and presently the fighting was among the tunnels of the Reserve Line. By half-past ten that also had vanished, and the British troops, with cavalry close behind, were advancing to their final objectives in open country.

The day closed with a remarkable record of success. Sir Julian Byng had carried the outposts, the Siegfried Line, and the Siegfried Reserve Line on most of his front, and had broken into the final line at Masnières. He had won nearly all his objectives; but at three points, and vital points, he had not succeeded. He had not got Rumilly and Crèvecoeur, and so had not yet obtained that defensive flank which he needed for his swing to the north. Nor had he won the crossings of the Scheldt canal, and breached the final line widely enough to let the cavalry through. Most important of all, he had not obtained the Bourlon ridge, the garrison of which had by now been reinforced. Only twenty-four hours remained to complete the work before the enemy would have received supports. In that time Bourlon might be won, and perhaps Rumilly and Crèvecoeur; but, now that the first shock of surprise had passed, the chance for the cavalry was gone.

With dawn on the 22nd the forty-eight hours of grace ended, the period during which the enemy must fight without his reserves. His reinforcements were hurrying up. Haig had now to decide whether to treat the action as a lucky raid, and hold himself fortunate for what he had already achieved, without risking more; or to regard it as a substantive battle, and press for a decision. Inevitably he leaned to the second alternative. To fall back when much has been won and still more seems within reach is possible for few commanders, even when they have less weighty reasons for their conclusion than were present to the mind of the British general. The choice which he now made had been really implied in his original plan. He was impressed by the acute significance of the Bourlon ridge. If he could only gain and hold it, the German front south of the Scarpe and Sensée would be turned, and the enemy must be compelled to abandon all the elaborate defences of that sector. It was such a nerve-centre as we had rarely before had the chance of striking at. In the light of subsequent events it is clear that the decision was unwise, since he had too small a force to achieve his purpose and to defend his gains against the attack which the enemy could develop. But to foresee the future with precision is not in the power of the most sagacious commander, and to take risks is of the essence of war.

On the morning of the 23rd came the serious assault on the Bourlon heights. For some days the battle was concentrated in the area about Bourlon Wood and village. The strife was fierce and bloody, and it became gradually clear that the enemy was growing in strength. Upon the 27th we held the salient formed like a rough rectangle, some 10 miles wide and 6 miles deep. It was a salient awkwardly placed, for we had not won either on north or east the positions which would have made it secure, and during that week the enemy, by means of his admirable communications, was hurrying up troops for a counter-stroke.

Cambrai had violently startled the German High Command. They had not dreamed of such an event, and they realised that only by the narrowest margin had they escaped catastrophe. The joy bells which rang prematurely in England woke uneasy thoughts in Germany, and the people for a moment were gravely depressed. It was Ludendorff's business to cheer his countrymen by a dramatic counter-stroke; for, knowing the immense sacrifice he was to demand from the nation in the coming spring, he could not afford to permit any check to their confidence. The British High Command were aware of this activity; and they took measures to prepare for the worst. Nevertheless, the enemy secured a tactical surprise. At 7.30 a.m. on the morning of Friday 30 November, a storm of gas shells broke out on the 10 miles between Masnières and Vendhuille. There was no steadily advancing barrage to warn us of the approach of the enemy's infantry, and the thick morning mist enabled him to reach our trenches when our men were still under cover. The result was that from the north end of the Bonavis ridge to Gonnelieu, and from Gonnelieu to Vendhuille, our line was overwhelmed. Isolated British detachments in advantageous positions offered a gallant resistance. But the advance could not be stayed. The batteries at La Vacquerie were taken – the first British guns to be lost since Second Ypres – and at 9 a.m. the enemy was in Gouzeaucourt. The situation was grave indeed, for our position in the front of the salient was turned in flank and rear. It was saved by the 29th Division at Masnières. Swinging back its right to form a defensive flank, it clung to Masnières and beat off all attacks. Its heroic resistance defeated the German plan of a frontal assault, and gave Byng time to attend to his broken right wing. Meantime, the other part of the enemy force had hurled itself against the front between Moeuvres and the Scheldt canal. A little after 9 a.m. the German infantry came on in wave after wave, so that as many as eleven waves advanced in one area during the day. The day was starred with heroic deeds. German waves broke and ebbed, leaving great numbers of dead, and by the evening the assault had most signally failed.

Little happened for the next two days but local fighting; but it was clear to Haig that, although the enemy's vigour seemed to be exhausted, the British front was in a highly unsatisfactory state. Either we must regain the Bonavis ridge, which meant a new and severe engagement for which we had not the troops, or we must draw in our line to the Flesquières ridge. He had no other course before him but to give up the Bourlon position for which his troops had so gallantly fought.

17

Last German Offensives

Ludendorff's Scheme – New German Tactics – The Attack of 21 March – The Somme Retreat – Foch appointed Generalissimo – America's Effort – Battle of the Lys – Ludendorff's Last Offensive – Foch's First Counter-Stroke – The Raid on Zeebrugge

At the beginning of 1918 the enemy once again took the initiative. The Eastern Front had gone out of existence, and Germany was able to bring westward sufficient troops to abolish the small Allied numerical superiority. Already she excelled their numbers, and she could at will call up a further reinforcement which would give her a margin of more than a quarter of a million men. On the Allied side there was no chance of such immediate increment. The American forces were slowly growing, but at the normal rate of increase several months must still elapse before they could add materially to the trained numbers in the field, and it would be the autumn at least before they could form separate armies. France could make no new effort. There had been as yet no adequate recruitment from Britain to fill the gaps left by Third Ypres and Cambrai. The mind of the Allies had become resigned to a defensive campaign for the spring, till America took her true place in the line, and it was assumed that the task would not be beyond their power.

Far other was the mood of the German High Command. They promised victory, complete and absolute victory in the field, before the autumn. The submarine campaign had not done all that had been expected of it, and it appeared that American troops could land in Europe. But they must come slowly, and during the next six months the Allies would have to fight their own battle. Now, if ever, was the hour to strike. The Reichstag blessed the enterprise. The news of it spread among the German people, and a wave of new confidence surged across Central Europe.

Ludendorff's aim was to secure a decision in the field within four months. To achieve this he proposed to isolate the British army, by rolling it up from its right and driving it into the sea or pinning it to an entrenched camp between the Somme and the Channel – a Torres Vedras from which it would emerge only on the signature of peace. This done, he could hold it with few troops, swing round on the French, and put them out of action. His first step, therefore, must be to strike with all his might at the point of junction of Haig and Pétain, which he assumed would be a weak point. Such being the general principles of his plan, what advantages could he command in its execution? The first was his powerful army. He had withdrawn six German divisions from Italy and several from the Balkans; he had ready for use half of the 1920 class of new recruits; and he had brought some ½ million men from the East. In the second place, his position on interior lines gave him the possibility of strategic surprise.

The conception was bold and spacious, and based on sound principles of the military art. Apart from the strategic advantages we have referred to, Germany relied for success upon new tactics. What that plan was may be briefly sketched. It was based primarily upon the highly specialised training of certain units, and may be described as the system of shock-troops carried to its extreme conclusion. The first point was the absence of any preliminary massing of troops near the front of attack. Divisions were brought up by night marches only just before zero hour, and secrecy was thus obtained for the assembly. In the second place, there was no long artillery 'preparation' to alarm the enemy. The attack was preceded by a short and intense bombardment, and the enemy's back areas and support lines were confused by a deluge of gas-shells. The assault was made by picked troops, in open order, or rather in small clusters, carrying light trench mortars and many machine guns, with the field batteries close behind them in support. The actual method of attack, which the French called 'infiltration', may best be set forth by the analogy of a hand whose finger tips are shod with steel, pushing its way into a soft substance. The picked troops at the fingers' ends made gaps through which others poured, till each section of the defence found itself outflanked and encircled. A system of flares and rockets enabled the following troops to learn where the picked troops had made the breach, and the artillery came close behind the infantry. The troops had unlimited objectives, and carried iron rations for several days. When one division had reached the end of its strength another took its place, so that the advance resembled an endless wheel or a continuous game of leap-frog. This method, it will be seen, was the very opposite of the old German massed attack, or a series of hammer blows on one section of front. It was strictly the filtering of a great army into a hostile position, so that each part was turned and the whole front was first dislocated and then crumbled. The crumbling might be achieved by inferior numbers; the value of the German numerical superiority was to ensure a complete victory by pushing far behind into unprotected areas.

The position of the Allies in the face of such a threat was full of embarrassment. The credit of foreseeing accurately the coming attack, which Mr Lloyd George claimed in April, in Parliament, for the Versailles Council, belonged in reality to Haig and to Haig alone. And Haig was acutely uneasy, for the British Army now held 130 miles of line, and these the most critical in the West, with approximately the same numbers as she possessed two years before, when her front was only 80 miles long and Russia was still in the field. Clearly this was a wildly dangerous extension for a weak force in an area which was one of the two possible objects of the coming enemy attack. The British Command attempted to atone for its weakness by organising a system of defensive zones. This was a defence in depth, elaborately wired and studded with redoubts and strong points. But with so few men at our disposal it was impossible to prepare alternative positions in rear.

On 21 March, at precisely a quarter to five, the whole weight of their many thousand guns was released against the British forward and battle zones, headquarters, communications, and artillery positions, the back areas especially being drenched with gas which hung like a pall in the moist and heavy air. The men in the outpost line, beaten to the ground by the bombardment, and struggling amid clouds of gas, were in desperate case. In the thick weather the enemy was beyond the places where the cross-fire of machine guns might have checked him long before the redoubts were aware of his presence. The first thing which most of the outposts knew was that the Germans were well in their rear, and they were overwhelmed before they could send back warning. The SOS signals sent up were everywhere blanketed by the fog. Presently the outposts were gone, and the Germans were battling in our forward zone.

For a fortnight the British Army was in retreat, a fortnight of sustained and marvellous heroism – outposts resisting to the last; batteries fighting with only a man or two in the gun teams; handfuls desperately counter-attacking and snatching safety for others with their own lives. After the second day we had no prepared lines on which to retire, and the rivers parallel to our front were useless from the drought. Again and again a complete disaster was miraculously averted. Scratch forces, composed largely of non-combatants, held up storm-troops; cavalry did work that no cavalry had ever done before in the history of war; gunners broke every rule of the text-books. Tanks saved many desperate situations, lying in ambush till the last moment and then, in the words of their commander, emerging 'like savage rabbits from their holes'. The retreat was in flat defiance of all precedent and law, and it succeeded only because of the stubborn valour of the British soldier. The situation was constantly critical. On the first day 40 miles of British line were overrun; within a week 40 miles distant the enemy were approaching the gate of Amiens. But by 5 April the fighting had died down.

The first bout was over; but there were others to come, and the Allies were far indeed from safety. The gate of Amiens had been shut, but the next blow might shatter it. One thing was already clear – the splendour of the British performance. The fight had begun with an attack by sixty-four German divisions on thirty-two British. By the end of March seventy-three German divisions had engaged thirty-seven British. By 9 April the total British force in action had grown to forty-six divisions of infantry and three of cavalry, and against them more than eighty German divisions had been launched. The disparity was in reality far greater than two to one, for, owing to the German power of local concentration, in many parts of the field the odds had been three or four to one. Whatever discredit attached to the Somme retreat it did not fall upon the British soldier. The cause of the disaster was simply that a long front had been imposed upon Haig, and that he had not been given sufficient men wherewith to hold it.

The ordeal, however, was the source of certain advantages, notably the complete unification of command. The moment was far too solemn for half measures. A divided command could not defend the long, lean front of the Allies against the organised might of Germany, directed by a single brain toward a single purpose.

One strong hand must be on the helm, and one only. It is fair to say that the opposition to the appointment of a generalissimo had not come from one Government alone; all the Allied Governments had fought shy of it. But now the iron compulsion of facts had broken down the barriers. On the 23rd Haig, after seeing Pétain, telegraphed to London asking that the Chief of the Imperial General Staff should come out at once. At the request of the Prime Minister Lord Milner also crossed the Channel on the 24th. On Tuesday the 26th, Milner and Sir Henry Wilson met Clemenceau and Poincaré, Haig, Foch, and Pétain at Doullens, the meeting being only achieved with difficulty owing to the confusion of the roads. That conference, held amid the backwash of the great retreat, marked in a sense the turning-point of the war. The proposal for a supreme commander-in-chief, strongly urged by Milner and supported by Clemenceau, was accepted by Pétain and welcomed by Haig. For the post there could be only one choice. Sir Henry Wilson's first idea that Clemenceau should be appointed the nominal generalissimo was abandoned, and Foch was unanimously chosen.

Other blessings came out of the ordeal. America increased her recruiting, and strained every nerve to quicken the dispatch of troops, so that she might soon stand in line with her allies. Mr Lloyd George and M. Clemenceau appealed to President Wilson, and no appeal was ever more nobly met. General Pershing postponed his plan of a separate American sector of operations, and offered to Foch every man, gun, and lorry which America had in Europe to do with as he pleased. France, unshaken by a menace which struck at her very heart, showed that quiet and almost prosaic resolution to win or perish which two years before had inspired her troops at Verdun. In Britain the threat of industrial strikes disappeared. The workers forewent their Easter holiday of their own accord in order to make up by an increased output for lost guns and stores.

It looked as if the good spirit of 1914 had been reborn, when men spoke not of rights or interests, but of what service they might be privileged to give to their country. On Wednesday 10 April, by a majority of 223, the House of Commons passed a Bill raising the limit of military age to fifty, and giving the Government power to abolish the ordinary exemptions, and to extend conscription to Ireland. Two divisions and other units were transferred from Palestine to France, and a contingent from Salonika. Moreover, the old doctrine of the necessity of keeping a certain force inside our shores to protect them from invasion was summarily abandoned, and within a month from 21 March 355,000 men were sent across the Channel.

***

Ludendorff, brought to a standstill on the Somme, prepared to put into effect the second part of his plan – to attack the depleted British front in Flanders, and roll up their line from the north. This had been regarded, in the original plan, as a strictly subsidiary operation. His aim was to push through between La Bassée and Armentières, capture Béthune, and then, directing his main pressure north-west, capture Hazebrouck and the ridge of hills north of Bailleul. This would utterly dislocate the whole British front towards the coast, and compel a general retirement. The British would be forced to fight hard to meet the peril, which directly menaced Calais and Boulogne; and when Foch had flung his last fresh troops into the breach, the time would be ripe for the final thrust for Amiens and the sea.

But the initial attack met with such startling success that the battle developed into a major operation. In three days Ludendorff advanced 11 miles. He met with stubborn resistance, although Foch delayed – wisely, as the event proved – in sending reinforcements. All available British reserves were hurried up, but with all our efforts we could not be otherwise than outnumbered, and, since the fight had become a major operation, we had to face continued drafts from the great German reserve. On the 11th Haig issued an order of the day in which he appealed to his men to endure to the last.

> There is no other course open to us but to fight it out. Every position must be held to the last man; there must be no retirement. With our backs to the wall, and believing in the justice of our cause, each one of us must fight on to the end. The safety of our homes and the freedom of mankind depend alike upon the conduct of each one of us at this critical moment.

The British Commander-in-Chief was not addicted to rhetorical speech, and these grave words from one so silent had a profound effect upon the Army and the nation.

The battle of the Lys came to an end at the end of April with the British line still intact. It had been for the enemy a tactical success but a strategic failure. He achieved no one of his principal aims, and in the struggle he weakened his chances of a future offensive by squandering some of his best reserves. By the end of April he had employed in that one northern area thirty-five fresh divisions and nine which had been already in action. These troops were the cream of his army, and could not be replaced. Moreover, an odd feature had appeared in the last stages of the Lys battle. The Germans seemed to have forgotten their tactics of infiltration, and to have fallen back upon their old methods of mass and shock. For the weakness of the new tactics was becoming clear. They could be used only with specially trained troops and with fresh troops; they put too great a strain upon wearied divisions and raw levies; therefore, as the enemy's losses grew, his tactics would deteriorate in the same proportion.

Ludendorff realised that he must try elsewhere. He was becoming desperate; his original strategical scheme had gone, and his efforts were now in the nature of a gambler's throw. On 27 May the new storm broke on the Aisne heights, and by the evening the French gains in three great actions had vanished like smoke, and the enemy was across the river. On the second day he was beyond the Vesle, and on the third his vanguard was looking down from the heights of the Tardenois on the waters of the Marne. It was the swiftest advance made in the West since the beginning of trench warfare. The situation was very grave, for the French line had been greatly lengthened, it bristled with vulnerable points, and there was scanty room to manoeuvre. Paris was dangerously near the new front, and the loss of Paris meant far more than the loss of a capital. Earlier in the campaign the great city might have fallen without bringing upon the Allies irreparable disaster; but in the past two years it was in the environs of Paris that many of the chief new munition factories had arisen. If these were lost the Allied strength would be grievously crippled, and after four years of war it was doubtful whether France had the power to replace them. Already the loss in *matériel* had been severe, for the country between the Aisne and the Marne was full of munition dumps and aerodromes. But the stubborn soul of him who was now Premier of France would not admit a tremor. On 4 June Clemenceau told the Chamber: 'Je me bats devant Paris; je me bats à Paris; je me bats derrière Paris.'

But Ludendorff could turn his startling success to no account. He tried to press westward but without success. On 9 June he made an attempt to cut off the salient which he had made in the Allied line and again failed. His last offensive, east and west of Rheims, began on 15 July. At midnight on Sunday 14 July, Paris was awakened by the sound of great guns. At first she thought it an air raid, but the blaze in the eastern sky showed that business was afoot on the battlefield. She waited for news with a solemn mind, for she knew that the last stage of the struggle for her possession had begun. Ludendorff, in fact, achieved nothing. He succeeded in crossing the Marne, but Foch was ready for him. He need no longer now wait on the defensive. Moreover he had his reserve, and the moment had come to use it. On 18 July he attacked the right flank of the new German salient. Ludendorff halted and began to retire. It was the beginning of his long retreat.

Foch at last had freedom of movement, for he had with him now the new American army. Already there were a million Americans in France. At Château-Thierry in June an American contingent had shown its worth, and on 15 July one American division and elements of another had rolled back the German assault. These were the troops who, according to the German belief, would not land in Europe unless they could swim like fishes or fly like birds. Like the doubting noble of Samaria, the enemy had declared, 'If the Lord would make windows in heaven, might this thing be?' The inconceivable had been brought to pass. Birnam Wood had come to Dunsinane.

The time had now come for Foch's counter-stroke. When he decided to stake everything on his attack, he took one of those risks without which no great victory was ever won. There were anxious consultations between Foch, Pétain, and Fayolle. But the general most intimately concerned, Sir Douglas Haig, had no doubts. He was prepared to weaken his own line rather than cripple Foch's great bid for a decision, and willingly consented to the withdrawal of the eight French divisions from Flanders. More, with the assent of his Government, he placed four British divisions unreservedly at Foch's disposal for use with Mangin or Berthelot. It was a courageous decision alike for Cabinet and Commander-in-Chief, for so far Foch had been frequently proved in error, and his record was still only of withdrawals and defeats.

On 18 May the French Tenth Army struck, and before the puzzled enemy could realise his danger the French and Americans were through his first defences. The advance of the 18th was like a great bound forward. At one point the advance was as much as 8 miles – the longest advance as yet made in one day by the Allies in the West. Foch had narrowed the German salient, crumpled its western flank, and destroyed its communications. He had wrested the initiative from the enemy, and brought the *Friedensturm* to a dismal close.

He had done more, though at the time no eye could pierce the future and read the full implications of his victory. Moments of high crisis slip past unnoticed; it is only the historian in later years who can point to a half-hour in a crowded day and say that then was decided the fate of a cause or a people. As the wounded trickled back through the tossing woods of Villers-Cotterets, spectators noted a strange exaltation in their faces. When the news reached Paris the city breathed a relief which was scarcely justified with the enemy still so strongly posted at her gates. But the instinct was right. The decisive blow had been struck. Foch was still far from his Appomattox, but he had won his Gettysburg. He had paralysed the nerve-centre of the enemy and driven him down the first stage of the road to defeat. The Allies on that July morning had, without knowing it, won the Second Battle of the Marne, and with it the war. Four months earlier Ludendorff had stood as the apparent dictator of Europe; four months later he and his master were in exile.

18

Zeebrugge and Ostend

The Control of the Submarine Peril – America's Naval Co-operation – Last Fight of the Goeben *and the* Breslau *– Sir Roger Keyes's Plan – The Attack on Zeebrugge – The Attack on Ostend –Paralysis of German Fleet*

The spring of 1917 had been the most critical period of the war, graver even than that stage we have just chronicled when the enemy stood at the gate of Amiens, for in April 1917 Germany seemed to have devised a weapon which the Allies could not parry and which struck straight at their heart. Their shipping was fast disappearing from the seas, and with it the sustenance of the British people and the munitionment of all the Allied armies. In that month there was food enough in Britain to last the civilian population six weeks and no more. Could Germany have realised earlier that marvellous chance, and have been in the position to keep more U-boats constantly at work on the great shipping routes, she would have sunk in a single month not 850,000 tons, but 2 million tons, and would have had the victory before the close of the year.

By the spring of 1918 the submarine menace was conclusively broken – broken at sea, without regard to the fortunes of the enemy by land. Partly it was done by weapons of offence – the destroyer, the decoy ship, the airplane, the bomb, and the depth-charge. All these we have already seen at work, but by now two other foes of the U-boat had declared themselves. One was the Allied submarine; there were only some hundred of them, but they sank twenty U-boats, and had therefore the best average (the 500 Allied destroyers sank thirty-four U-boats; the Allied auxiliary patrol craft, about 3,000 in number, sank thirty-one). The other was the American sub-chaser – little wooden vessels, displacing only 60 tons and manned by young men fresh from college. These tiny craft crossed the Atlantic under their own power in the face of fierce winter gales, and in the English and Irish Channels and at the mouth of the Adriatic by means of their listening devices located and hunted many U-boats to their doom. Partly the defeat was due to Allied methods of defence – the dazzle ship, the barrage, and the convoy. In November 1917 the American navy set to work to lay a barrage of mines across the 250 miles of the passage between Scotland and Norway. By the early summer of 1918 that barrage was at work, and the terror which it inspired in German submarine crews was in all likelihood a contributory cause of the mutinous spirit spreading in the German navy. As for the convoy system, it was the greatest single weapon which the Allies discovered. By the end of the war 607 homeward-bound convoys had been brought in, numbering 9,300 ships, and of these only seventy-three had been lost; there had been 527 outward-bound convoys, with 7,300 ships, and forty-five losses; the total loss was therefore 118 ships, or 0.7 per cent! Much of this success was due to the superb courage of our merchant seamen, of whom 15,000 lost their lives. 'No calculation in any shipping and supply programme included a margin for the human factor. Even when vessels unarmed and without wireless were required to proceed unescorted to waters infested with submarines, crews were always available and willing to sail.' (Salter, *Allied Shipping Control*, p. 129)

So much for the prevention of losses. There was also the positive side, the increase of mercantile tonnage, and its more economical handling, and here the civilian played a not less valuable part than the sailor. By the end of 1917 Britain, France, and Italy had at their disposal a mercantile marine of 18 million tons as compared with 24,500,000 before the war, and of this reduced tonnage 5,600,000 had to be employed in direct war service. In the first quarter of 1918 the excess of losses over new construction was 280,000 tons; in the second quarter there was a gain for construction of 283,000 tons, and in the third quarter a gain of 468,000 tons. In Britain by the end of 1917 there was a fairly scientific control of supplies, the various demands having been grouped under central authorities like the War Office and the Ministry of Munitions, so that the Ministry of Shipping in allotting transport had not to deal with a host of scattered specialists.

The next step was to group the various national controls together and give them an international character. This was done by the formation of international committees (on wheat, sugar, oils, etc.), and by the creation in the beginning of 1918 of an Allied Maritime Transport Council – the most useful fruit of the Paris Conference of November 1917. The new Council entered on its duties in the dark days of March 1918, and did invaluable work in allotting tonnage on sound principles, and preventing strife between the Allies over such questions as coal and foodstuffs, munitions and raw materials. It had no tonnage under its direct order except some 600,000 tons of chartered neutral shipping, but its recommendations were accepted by the various national governments. Beginning as an advisory body, it soon became in practice a vast and powerful executive.

The result of these and other measures was that in 1918 the Allies were amply confirmed in their command of the seas. The blockade of Germany was drawn tighter, for with American assistance the agreements with northern neutrals were made more drastic, and Germany, in spite of Russian supplies, was back in the position of 1916. The Allied naval strength had also increased. Britain had added, or was adding, to her Grand Fleet her new battlecruisers of the Renown class, which were capable of a speed of over 30 knots, as well as the battleships now completed from the 1913–14 programme. The United States sent a squadron of Dreadnoughts to Scapa – the *New York*, the *Wyoming*, the *Florida*, the *Delaware*, the *Arkansas*, and the *Texas*; and three others – the *Nevada*, the *Oklahoma*, and the *Utah* – to Berehaven, in Ireland, in case a German battle-cruiser should slip out and attack her troop convoys.

The events of the winter at sea had not been many. The loss of a convoy of eleven vessels in the North Sea on 17 October 1917 had been followed by the destruction on 11 December in the same waters of a convoy of fourteen. On the evening of 3 November there was a brilliant little action in the Kattegat, where we sank a German auxiliary cruiser and ten patrol boats. On 17 November our light cruisers were in action in the Heligoland Bight, and two enemy ships were damaged. On 14 January 1918, late in the evening, Yarmouth suffered her third bombardment from the sea. In the last week of that month the south end of the Dardanelles witnessed a curious affair. About 5.30 a.m. on Sunday 20 January, the British destroyer *Lizard*, being at the moment off the north-east point of Imbros, discovered the German cruiser *Breslau*, with the *Goeben* a mile astern, making for the harbour where British monitors were lying all unprepared. She engaged the enemy at a range of 11,000 yards, and came under heavy fire, so that she was unable to get within torpedoing distance. Another destroyer, the *Tigress*, came to her aid, and the two attempted to shield the monitors by smoke-screens. But their efforts were in vain, and the monitors *Raglan* and *M28* were speedily sunk, before the former could get her 14-inch American guns into action. The enemy then turned south, followed by the *Lizard* and the *Tigress*, and at

7 a.m. the *Breslau* ran into a mine-field, struck several mines, and promptly sank. Four Turkish destroyers appeared, accompanied by an old cruiser, and these the *Lizard* and the *Tigress* engaged and drove up the Straits. The *Goeben* continued southward till she found the attentions of our aircraft unpleasant, when she put about to return. In the act she struck a mine, which made her settle down aft and gave her a list of some 15°. The Turkish destroyers returned to protect her, and she managed to creep inside the Straits, followed by the *Lizard* and the *Tigress*, and assiduously bombed by British seaplanes. Her captain ran her ashore in the Narrows to the west of Nagara Point, where she lay for some days under the menace of our aircraft, till she was eventually tinkered up and refloated.

The opening of the German offensive on 21 March 1918 had been attended by the bombardment of Dunkirk from the sea. Meantime, a plan had been maturing to get rid of the intolerable menace presented by the use of the Flanders ports as German bases. A year before Jellicoe had declared his hope that the problem of the Belgian coast was not insoluble; and a new man had appeared who had the Elizabethan tradition of inspired audacity. Sir Roger Keyes had been the most trusted of Sir Rosslyn Wemyss's lieutenants in the Dardanelles campaign, and, like his leader, he interpreted generously the limits of what was possible for the British sailor. His appointment, first to the Plans department of the Admiralty, and then, in succession to Admiral Bacon, to the command of the Dover Patrol, augured well for a new phase of initiative and daring.

The strategical importance of closing up Zeebrugge and Ostend was patent. There nested the German destroyer flotillas which raided the Narrow Seas and occupied most of the time of the Dover Patrol. Our chief weapon against the U-boat was the destroyer, and the presence of German craft in these ports withdrew a large number of British destroyers from the anti-submarine campaign. Could Zeebrugge and Ostend be put out of action, the German naval base would be pushed back 300 miles to Emden, and the British east coast ports would become the natural bases from which to deal with the attacks by enemy surface craft on the Channel. It would not cut off the main bases of the U-boats, but it would release the forces of the Dover Patrol to hunt them down, and it would facilitate the construction of a new Channel mine barrage.

A plan had been under consideration since November 1917, and the advent of Sir Roger Keyes brought it rapidly to completion. Its purpose was to block the end of the Bruges Canal at Zeebrugge and the entrance of Ostend harbour – an operation such as in the Spanish-American War Lieutenant Hobson had attempted at Santiago. To understand the details it is necessary to examine the topography of the two places.

Zeebrugge is not a port so much as the sea end of the Bruges Canal, and in the canal the enemy submarines found perfect harbourage. Its mouth was flanked by two short piers or sea-walls with a lighthouse at the end of each, and ½ mile up the canal were the lock gates. A large mole had been built in a curve to the west of the channel – a mole about 80 yards wide and a mile long. At the land end, to allow for the flow of the tide, there were 500 yards of viaduct on piles. The Mole, as the vital defence of the harbour, had a normal garrison of 1,000 men, and bristled with artillery and machine guns, while all the coast was studded with long-range heavy pieces. On the Mole were the railway station and many newly built sheds for military and naval stores. The Ostend harbour was less elaborate. It was also the mouth of a canal to Bruges, but there was no mole as a flank guard. The problem for Sir Roger Keyes in both cases was to sink ships inside the canal, so that, aided by the silt of the tides, they should block the

entrance. It is no light task to clear an obstruction from a Channel port; about Christmas 1916 a rice-laden tramp sank in Boulogne harbour, and shut the place for a month. Could the operation be achieved the results were certain; but, in view of the strong defence, it seemed a desperate adventure, especially among the intricacies of Zeebrugge.

As it turned out, Ostend was the more difficult problem, for the very complexity of its safeguards made Zeebrugge vulnerable. The plan at Ostend was simply to get ships into the harbour and sink them far enough in to do the maximum of damage. It was a feat depending on secrecy and dash. At Zeebrugge the scheme was more elaborate. Three cruisers packed with concrete were to get as near the lock gates as possible before being sunk. To create a diversion, other vessels were to attack the Mole from its sea side, land men to engage the enemy garrison and prevent the guns there being used against the block-ships. At the same time, by means of a submarine laden with explosives, it was proposed to blow up the viaduct, which would isolate the German garrison on the Mole, the simultaneous attack on the viaduct and the later entry of the block-ships into the canal mouth. (In the expedition to Ostend in 1798, under Captain H. R. Popham, RN, troops were landed under General Eyre Coote to blow up the sluice-gates of the Bruges Canal. They succeeded in doing this, but could not re-embark through stress of weather, and were compelled to surrender.)

Twice Sir Roger Keyes's flotilla started, and twice it put back to port. It needed special weather conditions for success – an overcast sky, a drift of haze, a light wind, and a short sea. On Monday 22 April, the eve of St George's Day, the omens were favourable, and in the later afternoon, three hours before sunset, the expedition started, timed to reach Zeebrugge by midnight. It was a singular Armada. There were five old cruisers to act as block-ships – the *Intrepid, Iphigenia*, and *Thetis* for Zeebrugge, and the *Brilliant* and the *Sirius* for Ostend. A small cruiser, the *Vindictive* (5,600 tons, with a broadside of six 6-inch guns), was designed for the attack on the Mole, assisted by two Liverpool ferry-boats, the *Daffodil* and the *Iris*. There was also a flotilla of monitors, motor launches, and fast coastal motor boats for special purposes. Admiral Tyrwhitt's destroyers from Harwich covered the operations from the north, and there were present light covering forces from the Dover Patrol. The operations were commanded by Sir Roger Keyes in the destroyer *Warwick*, and he had also with him the destroyers *North Star* and *Phoebe*. The men for the block-ships and the landing-parties were bluejackets and marines, picked from a great number who had volunteered for the work. They were armed as for a land battle, with grenades and flame-throwers as well as rifles and bayonets; the *Vindictive* carried machine guns, Stokes mortars, and howitzers; and elaborate preparations had been made for the creation of an artificial fog to cover the attack.

It was a prodigious hazard to approach a hostile coast where navigation was difficult at the best of times, without lights, without knowledge of what new mine-fields the enemy might have laid, and at the mercy of a change in the weather which would expose the little fleet to every gun on the Flanders shore. There was only an hour and a half for the whole operation, for the shore batteries – 120 heavy guns, some of them 15-inch – had a range of 16 miles, and the return voyage must start at 1.30, to be out of danger before dawn. All went well on the outward voyage. Presently the *Sirius* and the *Brilliant* changed course for Ostend, and the smoke-screen, provided by the smaller craft, rolled landwards with the north-east wind ahead of the cruisers. Meantime the monitors and seaplanes had gone to work, bombarding the coast defences, as they had done often before. This device apparently deceived the enemy. He did not man the Mole, and his gunners retired to their bomb-proof shelters on shore, knowing well that in face of the smoke-screen they could not reply effectively to our fire. It was a case where an artillery 'preparation' lulled instead of awakening the enemy's suspicions.

But fifteen minutes before the *Vindictive* reached the Mole the wind changed to the south-west, and rolled back the smoke-screen so that the whole harbour was clear to our eyes and we to the enemy's. Instantly the darkness was made bright with star-shells and searchlights, and from the Mole and the shore an intense fire greeted our vessels. The action had begun, and Sir Roger Keyes signalled 'St George for England', to which the *Vindictive* replied, 'May we give the dragon's tail a damned good twist!' There was no time to be lost, and the *Vindictive*, under Captain A. F. B. Carpenter, laid her nose against the concrete sea-wall of the Mole. Her port side had been fitted with 'brows' – light hinged drawbridges which could drop their ends on the wall. A sudden sea had risen, which made the operation difficult; so after the *Vindictive* had let go an anchor she signalled the *Daffodil* to lie against her stern and keep it in position, while the *Iris* went forward to make fast to the Mole ahead of her. All the time a tornado of fire was beating on the three vessels, and to land men under such conditions might well have seemed impossible. But the marines and bluejackets, under their gallant leaders, swarmed over the splintering gangways, and dropped on to the shell-swept wall. The *Daffodil*, which should have landed her own men after berthing the *Vindictive*, was compelled to remain on the latter's starboard, pressing her into position, while her men crossed the *Vindictive* to join the storming-party; and the *Iris*, which should have made fast ahead of the *Vindictive*, found her grapnels too small, and had to fall in astern.

The storming-parties moved along the Mole, finding no Germans, but subject to the same withering fire from the shore end. Steadily, methodically, they blew up one building after another. A German destroyer lay on the harbour side of the Mole, and was promptly blown up by our bombs. And then suddenly ahead of them a column of flame leapt into the air, and they knew that the viaduct had gone. An old submarine, C3 (Lieutenant R. D. Sandford), had steered straight for the viaduct under the enemy's searchlights and under constant fire – an anxious task, for the thing was full of explosives. The viaduct itself was crowded with the enemy, who watched the little vessel approaching as if stupefied by its audacity. Apparently they thought that it was trying to get through the viaduct into the harbour. Lieutenant Sandford rammed his boat into the hole left for the tide in the steel curtain, touched the button, got into a skiff, and won clear away. There was no more gallant exploit in all that marvellous night.

The landing-parties on the Mole pushed on to the ragged edge of what had once been the viaduct, steadily pursuing the work of destruction. The lighthouse was taken, and there Wing-Commander Brock, who had organised the smoke-screen, was last seen desperately wounded, but still fighting. Suddenly the German fire seemed to be concentrated more on the harbour, and as they looked eastward they saw the reason. The block-ships were steering straight for the canal. The *Thetis* (Commander Sneyd) went first to show the way, but she had the misfortune to foul her propeller in the defence nets. She signalled a warning to the others, and then, pounded at by the shore batteries, was sunk in the channel some hundreds of yards from the canal mouth. Meantime the *Intrepid* (Lieutenant Stuart Bonham-Carter), with every gun in action, and belching smoke like a volcano, steered into the canal, and, resting her nose on the mud of the western bank, blew up and settled down neatly athwart the channel. The *Iphigenia* (Lieutenant Billyard-Leake) followed, a little confused by the *Intrepid*'s smoke, rammed a dredger, and continued, dredger and all, on her consort's heels. She beached on the eastern side, swung across the canal, and was blown up. The crews of these vessels retired in every kind of small craft, and, for the most part, were picked up by the destroyers sheltering behind the smoke-screen.

The signal arranged for re-embarkation had been a blast from the *Vindictive*'s siren. But the *Vindictive* had long ago lost her siren, so the *Daffodil* did the best she could with her hooter. What was left of the landing-parties clambered aboard; the *Daffodil* towed the *Vindictive* loose, and the flotilla turned for home. The intensity of the German fire redoubled, but the changed wind now served us well, and the smoke clouds cloaked our departure. The heavy guns between Zeebrugge and Ostend did not find their mark, and the raiders, led by the battered *Vindictive*, were presently in English waters.

The Ostend operation, under Commodore Hubert Lynes, was less successful, for there the block-ships could not be assisted by any containing action, such as that on the Zeebrugge Mole, to distract the enemy. Our motor boats lit flares on the ends of the piers, and concealed them from the shore end by a smoke-screen. Unhappily, the veer of the wind blew aside the screen and revealed the flares, which the enemy promptly extinguished by gun-fire. The *Brilliant* and the *Sirius* failed to find the entrance to the harbour, and were compelled to sink themselves 400 yards east of the piers and more than a mile from the true canal mouth.

By the morning of St George's Day the main part of the great venture had been successfully accomplished. Zeebrugge and the Bruges Canal were blocked, and it did not appear how, under the constant assaults of our aircraft, they could ever be cleared. The quality of the British Navy had been triumphantly vindicated, and in the darkest days of the war on land the hard-pressed Allies were given assurance that their fleet was still master of the seas, and the final barrier to a German victory. For the gallantry of all concerned – the marines on the Mole, the crews of the block-ships and of the *Vindictive* and her consorts, the men in the picket boats and motor launches – no words of praise are adequate. The affair will rank in history among the classic exploits of sea warfare. But in admiration for the human quality shown, the technical brilliance of the feat should not be forgotten. From its nature it could not be rehearsed. It demanded a number of conditions which involved for their concomitance an indefinite period of waiting, and in such a continued tension secrecy on the one hand and ardour on the other are not easy to preserve. It required an intricate plan, worked out to minute details, any one of which was at the mercy of unforeseeable accident. Sir Roger Keyes succeeded by taking every human precaution, and then trusting to the luck of the Navy; and it is hard to know whether the more to admire his admirable caution or his admirable hardihood.

The saga of the Flanders coast was not finished. To be forewarned is not always to be forearmed. A surprise may be achieved so audacious that it is confidently assumed that it cannot be repeated, but the mere fact of this assumption may be the occasion of a second surprise. The Germans at Ostend had removed all guiding marks for attacking ships, had cut gaps in the piers to prevent a repetition of the landing on Zeebrugge Mole, and had a flotilla of nine destroyers watching the bit of coast. A second attack there was to the enemy unthinkable, and therefore Sir Roger Keyes attempted it.

The second affair was planned as methodically as the first. It was, as before, under the command of Commodore Hubert Lynes, and Sir Roger Keyes was also present in the *Warwick*. About midnight on Thursday 9 May, they left the British coast with a number of monitors, destroyers, and motor boats, and, as block-ships, the old cruiser *Sappho* and the *Vindictive*, now on her last voyage. It was a windless spring night, with a quiet sea and a sky lit with faint stars. Unfortunately the *Sappho* broke down on the way and did not reach her destination on time, thereby halving the British chances. The commodore's destroyer hurried ahead, laid a light buoy, and then fell back, while the *Vindictive* in the charge of the smaller craft approached the shore. They saw before them a beacon burning, a flare which one of our coastal motor boats had hung in the rigging of the sunken *Sirius*.

There was no preliminary bombardment till fifteen minutes before the block-ships were due at the harbour mouth. At that moment two motor boats dashed in and torpedoed the ends of the high wooden piers, and on the signal the airplanes watching in the heavens began their bombardment, and the great shells from our monitors shrieked into the town. Our smoke clouds were loosed, and blinded the searchlights and the observation of the German batteries. And on their heels came the real thing, a dense sea fog, which blanketed everything, and forced our destroyers to use their sirens to keep in touch. The solitary block-ship, the *Vindictive*, was hard put to it to find the entrance. She wandered east and west under a hail of shrapnel fire from the shore, groping for the harbour mouth, and at last found it and steamed in. The enemy batteries had discovered her, and she was terribly wounded, while the machine guns on the piers raked her decks. She laid her nose to the eastern pier, and was preparing to swing across the channel when a shell destroyed her conning-tower. It appeared that she could not swing farther round, and there was nothing for it but to sink her, lying at an angle of some 25° to the eastern pier. There remained a passage between her and the western pier, too narrow to be used by destroyers or the larger submarines. Most of her crew were got off in motor launches, the commanders of which behaved with the utmost gallantry, and at 2.30 on the morning of Friday the 10th, the recall rockets went up and the flotilla turned for home. The nine German destroyers had been discreet, and had not shown themselves throughout the action. The *Vindictive* was triumphant in her death as in her life, and the second of the two great West Flanders bases was now lost to the enemy.

Zeebrugge and Ostend were the last nails in the coffin of the German navy. It seemed all but incredible that along with the great German land attack in France and Flanders there should not be some attempt at action by the ships from Kiel and Wilhelmshaven. If Germany was staking everything on victory, surely she must stake her fleet. It did not come. The British reserves were ferried across the Channel without interference. Britain herself attacked by sea two most vital bases and ruined them irrevocably, and still the great battleships gave no sign. At the moment it was a mystery, but six months later that mystery was explained. The German fleet had ceased to be more than a name. The sleepless activity of Sir David Beatty had paralysed its heart. In the first six months of 1918 over a hundred surface craft were lost in the Bight of Heligoland. Mine-layers, mine-sweepers, patrol boats – they were being driven from the seas; they mutinied, and the mutiny was suppressed; but the spirit and discipline necessary for the most arduous of human tasks had gone from their men. The use of foul weapons had ruined the moral of sailors who had done gallantly at Coronel and the Dogger Bank and Jutland, for the ancient law of Poseidon cannot be broken without disaster to the breaker. Already the British Admiralty knew what the German Marineamt only dimly guessed, that the first order given to prepare a fleet action would for the German navy be the signal for revolution.

19

The Turning of the Tide

Foch's Strategy for Final Battle – The Battle of Amiens – Panoramic View of the War – The Advance to Victory – Allenby in Palestine – Collapse of Bulgaria, Turkey, and Austria

The final battle had been joined, but it must develop slowly. Let us attempt to discover what was in Foch's mind.

The Second Battle of the Marne restored to the Allies the initiative. That is to say, they had now power to impose their will upon the enemy to the extent of deciding the form and the time of an action. Foch had now in addition a *final* superiority in men and material, and had, moreover – what is not necessarily the same thing – this superiority translated into a greater number of reserve divisions. He had, therefore, the means to his hand of using to the full the advantage of the initiative, and nothing but an incredible blunder could have lost him this crowning asset. All former Allied offensives had, after a shorter or longer time, come to a halt for the same reason – wearied troops were met by fresh enemy reserves. The battle became, as it were, stereotyped; the enemy was able to perfect his defence; and the action ended in stalemate. Foch drew the logical deduction from the tactics of surprise. He resolved to make the battle highly mobile. After striking a blow he would stay his hand as soon as serious resistance developed, and attack instantly in another place. His trust lay in a triple combination of which each part hinged upon the other – the weapon of the tank, the tactics of surprise, and the strategy of complete mobility.

But he was not yet ready for the grand climax, the decisive blow. It was still his business to wear down the enemy continuously and methodically by attacks on limited fronts, aiming at strictly limited objectives. The action must develop organically like a process of nature. From 21 March to 18 July he had stood patiently on the defensive; from 18 July to 8 August he had to win back the initiative, free his main communications, and dislocate Ludendorff's plans. From 8 August to 26 September it was his task to crumble the enemy's front, destroy the last remnants of his reserves, force him beyond all his prepared defences, and make ready for the final battle which should give victory.

By 4 August the Germans had been pressed back on to the line of the Aisne. Mindful of the Aisne defences of 1914 they turned to it as a natural refuge. But 1914 was not 1918; then Germany had had a great superiority in guns, and something not far from an equality in men; now superiority and equality had gone beyond recall. Foch had now a greater mass of manoeuvre than his antagonist. Moreover, the disastrous Second Battle of the Marne had played havoc with the German first-line troops. Indeed, so bad was the case that Ludendorff was compelled to appeal to Austria for men, and now for the first time an Austrian division was identified on the front in France.

The dreams of an attack on Amiens and an advance in Flanders were gone for ever. Ludendorff aimed at a winter front, running along the Ypres and Wytschaete heights, continuing on the low ridges between the Lys and La Bassée, and from Arras to the Oise holding the crest of the Bapaume and Lassigny uplands. He had now stabilised the position on the Aisne, and he hoped that the French would break their teeth on his new front, and that the battle would decline into one of those fruitless struggles for a few miles of trench in which the old actions had been wont to die away. He hoped in vain. Foch had no mind to waste one hour in operations which were not vital. It was his supreme merit that he saw the battle as a whole, and he was now preparing his deadly arpeggio on a far broader front. On Thursday 8 August, Sir Douglas Haig, south of the Somme, flung his Fourth Army against Prince Rupprecht.

The Battle of Amiens, which began on 8 August, was the true Allied counter-stroke. It was the preliminary to the long battle which was to culminate in the surrender of Germany. The conception and details of the attack were wholly British. During the final stages of the war, indeed, it was the British army which played the greatest part, Foch and Haig working together in perfect unity.

The Battle of Amiens was a conspicuous success. It was, in Ludendorff's phrase, 'the black day of the German army in the history of the war'. Success was due to the brilliant tactical surprise and the high efficiency of the new tanks which took the place of the preliminary bombardment. At one point the British tanks took captive a German regimental mess while it was breakfasting; at another the whole staff of a division was seized; in some villages the Germans were taken in their billets before they knew what had happened, and parties of the enemy were made prisoner when working in the harvest fields. The battle, the first phase of the Allies' offensive, closed upon the 12th. For they were in the old battle area, whose tangled wilderness gave unrivalled opportunities for defence, and the enemy had been heavily reinforced. He had a moment of respite; but it had been won at the expense of his waning reserves.

The effect of the Battle of Amiens had far greater importance than the material result. The mental condition of the enemy has been described by Sir Douglas Haig:

Buoyed up by the hope of immediate and decisive victory, to be followed by an early and favourable peace, constantly assured that the Allied reserves were exhausted, the German soldiery suddenly found themselves attacked on two fronts and thrown back with heavy losses from large and important portions of their earlier gains. The reaction was inevitable and of a deep and lasting character.

The effect upon their leaders was still graver. Ludendorff tendered his resignation, which was not accepted. At conferences at Spa on the 13 and 14 August with the Emperor and the Imperial Chancellor he urged that peace should be sought at once on the best terms obtainable; but the civilian statesmen did not dare as yet to undeceive their people. Meantime his one hope was a slow and stubborn retreat to the Siegfried system.

Foch had no intention of affording Ludendorff a leisurely retreat. It was his business to hustle him as soon as possible from the line he had chosen for his next stand. He must continue to play his deadly arpeggio along the whole line. Following Napoleon's maxim, he must 'keep the battle nourished until the moment came for the final stroke'.

***

The Allies were winning the war all over the world. But to appreciate the vastness of the struggle was a task possible only to some such celestial being as Thomas Hardy invented in *The Dynasts*. An observer on some altitude in the north, like the Hill of Cassel, on some evening that September, could look east and note the great arc from the dunes at Nieuport to the coalfields at Lens lit with the flashes of guns and the gleam of star-shells. That was a line of 50 miles – far greater than any battlefield in the old wars; but it was a mere fragment of the whole. Had he moved south to the ridge of Vimy he would have looked on another 50 miles of an intenser strife. South, again, to Bapaume, and he would have marked the wicked glow from Cambrai to the Oise. Still journeying, from some little height between the Oise and the Aisne, he would have scanned the long front which was now creeping round the shattered woods of Saint-Gobain to where Laon sat on its hill. From the mounts about Rheims he might have seen France's battle line among the bleak Champagne downs, and from a point in the Argonne the trenches of the Americans on both sides of the Meuse, running into the dim woody country where the Moselle flowed towards Metz. Past the Gap of Nancy and down the long scarp of the Vosges went the flicker of fire and the murmur of combat, till the French lines stretched into the plain of Alsace and exchanged greetings with sentinels on the Swiss frontier. Such a battle-ground might well have seemed beyond the dream of mortals, and yet it was but a part of the whole.

A celestial intelligence, with sight unlimited by distance, could have looked eastward, and, beyond the tangle of the Alps, witnessed a strange sight. From the Stelvio to the Adriatic ran another front, continuous through glacier-camps and rock-eyries and trenches on the edge of the eternal snows, to the pleasant foothills of the Lombard plain, and thence, by the gravel-beds of the Piave, to the lagoons of Venice. Beyond the Adriatic it ran through the dark hills of Albania, past lakes where the wild fowl wheeled at the unfamiliar sound of guns, beyond the Tcherna and Vardar and Struma valleys to the Aegean shores. It began again, when the Anatolian peninsula was left behind, and curved from the Palestine coast in a great loop north of Jerusalem across Jordan to the hills of Moab. Gazing over the deserts, he would have marked the flicker which told of mortal war passing beyond the ancient valleys of Euphrates and Tigris, up into the wild Persian ranges. And scattered flickers to the north would have led him to the Caspian shores, and beyond them to the table-land running to the Hindu Kush, which was the cradle of all the warring races. Passing north, his eyes would have seen the lights of the Allies from the Pacific coast westward to the Urals and the Volga, and little clusters far away on the shores of the Arctic sea.

The vision of such a celestial spectator, had it been unlimited by time as well as by space, would have embraced still stranger sights. It would have noted the Allied line in the West, stagnant for months, then creeping on imperceptibly as a glacier, then wavering in sections like a curtain in the wind, and at last moving steadily upon Germany. It would have beheld the old Eastern Front, from the Baltic to the Danube, pressing westward, checking and falling back; breaking in parts, gathering strength, and again advancing; and at last dying like a lingering sunset into darkness. Behind would have appeared a murderous glow, which was the flame of revolution. Turning to Africa, it would have noted the slow movement of little armies in west and east and south; handfuls of men creeping in wide circles among the Cameroons jungles till the land was theirs; converging lines of mounted troopers among the barrens of the German south-west, closing in upon the tin shanties of Windhoek; troops of all races traversing the mountain glens and dark green forests of German East Africa, till after months and years the enemy had become a batch of exiles. And farther off still, among the isles of the Pacific and on the Chinese coast, it would have seen men toiling under the same lash of war.

Looking seaward, the sight would have been not less marvellous. On every ocean of the world he would have observed the merchantmen of the Allies bringing supplies for battle. But in the North Atlantic, in the Mediterranean, in the Channel and the North Sea he would have seen uncanny things. Vessels would disappear as if by magic, and little warships would hurry about like some fishing fleet when shoals are moving. The merchantmen would huddle into flocks, with destroyers like lean dogs at their sides. He would have seen in the Scottish firths and among the isles of the Orkneys a mighty navy waiting, and ships from it scouring the waters of the North Sea, while inside the defences of Heligoland lay the decaying monsters of the German fleet. And in the air over sea and land would have been a perpetual going and coming of aircraft like flies above the pool of war.

The observer, wherever on the globe his eyes were turned, would have found no area immune from the struggle. Every factory in Europe and America hummed by night and day to prepare the materials of strife. The economics of five continents had been transformed. The life of the remotest villages had suffered a strange metamorphosis. Far-away English hamlets were darkened because of air raids; little farms in Touraine, in the Scottish Highlands, in the Apennines, were untilled because there were no men; Armenia had lost half her people; the folk of North Syria were dying of famine; Indian villages and African tribes had been blotted out by plague; whole countries had ceased for the moment to exist, except as geographical terms. Such were but a few of the consequences of the kindling of war in a world grown too expert in destruction, a world where all nations were part one of another.

***

The advance to victory, like the Somme retreat, cannot be painted on broad lines, for it was composed of a multitude of interlinked actions. The first stage, completed by the first week of September, was the forcing of the enemy back to the Hindenburg Line, an achievement made certain by the breaking by the Canadians on 2 September of the famous Drocourt–Quéant switch. In the south the Americans under Pershing cut off the Saint-Mihiel salient, and prepared for their drive northward. The next stage was the breaching of the Hindenburg defences, while Pershing attacked towards Mezières, and the Belgians, led by their King, attacked in the north towards Ghent – movements allotted to the last week in September.

On 26 September forty British and two American divisions faced fifty-seven weak German divisions behind the strongest entrenchments in history. By the 29th they had crossed the Canal du Nord and the Scheldt canal, and in a week were through the whole defence system and in open country. By 8 October the last remnants of the Hindenburg zone had disappeared in a cataclysm. Foch's conception had not been fully realised; Pershing had been set too hard a task and was not far enough forward, when the Hindenburg system gave, to pin the enemy to the trap which had been set. Nevertheless, by 10 October Germany had been beaten in a battle which Foch described as a 'classic example of the military art'. The day of doom was only postponed, and Ludendorff had now no refuge from the storm. Long before his broken divisions could reach the Meuse, Germany would be on her knees.

For she was now losing all her allies. They had been the guardians of her flanks and rear, and if they fell she would be defenceless. On 15 September the Allied armies moved forward at Salonika, and within a week Bulgaria's front had collapsed and she sought an armistice. On 19 September Allenby in Palestine opened an action which must remain a perfect instance of how, by surprise and mobility, a decisive victory may be won almost without fighting. This last crusade would have startled the soul of St Louis and Raymond and Richard of England could they have beheld the amazing army which undertook it. Algerian and Indian Moslems, Arab tribesmen, men of the thousand creeds of Hindustan, African negroes and Jewish battalions were among the liberators of the sacred land of Christendom. Breaking the defence in the plain of Sharon, Allenby sent his 15,000 cavalry in a wide sweep to cut the enemy's line of communications and block his retreat, while Feisal and Lawrence east of Jordan distracted his attention. The operations moved like clockwork. In two days the Turkish armies west of Jordan had been destroyed, while that on the east bank was being shepherded north by the Arabs to its destruction. By 1 October Damascus was in our hands, Aleppo surrendered on 26 October, and on the last day of the month Turkey capitulated. Meantime, on the anniversary of Caporetto, Italy had made her last advance, and the Austrian forces, which had suffered desperately for four years and were now at the end of their endurance, melted away. With her gallant army crumbled the country. On 4 November an armistice was arranged, and at the same time the Dual Monarchy broke up into fragments. The Emperor was left alone and unfriended in the vast echoing corridors of Schönbrunn.

The events of the last week on the Italian front were like the mad changes of a kaleidoscope. On the last day of October two Italian sailors entered the inner roadstead at Pola and blew up the Austrian dreadnought *Viribus Unitis*. It was a theatrical climax, for in that vessel, in June 1914, the Archduke Francis Ferdinand had travelled to the Dalmatian coast on the way to his death at Serajevo. On the evening of 3 November a detachment of Bersaglieri landed at Trieste, and the city passed under the control of Italy. Meantime the fleet at Pola was surrendered to the Southern Slavs, and everywhere throughout the Dual Monarchy there was revolution. New transient Premiers – Lammasch at Vienna, Michael Karolyi at Budapest – flitted across the scene, to give place to councils of soldiers and republican committees. Agram, Laibach, and Prague became suddenly the capitals of new states and the seats of new *de facto* governments.

The terms of the armistice put an end to Austria's army and navy, and placed all her territories at the disposal of the Allies for military operations. The vast straggling fortress of the Teutonic League had now been shorn of every outwork, and only the central keep of Germany remained. But that keep was already in desperate case, and was on the eve of hoisting the flag of surrender.

20

The Surrender of Germany

Peace Negotiations – Correspondence with President Wilson – Continued Allied Advance – Resignation of Ludendorff – Mutiny in German Fleet – German Revolution – Abdication of the Emperor – Last Days on the Western Front – The Armistice Signed

The destruction of the Siegfried defences broke the nerve of the German High Command, and when Ludendorff began to waver it was inevitable that the civilian statesmen should follow suit. The German people were dumbly determined that somehow or other the war should end before the winter. If the army was to be saved, by hook or by crook a way must be found to suspend hostilities, for every day made it clearer that retreat to a line of assured defence was beyond its power. Accordingly the High Command bade the politicians quicken the pace of their negotiations, and, discarding their old line of argument, beg unequivocally for an armistice. They were well aware that such a step would go far to wreck the *moral* of the troops, but they had no other choice.

On 5 October the Note was sent to President Wilson (the draft of which had been prepared by Ludendorff) asking him to take in hand the restoration of peace, and to invite the Allies to send pleni-potentiaries to open negotiations. He announced that Germany accepted the President's proposals set forth in his message to Congress of 8 January 1918 (the famous 'Fourteen Points'), and in his later pronouncements, as a basis for the discussion of peace terms. In order to prevent further bloodshed he asked for the conclusion of an immediate armistice on land and water and in the air. On 8 October Mr Wilson replied. He announced that America could not propose to her Allies a cessation of hostilities so long as the armies of the Central Powers were upon Allied soil. As a guarantee of good faith there must first be withdrawal from invaded territory. Germany made haste to answer, for by 12 October, the date of the reply, the last remnants of the Siegfried zone had gone. Their reply stated that Germany and Austria were willing to evacuate invaded territory as a preliminary to an armistice, and suggested a mixed commission to make the necessary arrangements. Small wonder that Germany assented. To get her troops back intact to her frontier was her dearest wish. She was in truth offering nothing and asking everything. There was nothing to prevent Germany, once safe inside her frontiers, from breaking off negotiations and instituting war on a new plan. It was clear that if an armistice came it must be one which was equivalent to surrender.

On 14 October Mr Wilson made his reply, and there was no dubiety about the terms.

It must be clearly understood that the process of evacuation and the conditions of an armistice are matters which must be left to the judgment and advice of the military advisers. The President feels it his duty to say that no arrangement can be accepted by the Government of the United States which does not provide absolutely satisfactory safeguards and guarantees of the maintenance of the present military supremacy of the armies of the United States and of the Allies in the field.

This was final. Foch, Haig, and Pershing were not likely to fling away the predominance which was now assured to them.

The history of events runs now in two parallel streams, one of diplomacy and one of war. By the evening of 10 October Haig was in the western skirts of Le Cateau, and our troops held the very slopes where in August 1914 Smith-Dorrien had fought his great battle against odds, and bluffed Kluck at a moment when that General had victory in his hands. On the 17th it was found that Ostend had been evacuated. And on the same day it was reported by our airmen that the enemy was retiring from Lille, and had sent out some thousands of civilians towards our lines. A patrol entered the city, to be received with frenzied joy by the inhabitants. Next day Lille was occupied by our troops, and the 15th Corps pressed on to the east, taking Roubaix and Tourcoing. The capital of the north-east was restored to France, and its statue in the Place de la Concorde could once again be garlanded with flowers.

The progress of that week was not less conspicuous farther south. By 23 October the Allied centre and left were everywhere in open country, and facing hastily prepared field defences; but in the south the French and Pershing had still to carry the final system fortified on the old enemy plan.

The problem before Pershing had now become the most difficult of that of any army commander. The German position in the Argonne was nearly invulnerable to frontal attack, and the plan of pressing forward on both sides of the wooded ridge was foreseen by the enemy, and made difficult by prepared defences of the greatest strength and the intractable nature of the terrain. The American First Army was given a task like the British at the Battle of the Somme, and, like the British, suffered from its lack of experience and its too audacious gallantry. It had not yet learned, as the commands of Haig and Pétain had learned, caution and wiliness by bitter experience. Pershing's front of 18 miles between the Meuse and the Argonne was miserably supplied with roads – one along the Meuse, one on the edge of the Argonne, one by

Montfaucon in the centre, all bad, and too much exposed to enemy fire. The finest transport system in the world must have broken down under such handicaps. But for the engineers to construct a new road system meant delay, and the problem was therefore that, if the war was not to drag into 1919, the splendid fighting stuff of the American infantry must be used in spite of all disadvantages. It was a bold decision for the commander to take, but it was essentially wise, and it was a decisive factor in victory. But the price paid was high. By 28 September the Americans had penetrated 7 miles inside the enemy's lines; it took them eleven days to advance 2 miles more. They were now in direct contact with the Kriemhilde system, and the attack of 14 October failed to break it. When the second phase of Pershing's attack closed on 31 October the last Kriemhilde position had not been taken. The American First Army had fought a new Wilderness Campaign which may well rank for valour and tenacity with the old.

Against Haig, now approaching the Mormal forest, the other great German defensive effort was made. The weather was bad, and the misty air made it hard to locate enemy batteries, while the undevastated woods and hamlets gave endless chances for machine-gun resistance. The Mormal forest, too, afforded a perfect screen for counter-attacks. Yet in two days the British Fourth, Third, and First Armies advanced 6 miles.

The condition of Ludendorff's forces was becoming tragic. If those of the Allies were tired, his were in the last stages of fatigue. On 21 March he had possessed a reserve of eighty fresh divisions, and during April, May, and June divisions were not sent back to the line without at least a month of rest and training. On 31 October he had but one fresh division, and the intervals of rest had shrunk to nine days – far too short to permit of recovery. Moreover, these wearied units were returned to the front without being brought up to strength, and divisions entered the line numbering less than

1,000 rifles. Ludendorff was fighting with the fury of despair to delay his retirement, so that he might move his vast quantities of material, and consequently he could give his broken troops no rest. The result was that their discipline was breaking, and the whole enemy *moral* was on the brink of collapse. Prodigies of gallantry and sacrifice were performed by the remnants of the old officer class, and notably by the machine-gunners, but no valour could prevail against overmastering physical weakness.

To make matters worse, it was clear that there was no city of refuge in the shape of a shorter line to which he could retreat and find a breathing space. The Meuse was already turned. It needed but a final bound to set the Americans astride the Metz railway. With Haig pressing fiercely in on the centre it was inevitable that the retreat would be largely shepherded northward, with appalling losses, into the gap of Liége, and there, on the scene of her worst infamies, Germany would meet her fate. The men who had outraged Belgium were mostly dead in dishonoured graves, but justice would be done upon their haggard successors. The shadow of a far more terrible Sedan brooded over the proud German High Command.

In such circumstances it was small wonder that Germany strove feverishly for peace. She flung dignity to the winds, blasphemed her old gods, and recanted with indecent haste her former creeds – not as a penitent, but as a criminal who stands condemned and seeks to ingratiate himself with his judges. On 20 October a second Note was addressed to Mr Wilson, agreeing to leave the conditions of armistice to the military advisers of both sides, and to accept the present relative strength on the fronts as the basis of arrangement, trusting to the President to approve no demand 'irreconcilable with the honour of the German people'. On 23 October Mr Wilson replied. His answer left no loophole of escape. In effect it demanded the abdication of the Emperor and the destruction of all for which he had stood; it asked that the Great General Staff should be deposed from their autocracy and placed under civilian control; it declined to treat save with new men bearing a popular mandate. To accept these demands was tantamount to an admission of final defeat in the field. Germany accepted them on 27 October, declaring that peace negotiations would be conducted by a people's Government to which the military powers were subject.

On Saturday 26 October, Ludendorff resigned. Few friends now remained to him. The German people at large saw in his military dictatorship of the past two years the cause of their misfortunes and especially they blamed him for the rash optimism which had led to the March offensive; while the reactionaries reprobated him as the originator of the first armistice proposals, which had taken the heart out of the army. Upon Ludendorff and his world the Twilight of the Gods was falling. In the wild legends of the Northern races the shades of the dead appeared to those on the brink of doom, and the heavens were filled with the Shield-maidens riding to choose the slain. The superstitious among Germany's rulers had in those days the spectacle of many portents to convince them of approaching calamity. Everywhere the wheel was coming full circle. The Belgians were approaching the dark land where each village spoke of German crimes. The British were almost within sight of the region where they had first met the enemy, swinging south, as he thought, to victory before the leaves fell. The French and the Americans had but a little way to go till their eyes beheld the wooded hills of Sedan. The alliances of which Germany had boasted were now utterly dissolved. More ominous still, that Eastern Europe which had seen her most spectacular triumphs was like to prove her worst undoing. The poison of Bolshevism, with which she had sought to inoculate her opponents, was beginning to creep into her own veins. Whatever crimes she had committed in the long war were now blossoming to her hurt.

***

Ludendorff had gone, and the Supreme Command was in commission. Foch was on the eve of his last step. Pershing and Gouraud advanced to cut the Metz–Montmédy-Mézières line and limit the avenue of German retreat. Haig took Valenciennes and pushed on down the Sambre towards Namur. On Tuesday 5 November, the enemy's resistance was finally broken. Henceforth he was not in retreat but in flight. Moreover, Foch had still his trump card to play, the encircling swing of his right by way of Metz to close the last way of escape. If a negotiated armistice did not come within a week there would be a *de facto* armistice of complete collapse and universal surrender.

During that week in Germany the mutterings of the storm of revolution were growing louder. Some issued heated appeals for a patriotic closing up of ranks in a last stand against the coming disaster; others attempted to make a scapegoat of the fallen Ludendorff; and everywhere was apparent a rising anger against the Imperial House. The Emperor had fled to the army, but the army was in no case to protect him. Everywhere there reigned a frantic fear of invasion, especially in Bavaria, where the collapse of Austria made the populace expect to see at any moment the victorious Italians in their streets; and invasion was no cheerful prospect to Germany when she remembered her own method of conducting it, and reflected that for four years she had been devastating the lands and dragooning the peoples of the Powers marching to her borders.

Strange things, too, were happening within her own confines. In the first days of November the stage had been set for a great sea battle. Her High Sea Fleet was ordered out, but it would not move. The dry-rot, which had been growing during the four years' inaction, had crumbled all its discipline. 'Der Tag' had come, but not that joyous day which her naval officers had toasted. She had broken the unwritten laws of the deep sea, and she was now to have her reward. On 4 November the red flag was hoisted on the battleship *Kaiser*. The mutiny spread to the Kiel shipyards and workshops, where there had always been a strong socialist element; a council of soldiers, sailors, and workmen was formed; and the mutineers captured the barracks, and took possession of the town. The trouble ran like wildfire to Hamburg, Bremen, Lübeck, and adjacent ports, and it was significant that in every case the soldiers and sailors took the lead. Deputations of Social Democrats were sent down post-haste by the Government, and succeeded in temporarily restoring order, but the terms on which peace was made were the ruin of the old régime. In Cologne, in Essen, and in other industrial centres there were grave disturbances, and everywhere the chief outcry was against the Emperor and the Hohenzollerns. He who had been worshipped as a god, because he was the embodiment of a greater Germany, was now reviled by a nation disillusioned of dreams of greatness. At the same time the Empire was dissolving at its periphery. The Polish deputies from Posen and Silesia seceded from the Reichstag, and Schleswig demanded liberation.

It was hard to tell where in Germany now lay the seat of power. On the 5th the Army Command invited to Headquarters representatives of the majority parties in the Reichstag to discuss the next step, and search was made for military officers who might be least unacceptable to the Allies. On that day the Government at Washington transmitted to Germany, through Switzerland, the last word on the matter of negotiations. This Note gave the reply of America's allies to the correspondence which had been formally submitted to them. They had accepted the President's Fourteen Points as a basis on which they were willing to negotiate peace – with two provisos: first, they reserved their own liberty of action on the question of the freedom of the seas, since that phrase was open to so many interpretations; second, by the word 'restoration' in the case of invaded territories, they declared that they understood 'compensation by Germany for all damage done to the civilian population of the Allies, and to their property, by the aggression of Germany by land, by sea, and from the air'. Mr Wilson signified his assent to these provisos, and announced that Marshal Foch had been authorised by all the Allies to receive properly accredited representatives of the German Government, and to communicate to them the terms of an armistice.

At the front during those last days the weather was wet and chilly, very different from the bright August when British troops had last fought in that region. The old regular forces which had then taken the shock of Germany's first fury had mostly disappeared. Many were dead or prisoners or crippled for life, and the rest had been dispersed through the whole British Army. The famous first five divisions of the Retreat from Mons were in the main new men. But some were there who had fought steadily from the Sambre to the Marne, and back again to the Aisne, and then for four years in bitter trench battles, and who now returned after our patient fashion to their old campaigning ground. Even the slow imagination of the British soldier must have been stirred by that strange revisiting. He was approaching places which in 1914 had been no more than names to him, half-understood names heard dimly in the confusion of a great retreat. But some stood out in his memory – the fortress of Maubeuge, on which France had set such store; above all, the smoky coal-pits of Mons, which had become linked for ever in the world's mind with the old 'Contemptibles'. Then he had been marching south in stout-hearted bewilderment, with the German cavalry pricking at his flanks. Now he was sweeping to the north-east on the road to Germany, and far ahead his own cavalry and cyclists were harassing the enemy rout, while on all the packed roads his airmen were scattering death. On the night of the 7th the line of the Scheldt broke, and on the 9th the Guards entered Maubeuge, while the Canadians were sweeping along the Condé canal towards Mons. Next day the Belgians had Ghent. In the south the Allied advance was even more rapid. Indeed the record of places captured had become meaningless.

These were feverish days both for the victors and the vanquished. Surrender hung in the air, and there was a generous rivalry among the Allies to get as far forward as possible before it came. This was specially noted among the British troops, who wished to finish the war on the ground where they had started. Take as an instance the 8th Division in Horne's First Army. It had spent the winter in the Ypres salient; it had done gloriously in the retreat from Saint-Quentin; it had fought in the Third Battle of the Aisne; and from the early days of August it had been hotly engaged in the British advance. Yet now it had the vigour of the first month of war. On 10 November one of its battalions, the 2nd Middlesex, travelled for seven hours in buses and then marched 27 miles, pushing the enemy before them. They wanted to reach the spot near Mons where some of them (then in the 4th Middlesex) fired almost the first British shots in the war, and it is pleasant to record that they succeeded. Likewise the 2nd Royal Irish, who had fought with the 3rd Division in the loop of the canal north-east of Mons on 26 August 1914, were, with the 63rd Division, entering the same loop on the last day of war.

Meantime in Germany the conventions which for generations had held her civilian people was patently dissolving. There were few mutinies like that of the northern ports. The old authorities simply disappeared, quietly, unobtrusively, and the official machine went on working without them. Kings and courts tumbled down, and the various brands of socialists met together, gave themselves new names, and assumed office. There was as yet nothing which approached a true revolution, nothing which involved a change of spirit. Deep down in the ranks of the people there was a dull anger and disquiet, but for the moment it did not show itself in action. They stood looking on while the new men shuffled the old cards.

But it was essential for Germany to get rid of the signposts of the old régime. Bavaria took the lead, and on Friday the 8th a meeting of a workmen's and soldiers' council, under the leadership of a Polish Jew, Kurt Eisner, decreed the abolition of the Wittelsbach dynasty. In Frankfort, Cologne, Leipzig, Bremen, Hanover, Augsburg, and elsewhere, similar councils were formed, who took upon themselves the preservation of order, and declared that they held their power in trust for the coming German Socialist Republic. So far there had been few signs of despotic class demands on the Russian model; in most places the change was made decently and smoothly. Saturday the 9th saw the crowning act in the capital. Bands of soldiers and enormous assemblies of workmen patrolled the streets, singing republican songs. There was a little shooting, and a certain number of windows were broken. Soldiers flung away their badges and iron crosses; everywhere the royal arms were torn down, and red flags fluttered from the balcony of the Imperial Palace, whence, in the first week of August 1914, the Emperor had addressed his loyal people.

Yet, orderly as was the first stage in Germany's revolution, and strenuous as were the efforts made to provide administrative continuity, on one side the revulsion was complete. The old absolutism was gone, and monarchy within the confines of Germany had become a farce – hated in some regions, in all despised as an empty survival. For centuries the pretensions of German kinglets had made sport for Europe. Now these kinglets disappeared, leaving no trace behind them. In Bavaria, Saxony, Würtemberg, the Mecklenburgs, Hesse, Brunswick, Baden, the dynasties fell with scarcely a protesting voice. With the lesser fell the greater. On Saturday the 9th it was announced that the Emperor had decided to abdicate, and that the Imperial Crown Prince renounced the succession. With a revolution behind him and his conquerors before him, there was no place left for him in the world. He did not stand upon the order of his going. On Sunday the 10th he left Main Headquarters at Spa, crossed the Dutch frontier, and sought refuge in the house of Count Bentinck at Amerongen. Prince Rupprecht retired to Brussels to await the victors, and the Imperial Crown Prince fled from his armies, and, like his father, found sanctuary in Holland.

History has not often recorded a fall from greater heights to greater depths. The man who had claimed to be the vicegerent of God on earth, and had arrogated to himself a power little short of the divine, now stole from the stage like a discredited player. Other kings and leaders who have failed have gone down dramatically in the ruin they made, but this actor of many parts had not the chance of such an exit. His light, emotional mind and his perverse vanity had plagued the world for a generation, and had now undone the patient work of the builders of Germany. Tragic, indeed, was the cataclysm of German hopes, and tragic, but in a lesser sense, was the fall of William the Second, King of Prussia, Margrave of Brandenburg, and Count of Hohenzollern. Like Lucian's Peregrinus, his life had been dominated by a passion for notoriety; but, unlike that ancient charlatan, he could not round off his antics on a public pyre. In fleeing from his country he did the best he could for his country's interests, and no humane man will wish to exult over the spectacle of broken pride and shattered dreams. In such an end his ὕβρις had received the most terrible of retributions.

***

The German delegates, who left Berlin on the afternoon of Wednesday the 6th, arrived in the French lines at ten o'clock on the Thursday night, and were given quarters in the château of the Marquis de Laigle at Francport, near Choisy-au-Bac. On Friday morning they presented themselves at the train in the forest of Compiègne which contained Marshal Foch and Sir Rosslyn Wemyss. The French Marshal asked, 'Qu'est-ce que vous desirez, Messieurs?' and they replied that they had come to receive the Allied proposals for an armistice. To this Foch answered that the Allies did not propose any armistice, but were content to finish the war in the field. The delegates looked nonplussed, and stammered something about the urgent need for the cessation of hostilities. 'Ah,' said Foch, 'I understand – you have come to seek an armistice.' Von Gündell and his colleagues admitted the correction, and explicitly asked for an armistice. They were then presented with the Allied terms, and withdrew to consider them, after being informed that they must be accepted or refused within seventy-two hours – that is to say, before eleven o'clock on the morning of Monday the 11th. They asked for a provisional suspension of hostilities, a request which Foch curtly declined. The terms were telephoned to Berlin, and a conference of the new Government was held that morning. The hours of grace were fast slipping away, and Foch was adamant about the time limit. The delegates were instructed to accept, and after a protest they submitted to the inevitable.

The terms were so framed as to give full effect to the victory on land and sea which the Allies had won. All invaded territory, including Alsace-Lorraine, was to be immediately evacuated, and the inhabitants repatriated. Germany was to surrender a large amount of war material, specified under different classes. The Allies were to take control of the left bank of the Rhine and of three bridgeheads on the right bank in the Cologne, Coblenz, and Mainz districts, and a neutral zone was to be established all along that bank between Switzerland and the Dutch frontier. A great number of locomotives and other forms of transport were to be immediately delivered to the Allies. All Allied prisoners of war were to be repatriated forthwith, but not so German prisoners in Allied hands. German troops in Russia, Rumania, and Turkey were to withdraw within the frontiers of Germany as these existed before the war. The treaties of Brest-Litovsk and Bucharest were cancelled. German troops operating in East Africa were to evacuate the country within one month. All submarines were to repair to certain specified ports and be surrendered; certain units of the German fleet were to be handed over to the charge of the Allies, and the rest to be concentrated in specified German ports, disarmed, and placed under Allied surveillance, the Allies reserving the right to occupy Heligoland to enforce these terms. The existing blockade was to be maintained ... Such were the main provisions, and the duration of the Armistice was fixed at thirty-six days, with an option to extend. If Germany failed to carry out any of the clauses, the agreement could be annulled on forty-eight hours' notice. The acceptance of such terms meant the surrender of Germany to the will of the Allies, for they stripped from her the power of continuing or of renewing the war.

It is necessary to be clear as to the exact significance of the terms of capitulation, for strange conditions have since been read into them by critics of Allied policy. These terms meant precisely what they said – so much and no more. Mr Wilson's Fourteen Points were not a part of them; the Armistice had no connection with any later treaties of peace. It may be argued with justice that the negotiations by the various Governments between 5 October and 5 November involved a declaration of principles by the Allies which they were morally bound to observe in the ultimate settlement.

But such a declaration bore no relation to the Armistice. That was an affair between soldiers, a thing sought by Germany under the pressure of dire necessity to avoid the utter destruction of her armed manhood. It would have come about though Mr Wilson had never indited a single note. In the field since 15 June Germany had lost to British armies 188,700 prisoners and 2,840 guns; to the French, 139,000 prisoners, and 1,880 guns; to the Americans, 44,000 prisoners and 1,421 guns; to the Belgians, 14,500 prisoners and 474 guns. In the field, because she could not do otherwise, she made full and absolute surrender.

* * *

In the fog and chill of Monday morning, 11 November, the minutes passed slowly along the front. An occasional shot, an occasional burst of firing, told that peace was not yet. Officers had their watches in their hands, and the troops waited with the same grave composure with which they had fought. At two minutes to eleven, opposite the South African brigade, which represented the easternmost point reached by the British armies, a German machine-gunner, after firing off a belt without pause, was seen to stand up beside his weapon, take off his helmet, bow, and then walk slowly to the rear. Suddenly, as the watch-hands touched eleven, there came a second of expectant silence, and then a curious rippling sound, which observers far behind the front likened to the noise of a light wind. It was the sound of men cheering from the Vosges to the sea.

After that peace descended on the long battlefield. A new era had come and the old world had passed away.